London's Armed Police

LONDON'S ARMED POLICE

1829 to the present

Robert W. Gould, MBE
and
Michael J. Waldren

ARMS AND ARMOUR PRESS
London   New York   Sydney

First published in Great Britain in 1986
by Arms and Armour Press Limited, 2–6 Hampstead High Street, London
NW3 1QQ.

Distributed in the USA by Sterling Publishing Co. Inc., 2 Park Avenue, New
York, NY 10016.

Distributed in Australia by Capricorn Link (Australia) Pty. Ltd., P.O. Box 665,
Lane Cove, New South Wales 2066, Australia.

British Library Cataloguing in Publication Data:
Gould, Robert W.
London's armed police
1. Metropolitan Police – History
2. Firearms – England – London – History
I. Title II. Waldren, Michael
363.2'3 HV8196.L6

ISBN 0-85368-880-X

Jacket illustrations. Front: armed police cover the front of the flat in Balcombe
Street, where IRA terrorists were besieged in December 1975. Back: 64 years
earlier, armed police return fire at the siege of Sidney Street. Both illustrations
courtesy of Syndication International Ltd. Colour simulation by Robert W.
Phasey.

Acknowledgements: The authors are indebted to the following for their expert
assistance. The Curator and staff of the Metropolitan Police Historical
Museum; Mr William Waddell, Curator of the Black Museum, New Scotland
Yard; Mr Frederick Wilkinson; and Mr Victor L. H. Wilkinson.

Key to illustration credits: *Black Museum*, Black Museum, New Scotland Yard;
Illustrated News, London Illustrated News; *Met*, Metropolitan Police; *Met H*,
Metropolitan Police Historical Museum; *PRO*, Public Records Office; *Enfield*,
Pattern Room, Royal Small Arms Factory.

Plans by Susan Waldren. Photography (illustration sections) by Brian J. Turner.
Pen and ink illustrations by Robert J. Marrion.

Designed by David Gibbons; edited by Michael Boxall; typeset by Typesetters
(Birmingham) Ltd., camerawork by Anglia Repro Ltd., Rayleigh; printed and
bound in Great Britain.

Contents

List of Maps

Preface

One of the many myths about the Metropolitan Police, perpetuated by sections of the Press and fostered by some senior police officers, is the premise that London's policemen have always been unarmed. In fact Metropolitan Police officers have always had access to, and occasionally used, a variety of arms. Unfortunately, at least until the last decade, these were usually inferior in performance to the weaponry available to their assailants.

The attitude of London's public and Press on this emotive question of arms for police has tended to vary from generation to generation, but has always been coloured by whether their police force, as a body, was in or out of favour. Thus, acts of heroism by individual officers or policemen killed or maimed while keeping the peace, or saving life, tend to bring all the members of that Force into public favour. On the other hand, corruption or malpractice very rightly brings them into disrepute; but not just the officers concerned. Odium attracted by the few is temporarily shared by all their colleagues. This pattern of ebb and flow in public opinion is strongly marked as are the incidents which have led the Metropolitan Police, often unwillingly, from flintlock pocket pistols and cutlasses to submachine-guns and gas. In an ideal world policemen would not need guns, but in an ideal world neither they nor innocent members of the public would be murdered.

Although this book is called 'London's Armed Police' it deals primarily with London's Metropolitan policemen and not their colleagues in the City of London. Mike Waldren, still a serving police officer, has provided the earlier chapters but the latter part of the book is solely my responsibility. In any case none of the comments reflect official views of the Commissioner of Police of the Metropolis.

Robert W. Gould

1

The Early Years

In 1829 George IV sat on the throne and an estimated 115,000 inhabitants in his capital city supported themselves by pursuits either 'criminal, illegal or immoral'. This was rather more than one in ten of the entire population of London, including men, women and children. Of that total about 50,000 were prostitutes, many of whom supplemented their earnings by picking their clients' pockets, or worse, which left approximately 65,000 living openly by crime.

Despite more than 200 capital offences, including impersonating a Chelsea Pensioner and chipping bits off Westminster Bridge, law enforcement was generally chaotic or non-existent. The mounted and foot Bow Street patrols, which totalled 190, was too small a force to be effective and the Watch was generally useless or corrupt, or both. Eighteen different police authorities existed within the parish of St. Pancras alone while the whole of Kensington was guarded by three watchmen of whom it was reported that one was drunk all the time and the other two most of the time. The state of the Watch was examined in 1828 by a Select Committee which found 'Persons are selected as watchmen who will bring the lowest expense on the parish – the labourer, who has worked all day and must sleep in his box at night, or the aged pauper, whose infirmities would make him the object of relief'. In any case many London parishes, including Fulham, Ealing, Wandsworth, Stratford and Bow were without watchmen of any sort, even aged paupers.

On Wednesday 15 April 1829 the Home Secretary, Sir Robert Peel, begged leave to bring before the House of Commons a Bill for 'Improving the Police in and near the Metropolis'. If accepted it would eventually unite under one roof all the many parochial police authorities and their various law enforcement agencies. He pointed out that if a police force were established on the lines he suggested there would be no necessity for the military to preserve 'the tranquility of the Metropolis'. The Duke of Wellington sanctioned the measure and shepherded the Police Bill through the House of Lords. In order to ensure that the Bill was passed, Peel's political horse-trading with the Whig opposition left the square mile of the City of London, still guarded by the Watch, firmly embedded in the middle of the Metropolitan Police area.

The Act became law on 19 June 1829 and two Justices of the Peace, directly answerable to the Home Secretary, who became the Police Authority for the Metropolitan Police, were appointed to control the newly formed police. They were Colonel Rowan, a veteran of the Peninsula and Waterloo, and Richard Mayne, a barrister and son of a judge. Although they referred to themselves, and were addressed, as Commissioners, it was not until 1839 that the title was made official. A serious suggestion that the police should wear civilian clothing, marked by a distinguishing brassard, was debated at length and finally discarded in favour of a non-military uniform. Contracts were accordingly awarded on 3 August 1829 for various items of uniform and equipment which included hats from Mr Moore of Piccadilly and swords and belts from Mr Tatham at Charing Cross. Robert and William Parker, from their separate shops in Holborn, supplied rattles, truncheons, staves and handcuffs to the value of £454 10s 8d.

Peel's police force comprised eight Superintendents, twenty Inspectors, 88 Sergeants and 895 Constables formed into companies and distributed in five Divisions. The Constables were clad in a blue swallow-tail coat, white duck trousers (blue cloth in winter) and a black top hat lined with leather. Each man was equipped with a wooden rattle (to summon assistance) and carried a truncheon, 18½ inches long, made from male bamboo or lancewood, in the tail pocket of his coat. Two-thirds of the men were to be employed on night patrols and the first contingent marched out on duty at 6 p.m. Tuesday, 29 September 1829.

Unfortunately the new police were not exempt from the 'scourge of the working classes', as one writer had described intoxicating liquor, and William Atkinson, the proud holder of warrant No. 1, was dismissed for drunkeness that same evening. On the next day Constable Patrick Haggerty, still wearing his uniform (until 1869 policemen were obliged to wear uniform whether on or off duty) was apprehended by the Watch in Mile End Road for being drunk and disorderly and offering to fight all comers – including the Watch. As there were no takers Haggerty contented himself with hitting his sergeant over the head with his brand-new truncheon. A few days later it is to be hoped that the 'graveyard' constables armed with cutlasses remained sober. In October these men were posted to burial grounds around inner London to combat the activities of 'body snatchers' who stole corpses and sold them to hospitals for medical research.

After a shaky start the force began to settle down although of the first 2,800 men recruited, 2,238 were dismissed, 1,790 of them for being drunk on duty. On 21 December 1829 Richard Mayne wrote to the Receiver, the man responsible for supervising police expenditure from public monies, advising him that a further supply of staffs, rattles and handcuffs was needed for the expanding police force. Included in the requisition was an item for fifty pairs of pistols. This order was filled by a flintlock pocket pistol, sometimes termed the Police model, made specifically for the Metropolitan Police. The weapon measured 6½ inches overall and was fitted with a folding trigger (no trigger guard) and a top safety catch. These pistols were made in London, probably by William Parker.

However, many of London's populace did not take kindly to their new guardians of law and order, whether armed or unarmed. In September 1830 one of the milder worded posters addressed to 'ye grievously oppressed and overburdened Parishioners of St. Pancras' urged them to attend a meeting for the purpose of petitioning the King (now William IV) for 'the abolition of the present military and grievously EXPENSIVE SYSTEM OF POLICE'. More inflammatory in tone was the wording on another placard which appeared in November 1830.

'Peel's Police, Raw Lobsters, Blue Devils, Or by whatever other appropriate name they be known. Notice is hereby given That a subscription has been entered into, to supply the PEOPLE with STAVES of superior Effect, either for Defence or Punishment, which will be in readiness to be gratuitously distributed whenever a similar unprovoked and therefore unmanly and bloodthirsty Attack be Again made upon Englishmen by a Force unknown to the British Constitution, and called into existence by a Parliament illegally constituted, legislating for their individual interests, consequently in opposition to the Public good.'

In the same year, when the King was to attend the Guildhall on Lord Mayor's Day, another rash of posters appeared.

'Liberty or Death. Englishmen! Britons!! and Honest Men!!! The time has at length arrived. All London meets on Tuesday. Come Armed. We assure you from ocular demonstration that 6,000 cutlasses have been removed from the tower, for the use of Peel's Bloody Gang. Remember the cursed speech from the throne!! These damned Police are now to be armed. Englishmen, will you put up with this?.'

6,000 cutlasses would have armed each man in the Metropolitan Police three times over, but presumably the author believed the truth of the old saying 'One for wear, one for spare and one for Sunday'. Although the House of Commons was assured that the King would be safe and anything happening at the Tower of London was a routine check, fainter hearts prevailed and the procession was cancelled. Future agitators had learned a valuable lesson. If enough wild accusations are made about Police, those in authority may back down.

Unfortunately, attacks on the new police were not always verbal for by now the first two policemen had been murdered on the streets of London. On 27 June 1830 Police Constable 169 Grantham was called to a dispute in Skinner Street, Somers Town. He was knocked to the ground by the disputants and one of the men involved, Michael Duggan, a bricklayer, repeatedly kicked him in the head. P.C. Grantham had the melancholy distinction of being the first Metropolitan policeman killed on duty; he also became the father of twins on the day he died. The second death followed two months later on the night of 17 August in Macklenburgh Square, just off the newly gas-lit Grays Inn Road. P.C. 43G Long approached three men who appeared to be acting suspiciously. One of the trio, William Sapwell, plunged a shoemaker's razor-sharp knife into Long's chest. The six-inch blade was so firmly lodged that the hilt broke off when an attempt was made to remove the knife. Long, the father of five children, died almost immediately.

However, the Metropolitan Police was beginning to gather support from some sections of the community who suggested that constables should be armed with something more lethal than a wooden stave. Following an incident on 15 November 1830 in which P.C. Berry was both shot and stabbed while attempting to arrest two burglars, residents of Tulse Hill signed a letter to the Commissioners suggesting '. . . the propriety of the Police Constables in our neighbourhood being furnished with a sword or cutlass and at least one pistol, each man, from a conviction that the men are not sufficiently protected for the fearless discharge of their duty in the dead of night, in such a neighbourhood as ours and particularly as it appears there are a gang of desperate ruffians about. We are decidedly of the opinion that had Policeman Berry been armed with the above mentioned weapons he would have taken both ruffians into safe custody without having been so barbarously attacked.' The letter ends by expressing satisfaction at Berry's 'spirited conduct' and wishes for his speedy recovery.

This letter was referred to the Home Secretary for a decision and the Commissioners were answered on 25 November, 'I am directed . . . to inform you that, upon the recommendation of the inhabitants, and in consideration of the circumstances they have stated, he approves of the proposal that each Police Officer in the district should be provided with a cutlass for his defence.' This would have been the standard police steel-bladed cutlass with brass grip and guard and only carried by men on night duty.

A similar application on behalf of his local police was made by a Mr Whiting from Battersea who wrote on 10 February 1831, '. . . considering the lonely and unfrequented situation of several of the rounds in this neighbourhood I think it desirable they should be armed with a cutlass, and indeed cannot consider them completely effective without'. However, it seems probable that some constables were already carrying arms for the following order, in the form of a memorandum, was issued by Richard Mayne on 8 November 1831. 'The Super-intendents are to take particular care that the Constables do not carry Pistols about them, nor in fact Arms of any kind without the express permission of the Commissioners thereto.' This order is interesting in that members of the public could still lawfully carry arms, including a firearm, for self-defence, but this was not permissible for police.

The growing appreciation of suburban householders for their still new police force was not echoed by other sections of the community. An extreme militant group called the National Political Union proposed to hold a public meeting on 12 May 1833 at Coldbath Fields, near the House of Correction in Clerkenwell. Handbills had been distributed previously preaching revolution and urging supporters to come armed on the day. This they did with knives, weighted cudgels, macaroni lances (folding daggers affixed to poles) and an ample supply of brickbats and stones. Lord Melbourne, who had succeeded Peel as Home Secretary in 1830, issued posters prohibiting the meeting, but the posters were not signed. Colonel Rowan, with verbal instructions from Melbourne to disperse the crowd if speeches were made, took personal charge of about 500 police who remained out of sight in some nearby stables. Another 70 men of 'A' Division, under a superintendent, policed the meeting-place. Owing to the content of the speeches, which advocated overthrowing the Government by force, Rowan ordered his men to clear the mob and arrest the speakers. In the running battle which then ensued, the police, armed with staves and outnumbered by more than ten to one, sustained many casualties including two seriously injured, and P.C. Robert Culley who was killed by being stabbed in the chest.

At the subsequent inquest the coroner's jury returned a verdict of justifiable homicide on the grounds '. . . that no Riot Act was read nor any proclamation advising the people to disperse; that the Government did not take proper precautions to prevent the meeting assembling; and that the conduct of the Police was ferocious, brutal and unprovoked by the people'. Members of the jury were each presented with a silver loving-cup to commemorate 'this glorious verdict' and were treated to a torchlight procession and a steamboat excursion up the Medway. The verdict was overturned by the King's Bench and the Government was shocked into the unprecedented step of allowing Culley's widow £200 compensation. A debate in the House of Commons which began on 13 June 1833 raged on and off for two months. William Cobbett, the member for Oldham and an uncompromising Radical champion, was particularly vociferous. '. . . it was something new in England to see peace officers in uniform embodied in companies and battalions marching in rank and file, commanded by Sergeants and Colonels – under the mock name of Superintendents'. He also alleged that the police had carried pistols and swords (despite the absence of injuries from such weapons) and added that unless the House got rid of these gendarmerie and returned to the old system 'the people must arm themselves'.

Opponents of the Metropolitan Police continually raised the spectre of a uniformed force, trained on military lines and chiefly composed of ex-soldiers – reviving the post-Cromwell abhorrence of the standing army. In fact training for the police, military or otherwise, was virtually non-existent. According to P.C. 149K Henry Wood, in his written report dated 29 April 1834, he joined the Force on 25 March that year. He was issued with his uniform at Scotland Yard and then walked to Poplar police station to which he had been posted. He was there instructed in his duties and the next night found him walking his beat from the Ferryhouse Mill wall as a fully fledged constable! Insofar as ex-soldiers were concerned they numbered only 402 out of a total of 3,308 policemen. This figure appears in a return dated 23 April 1834 submitted by a vestryman of St. Anne's who listed the previous occupation of every constable.

On 13 August 1836 the Bow Street Mounted Patrol was re-named the Mounted Police and officially transferred to the Metropolitan

Police. This force had been revived in 1805 and, at the date of its transfer, comprised a principal inspector, four inspectors and 68 constables, mainly ex-cavalrymen (of whom only three were Londoners) who covered the main highways within a radius of twenty miles from the centre of the Metropolis. This Horse Patrol was London's first uniformed and armed police force. Each man wore a blue double-breasted coat with yellow metal buttons, white leather gloves and a black leather stock, hat and wellington boots, with steel spurs. Their distinctive scarlet waistcoat earned them the nickname of 'Robin Redbreasts'. Armed with a pistol, sabre and truncheon, transferees to the new mounted police were to retain the pistol for at least the next thirty years and the sabre until 1868. In 1886 the designation 'Mounted Police' was changed to 'the Mounted Branch'.

A Dismounted Horse Patrol, 100 strong, had been established in 1821 to train men and provide a reserve for the Horse Patrol. The men were similarly uniformed, less the spurs, but wore a black felt hat instead of leather and carried a cutlass in place of a sabre. They patrolled on foot within a radius of six miles from Charing Cross and, in common with their mounted colleagues with whom they liaised, usually worked at night. Their daytime counterparts, the Bow Street Foot (or Day) Patrol numbered 27 men who covered the City and Westminster as a preventive force against robbery and housebreaking. The Foot Patrol had been abolished in 1829, but the Dismounted Patrol may have been disbanded or absorbed at a later date commensurate with the spread of the Metropolitan Police district. Unfortunately neither body is mentioned in the 1829 Act which only refers to 'the night watch and other night police'.

At this time the Metropolitan force was the only efficient police in the kingdom and large groups of London policemen were often temporarily drafted to other areas in order to keep the peace. Thus the first recorded occasion when Metropolitan constables used their sidearms occurred during the Chartist riots in Birmingham in the summer of 1839. (Chartism was a national movement for the extension of political power to the working classes, including annual parliaments.) Forty London constables were besieged in a police yard by a raging mob for nearly two hours while other rioters went on the rampage sacking shops and warehouses. Eventually the police with drawn cutlasses, and backed by mounted dragoons, fought their way onto the streets and restored order. There were heavy casualties on both sides and

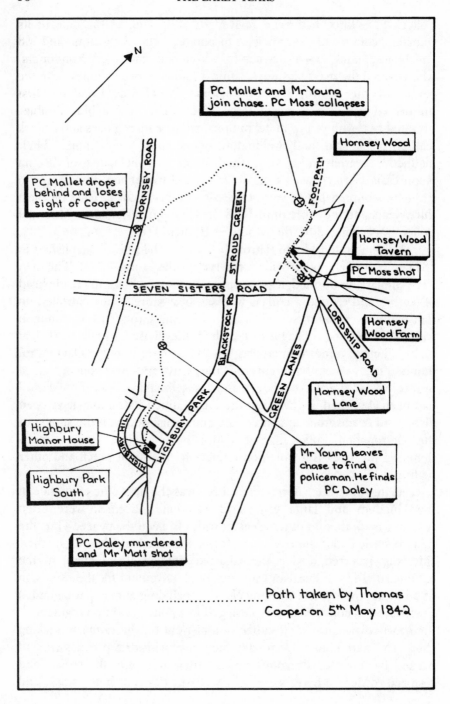

PC Mallet and Mr Young join chase. PC Moss collapses

Hornsey Wood

PC Mallet drops behind and loses sight of Cooper

Hornsey Wood Tavern

PC Moss shot

SEVEN SISTERS ROAD

Hornsey Wood Farm

Hornsey Wood Lane

Highbury Manor House

Highbury Park South

Mr Young leaves chase to find a policeman. He finds PC Daley

PC Daley murdered and Mr Mott shot

.... Path taken by Thomas Cooper on 5th May 1842 afterwards the General Convention of Chartists issued a proclamation declaring that 'a flagrant, wanton, and unjust outrage has been made upon the people of Birmingham, by a bloodthirsty and unconstitutional force from London . . .'

In the same year the Metropolitan Police Act of 1839 incorporated the marine or river police into the Metropolitan Police as the Thames Division. The river police had been created in 1798 to combat the estimated 10,000 thieves, both ashore and afloat, who pillaged goods from riverside quays and anchored ships to the tune of £500,000 annually. Multiply this figure by at least seventy to reach a comparable sum for the 1980s. Although not uniformed, it was the first London force to be paid and maintained by central authority. On amalgamation the Division's fearsome arsenal of blunderbusses was handed in, although a number of sea-pattern pistols were retained and the men apparently continued to wear their cutlasses.

By the 1840s a clear ebb and flow pattern was apparent in the attitude of London's populace and Press towards their police force. Accusations of police brutality, the inevitable aftermath of riots and street disturbances, caused the tide to ebb, but the murder on duty of an unarmed policeman reversed the flow, invariably accompanied by demands for better protection, usually firearms.

The case of Thomas Cooper was typical of the period. Cooper, a bricklayer by trade, lived in Clerkenwell and was fascinated by pistols to the extent of going without food in order to add to his collection. By the time he was 23 years of age he appears to have shot most of the cats in the neighbourhood and even tried to persuade his younger brother and a friend to stand against a wall and be used as targets. He had also been convicted nine times for trivial thefts and assaults and on the last occasion told the arresting officer that 'he should never be happy till he killed one of the Police'.

An outbreak of armed robberies in April 1842, which followed the traditional pattern of 'Your money or your life', led to an extra concentration of police in the area concerned. Just before 4 p.m. on 5 May 1842, P.C. 162N Moss saw Cooper (whose description answered that of the wanted man), with a long-barrelled cavalry pistol in each hand, emerge from Hornsey Wood, Highbury. Cooper apparently saw the officer for he ran back and attempted to hide in a ditch. Moss approached and asked Cooper to give an account of himself. Cooper's reply took the form of a shot fired at the P.C.'s head from the right-hand pistol. In fact the ball passed through the officer's left arm which he had lifted to protect his face. When Moss later received medical treatment small pieces of grass were found embedded in the wound; unable to find paper for wadding the charge, Cooper had used grass. Cooper then fired the pistol in his left hand which flashed in the pan (the priming powder fired but failed to ignite the main charge) and Moss leapt at him. Since he was unable to use his left arm the fight was one-sided and Cooper tore himself free. As he ran off he flourished a long knife threatening that he 'would do for' the constable if he attempted to follow. Moss did follow, but finally collapsed through loss of blood which gave Cooper time to reload his first pistol and re-prime the second.

The pursuit was then taken up by P.C. 41N Mallett who had heard the shots, and several people joined the hue and cry including Charles Mott, a journeyman baker, and John Young, a waiter from Hornsey Wood Tavern. After a chase of two miles Cooper was eventually cornered against a fence in Highbury Park South. The first officer had dropped behind, but Mott, who had armed himself with a stick, and Young had been joined by P.C. 65N Daley. Daley asked Cooper if his pistols were loaded and Mott, taking advantage of this slight distraction, attempted to seize the gunman. Cooper shot him in the shoulder and turned the muzzle of his second pistol on Daley who was about to grapple him. The policeman was not so fortunate as the baker and Cooper shot him at point-blank range; the ball went through his heart and out of his back – he died instantly. With both pistols empty Cooper surrendered, pleading that he should not be 'ill used'. His wrists were tied with strong cord and his captors took him to Islington Police Station. By the time they arrived the group was followed by a mob, several hundred strong, all baying for the killer's blood.

Many newspapers the next morning demanded to know how a constable was supposed to defend himself with a piece of wood 'against the discharge of a pistol' and asked why the men had not been equipped with cutlasses or firearms. *The Times* did not enter the debate, but contented itself with reporting that '. . . the neighbourhoods of Hornsey, Highgate and Islington were thrown into a state of the most painful alarm and excitement . . .' On 18 June 1842 Cooper was found guilty of the murder of P.C. Daley after the jury had considered the evidence for less than two minutes. Before his execution Cooper confessed to the prison chaplain that he had committed about thirty highway robberies, sometimes with violence, and explained how he had escaped detection for so long. He never worked with an accomplice and stayed away from pawnbrokers as these 'were the very worst enemies a poor thief could have'.

By 1850 the pattern of crime in London and the other big cities was changing. Highwaymen had been displaced by footpads armed with a weighted cosh – although burglars and housebreakers still favoured a firearm. A gun was not necessary to a footpad who usually approached his victim from behind and stunned him, or her, before rifling pockets and purses. Burglars on the other hand were liable to be confronted by a householder who, alarmed by the growing number of criminals carrying guns, had taken the precaution of arming himself and his staff. Cause and effect. Several intruders met a gory end at the hands of armed citizens or their servants – and vice versa.

The Great Exhibition of 1851 included percussion cylinder revolvers from two competitors, Robert Adams, who was British, and an American, Samuel Colt. Both weapons had the advantage of chambering a number of rounds, instead of one, but none of these revolvers was purchased for police use and the most modern firearm available to the Metropolitan Police had been delivered in 1844. This was a single-shot percussion belt pistol with a steel barrel, six inches long, and fitted with a swivelling rammer, but without the belt hook as issued to the Royal Navy and coastguard service. However, one concession had been made – the issue of paper cartridges. A stiffened paper tube (hence cartridge paper) held both powder and ball and the paper was then used as a wad, obviating the need to carry the three components separately.

Although foot police sometimes carried pistols for certain duties (mounted men habitually carried them) there was no facility to reload once the single shot had been fired. Labalmondiere, the Inspecting Superintendent, in a report dated 8 August 1852, wrote to the Home Office: 'Hitherto, although each mounted man has been supplied with a Pistol, he has had no way of carrying ammunition. I have therefore submitted for your approbation a method of fitting up the holster pipe in which the truncheon is now carried, and without interfering with it, so that in case of necessity half a dozen cartridges may be carried with it. The cost of the fittings will be four shillings for each saddle, for which authority is required.' Mr Secretary Walpole agreed to the expenditure.

A contract covering the years 1857 to 1859 itemizes the cost of various police arms and accoutrements. These include cutlasses for dismounted men at thirteen shillings each, and pistols with swivel ramrods for inspectors costing £2 6s. Similar pistols for mounted men were much cheaper at £1 15s each. As the inspectors' pistols were nearly a third dearer than those for mounted constables, it has been suggested that they were either double-barrelled or of a better quality, but as none of these pistols has survived the answer will never be known. Powder flasks at five shillings each indicate that the issue of paper cartridges was not universal throughout the Metropolis. A new item, costing 3s 6d each, was the 17-inch truncheon which in 1856 replaced the 18½-inch stave carried by foot constables.

The year 1863, foreshadowing events in Ulster more than a century later, saw the first occasion when a policeman was killed in his own home and in front of his wife. On 19 January at about 4 p.m., P.C. 84T Davey was working his beat in Acton when he caught two brothers, Isaac and Joseph Brooks, aged respectively 25 and 23, stealing timber. The two men, who were well known to local police, dropped the wood and decamped. Davey reported the incident to his section sergeant when they met at 6 p.m. and two hours later was given permission to go home, a short distance from his beat, for a meal. The Brooks brothers also returned home to 1 Chapel Place, Acton, whence Joseph's woman, Jane Lake, was sent with a pair of his trousers to Mr Ayre's pawnshop in Hammersmith. There she used the garment to redeem her lover's gun, a single-barrel percussion fowling piece, which was in pledge. At 8.30 that evening Joseph Brooks took his gun to Davey's home and knocked on the door. It was opened by the constable's wife, Martha, who called her husband. As he came to the door Brooks placed the muzzle to Davey's head and fired, blowing away a large piece of his skull. The gun had been loaded with no. 5 shot (pinhead pellets), intended for birds, but at point-blank range it would have the effect of solid shot.

Both brothers were arrested at their home in the early hours of the following morning. Inspector Searle, the senior officer present, found the gun hidden in Joseph's bed and established that it had recently been fired by sticking his little finger into the muzzle and smelling the percussion cap nipple. As Joseph was getting dressed a powder flask fell out of his jacket pocket and a quantity of No. 5 shot was discovered in a box under the bed. Both men were tried on 8 April; Isaac was aquitted but Joseph was convicted and hanged.

The entry in Police Orders had been brief and to the point, 'Death – T. P.C. 84 Davey; pay to 19th'. A small pension and an award of £15 was awarded to the widow by the Home Office. The pension is interesting in that it was intended to reassure police officers that their families would be cared for should they be killed on duty. However, very little money was involved. In 1869, for example, a total of £212 a year was being paid to the widows and orphans of the fifteen men killed on duty – an average of £14 per annum for each family. At that time a constable's pay had remained unchanged since 1829; £1 1s per week, but presumably as far as the widows were concerned a small pension was better than none at all.

By 1864 the strength of the force had increased to 7,113 and in the same year the swallow-tail coat and beaver hat were scrapped and replaced by a tunic and the predecessor of the present distinctive helmet. The truncheon was transferred to a black leather spring-loaded case and suspended from the waist belt on the right-hand side. Certainly the original uniform was sadly out of date, but the real reason for the change was quite astonishing – the pendulum had swung the other way. From being too military it now appeared that the Metropolitan Police was too civilized. An orchestrated Press campaign unfavourably compared the police with the army (which must have startled Tommy Atkins) and suggested that military discipline and bearing were essential if London's police were to restore good relations with the man in the street. Guards NCOs organized drill parades and the new tunic was patterned on those worn by British infantry of the line. Admittedly relations between police and public were low and police morale was even lower. In the previous year alone, three sergeants and 212 constables had been dismissed for drunkeness on duty – but worse was to come.

In June 1866 the radical Reform League announced a public demonstration in Hyde Park. Spencer Walpole, the new Home Secretary, decided to ban the meeting and the surviving Commissioner, now Sir Richard Mayne, took personal command of 1,613 police armed only with their truncheons. The peaceful procession of Reform Leaguers arrived at Hyde Park Corner and, confronted by a strong police cordon, turned away to Trafalgar Square to listen to the inevitable speeches. However, the mob, many thousands strong, which had attached itself to the procession, had not come to listen to speeches, it had come for trouble. The stage was now set for what was to be known as 'Bloody Sunday'. Armed with Hyde Park railings, torn out and used as makeshift spears, scaffold poles, knives and cudgels the rabble went to war. Order was finally restored when the heavily outnumbered police were reinforced by two companies of Guards. Mayne himself was injured by a brickbat as he sat on his horse and 265 of his men were also injured – 28 of them crippled for life.

Predictably, Mayne was accused of 'ruthless abuse of his authority' and of 'disgraceful provocation by inviting the support of soldiers'; the Metropolitan Police generally was censured for 'brutal and barbarous conduct'. Once again alleged police brutality had resulted in a scale of injuries to police at least twice as serious and ten times more numerous than those inflicted on the peaceful citizens exercising their civil rights and liberties. This phenomenon had first been observed after the Battle of Coldbath Fields and would invariably reappear in the aftermath of future public disturbances.

2
Bombs and Burglaries

By 1867 the Fenian Brotherhood, sworn to liberate Ireland from England's yoke, had enlisted many American Civil War veterans who were familiar with guns and explosives. A plan to attack Chester Castle on 11 February 1867, clear the armoury, and use the weapons to support a rebellion in Ireland was frustrated and the 1,400-strong Fenian army scattered. There were a number of arrests but two of the Fenian leaders were freed from custody by an armed raid in which a Manchester police sergeant was shot dead. There were other shooting incidents and bomb attacks and the *Illustrated London News* reported on 19 October 1867:

'The frequent repetition of murderous attacks on the Police in these days of Fenian fury makes it expedient that the civil guardians of our peace should be taught how to use more formidable weapons than the truncheon, in case of need, for the purpose of self-defence. Arrangements have, indeed, been made for the instruction of Officers and Constables of the Metropolitan Police Force in the cutlass exercise; and a portion of the ground belonging to the Wellington Barracks, St. James's Park, has been placed at the disposal of Sir Richard Mayne.'

The article went on to add that squads of 20 to 30 inspectors and sergeants would be instructed daily and they in turn would instruct the constables under their command. It is not clear which aspect of the cutlass exercises was intended to provide a defence against guns and gunpowder.

London was to be the next target for the bombers. Two Fenians named Burke and Casey had been arrested and were in Clerkenwell Prison awaiting trial. On 12 December 1867 the Commissioner received a letter from Dublin Police Office giving details of a plot to rescue the two terrorists by blowing down the 25-foot-high prison wall while they were exercising in an adjoining yard. Other than alerting the prison governor, who moved the two prisoners to another part of the building, Mayne failed to pass the information to the Division concerned. On 12

December two men rolled a barrel of gunpowder against the prison wall in Corporation Row, lit the blue touch-paper and retired. The fuze, however, was damp and failed to ignite the main charge, so the men collected their barrel and drove away in a horse and cart. There was a repeat performance the following afternoon with a tragic difference. The powder exploded at 3.45 p.m. demolishing a number of private houses, killing four innocent people and injuring forty more, including children. Four of the conspirators were convicted and one of them, Michael Barrett, had the doubtful distinction of being the last man to be publicly executed in England.

In the panic which followed the Clerkenwell outrage, thousands of special constables were sworn in, an increase in police strength was sanctioned, and the inevitable questions were asked about arming the Metropolitan Police. The old-style pistols, powder flasks and bullet moulds had been withdrawn in January 1866 and, in consequence, some revolvers were borrowed and issued as a temporary measure. Nothing is known for certain about the number, or model of these weapons, but they may well have been Adams's percussion revolvers on loan from the army. A week after the explosion five constables from each of ten Divisions were directed to attend Wormwood Scrubs at 11 a.m. on the 23rd to be instructed in revolver drill by Inspector Nightingale of 'A' Division. The course lasted two hours and each man actually fired ten rounds. This appears to have been the first police firearms course, but there was no provision for refresher training. At 2 p.m. on Christmas Eve another fifty men attended a similar course together with a superintendent and three inspectors who were required to learn how to instruct in revolver drills. With the increased firearms training more ranges were required and Police Orders for 27 December 1867 asked for a return to be submitted the next day '. . . shewing the position or name of place where each Rifle Range or Butts, or other place which would be available for revolver practice, is situate on each Division'.

On 28 August 1868 a Police Order informed the Force that 'The Secretary of State has, upon the recommendation of the Commissioner, authorized the supply of Adams's Breech Loading Revolvers, with boxes for the safe keeping of the same'. A total of 622 revolvers were supplied from the Tower of London, in three batches, between 28 August 1868 and 29 January 1869. These weapons were probably ex-army, but it is not possible to identify which model of Adams's .450 calibre revolver was actually purchased by the Metropolitan Police. Tower records are not available and no revolvers of this type bearing a police stamp appear to have survived, if indeed they were ever marked. They were issued to the twenty Divisions which then constituted the Metropolitan Police District and stored at 63 different police stations. There was a considerable difference in the numbers allocated to each Division. 'K' Division, which at that time covered Stepney, Poplar, Shadwell, Bethnal Green, Bow Road, West Ham, Barking Road (later East Ham) and the Isle of Dogs, had the highest number with 51 revolvers. The smallest figure, 16, was apportioned to 'V' Division which only policed Battersea and Wandsworth. Ten rounds of ammunition were supplied with each new weapon and directions were issued that 'the greatest care will be taken with them' and that 'Superintendents are to see that they are kept under lock and key in a safe place.'

During this period one of the more minor problems concerned the weight of truncheons which apparently varied between 12 and 15 ounces, instead of 13 as provided in the contract. The episode (and there must have been one) which sparked off the inquiry is not recorded, but in February 1868 Captain Harris, the Deputy Commissioner, directed that truncheons supplied by the firm of Parker Field should all be inspected to ensure that each was of acceptable weight. John Field replied directly to Sir Richard Mayne on 29 February pointing out the difficulties and adding '. . . I find that many of the staves now finished are ½ an ounce below the weight of the pattern and if they are to be rejected we shall be a long time getting 1,100 all to one weight'. On 10 March the Commissioner, annoyed because he had not been consulted in the first instance, wrote to the Receiver 'By whom are the truncheons examined and under what regulation? I have not heard any question as to their being weighed.'

As 1868 drew to a close Sir Richard Mayne, still in office, died on 26 December. It was the end of an era. During his forty years, first as joint and then as sole Commissioner, he had seen his police force, and there is no doubt that he considered the Metropolitan Police as *his* force, grow to a strength of nearly 8,000 men. It policed a population nearly double that of Paris, four times that of New York and eighteen times that of Rome. The 1840s had seen the Force assume police responsibility for 'all the Royal palaces and a 10 miles radius thereof', the Houses of Parliament, London Docks, Deptford Yards, the Tower of London and Woolwich Arsenal. Since 1860 it had also guarded the magazine stations in the Royal dockyards of Portsmouth, Devonport, Chatham and

Pembroke Dock. Peel's 'bloody gang' had become a bulwark of Victorian society.

Colonel Labalmondiere held the reins until 13 February 1869 when another colonel, Edmund Henderson, a regular officer of the Royal Engineers, was appointed Commissioner. The new broom swept briskly, wringing from the Home Office a pay rise of one shilling per week for constables and allowing them to wear beards and moustaches on duty and civilian clothes when off duty. However, the provision of a weekly rest day proved a grave disappointment to Henderson who reported 'the constable becomes unhinged and unsettled by constant interruption of duty', i.e., by having one day off in seven on a rota system. At least the unhinged and unsettled constabulary fared better than their colleagues whose names appeared each week in Police Orders under the heading 'Dismissed the Force – worn out – pay to . . .'

Henderson survived the scandal of a police strike in 1872 and an even bigger scandal in 1877 involving three out of the five senior officers in the Detective Force. In the ensuing upheaval Howard Vincent, a barrister, was appointed to the newly created post of Director of Criminal Investigations. The increasing number of burglaries doubtless concerned the new Director as much as they worried the public and the Press. None was more concerned than little Mr Thompson, of independent means, who lived at 5 East Terrace, Nunhead, with his wife Susan and her sister Hannah. But appearances are often deceptive. In fact Mr Thompson was Charles Frederick Peace who earned his living by burglary; Hannah was his legal wife and not his sister-in-law, and Susan (Grey) was his mistress and not his spouse.

Peace had fled to London two years previously after murdering a man named Dyson in Manchester and he was also responsible, although it was not known at the time, for the killing of P.C. Cooke, also in Manchester. Both victims had been shot. In the handbill which offered a reward of £100 for information leading to his capture he was described as 'almost a monkey of a man, with the power of pulling about and altering his features so as to make his face unrecognizable even by his relations and intimates'. Peace, who invariably carried a gun and had sworn not to serve another prison sentence, burgled a house at 2 St. John's Place, Blackheath, during the night of 9/10th October 1878. The owner was absent and P.C. 202R Robinson, posted to the beat, had been instructed to check the house as often as possible. In the official version of what followed, Robinson noticed a light in the drawing-room of the unoccupied house and went in search of another constable, William Girling, and they were then joined by Brown, the section sergeant. What actually happened was related by Robinson before he died at Greenwich in 1926, an old man of 78. Robinson had stopped for a quiet smoke in a sheltered byway at the back of the house and was joined by Girling who had left the adjoining beat for a similar purpose. They were caught by Sergeant Brown, who had been looking for them, and threatened with a disciplinary report for idling and gossiping and failing to work their respective beats. At that point all three saw a flicker of light in the drawing-room and from then on both versions coincide. Robinson climbed over the back wall, followed by Girling, and the sergeant went round to the front door and rang the bell. Peace doused his light and jumped out of the ground floor back window only to be confronted by Robinson. Shouting 'Keep back or by God I'll shoot you,' he fired four shots which all missed, from a revolver which was tied to his wrist. Muttering 'I'll settle you this time,' the burglar took careful aim at Robinson's head. The constable shielded his face with his arm and the bullet passed through his elbow. As they struggled together on the ground Peace attempted to draw a knife, but was knocked senseless by a 'sweeping downward blow' delivered by Girling's truncheon. Peace at first gave the name of John Ward, but his true identity was discovered thanks to his mistress, despite her sworn oath to Peace that she would never speak his true name. She wrote it on a piece of paper instead and later claimed the £100 reward.

On 19 November 1878 the burglar was sentenced to life imprisonment for the attempted murder of P.C. Robinson and the judge gave the officer Peace's revolver as a souvenir. While being transferred to Manchester, to stand trial for the killing of Dyson three years previously, Peace made a daring but unsuccessful attempt to escape from a moving train. He was sentenced to death at Leeds Assizes for Dyson's murder and on the eve of his execution confessed to shooting P.C. Cook. The auction of Peace's collection of fiddles, stolen over many years, was apparently well attended by curious buyers.

During the next three years, as burglaries continued and injuries to police increased, there was mounting and vocal concern, especially from night duty constables in urban areas, for some better protection than that afforded by a truncheon. Obviously the 'greatest care' was being taken of all the Adams revolvers – they remained securely locked in their boxes. Complaints from their men were ignored by senior police officers until the slaying of P.C. 356V Frederick Atkins. The case of Atkins was in a different category from those of his colleagues who had been killed or injured while attempting to arrest armed criminals. On 22 September 1881, P.C. Atkins was on night duty in the neighbourhood of Kingston Hill, and at about 1.15 a.m. made a routine visit to one of the large houses on his beat. It was a fairly common practice in those days for the beat man to check the doors and windows of the larger residential properties. As Atkins walked up the drive he was ambushed by an unseen gunman who shot him in the abdomen, chest and groin. In a lucid period before he died Atkins told his colleagues that he neither saw nor heard anything before the shots. A search later revealed that the protective bar had been removed from a small window on the ground floor, beneath which lay a cold chisel and a lantern. Atkins's killer, who was never found, was obviously an armed burglar who had ensured his escape by coldbloodedly shooting a policeman three times.

The effect on police, public and Press was electric. More than 1,500 officers from different Divisions attended the funeral, local shopkeepers closed their premises as a mark of respect, the newspapers were in full cry and *Punch* entered the lists with a cartoon captioned 'An Unequal Match'. The noise reached the ears of the Home Secretary who asked the Commissioner whether his men wished to carry firearms. Henderson consulted his superintendents who were unanimous that arming the police would damage their public image and, furthermore, the constables themselves did not wish to be armed. This view was duly passed to the Home Secretary who was obviously receiving information from another source for he was not satisfied that the Commissioner's reply truly reflected the opinion of constables. He directed that inspectors should be consulted as to the wishes of their men.

Colonel Henderson's reply took the form of a nine point memorandum which was presented to the Home Secretary towards the end of 1882. The Commissioner stated that the rank and file generally agreed with their superintendents that a revolver would not afford much protection. He added that an officer would be at risk in law if he used the weapon with fatal results and would therefore be afraid to use it at all. This line of reasoning was rather flawed by Henderson's admission that a similar argument could be applied to the use of a truncheon. He also suggests that the feeling that police should be armed was much stronger on the magistrates' bench and in the Press than among the constables. However he admits to a 'certain sense of insecurity among the men who patrol at night in the suburban districts, visiting all kinds of lonely places where no help is to be got in an emergency'. Henderson concludes with a suggestion that patrols should be doubled 'in the secluded localities which are naturally selected by burglars for their operations'. Finally, a committee of the two district superintendents and the superintendents of the outer divisions 'are to go carefully into the matter and report'.

Two days after the Commissioner's memorandum was delivered to the Home Office yet another policeman was killed by an armed burglar. Thomas Henry Orrock embarked on his career of crime equipped with two chisels, a wedge, a bulls-eye lantern and a revolver; the latter bought for 10s 6d as a result of an advertisment in *Exchange and Mart.* One of the chisels had recently been sharpened and the grinder had scribed the owner's name on the blade. Orrock chose the foggy night of 1 December 1882 for his first venture, which was to break into the chapel which he had attended as a child. He forced a window and was about to climb in when he was arrested by P.C. George Cole. During the struggle Orrock dropped his tools but not the gun, which was under his jacket. *En route* to the police station he managed to draw the revolver, shoot Cole four times and escape. Orrock was eventually brought to justice, but not until more than three years later. His downfall was largely due to the tenacity of the murdered officer's section sergeant, Cobb, who traced his man to Coldbath Fields Prison where he was serving a sentence for burglary.

On 15 March 1883, in the midst of the controversy about firearms for police, a bomb exploded beside the Local Government building in Charles Street, off Whitehall, and later that evening another device was found outside the offices of *The Times* newspaper. In the panic that followed, armed constables guarded the more important Government offices while nearly another 1,000 Metropolitan constables, usually unarmed, were posted to other places considered as likely targets. These ranged from the Houses of Parliament to the Royal Gunpowder Factory at Waltham Abbey and included all Royal palaces, London bridges, prisons and public buildings. A total of 93 sergeants and constables acted as protection officers to important figures and these varied from the Home Secretary, who was allotted fourteen, to the German Ambassador who had to be content with one.

During the next two years twenty-two bomb attacks were delivered against buildings and monuments including the Tower of London,

Nelson's Column and Scotland Yard itself. The Royal Irish Constabulary sent thirteen armed officers on loan to the Metropolitan Police
to assist the hastily established Special Irish Branch. When the
campaign was over the word 'Irish' was dropped from the title and the
department was known simply as the Special Branch, or more familiarly
the Branch.

The first bombs had temporarily diverted public and Press
attention from armed burglaries, but in August 1883 two burglars fired a
number of shots at police and escaped from a ransacked house in
Holloway. On the 28th of that month another two burglars, this time in
Wimbledon, were disturbed by P.C. Boans. In a running fight the officer
struck his assailants with his rattle and attempted to arrest them until he
was shot and severely wounded. The burglars dropped a six-chambered
pin-fire revolver (the firing pin formed part of the cartridge and not the
gun) used in the shooting and made good their escape.

On 29 August the *Evening Standard* editorial was very much to the
point on the question of arming police.

'For the second time in the course of a few days persons endeavouring to arrest burglars
have been shot at by them, the criminals in each case making their escape. Parliament
occupies itself in fighting over theoretical crotchets, and entirely overlooks the really
urgent problems of the day. One of these is the manner in which persons who meditate a
crime arm themselves with revolvers, and go about their work with the resolution of
murdering anyone who may interrupt them . . . It is not only foolish but absolutely cruel
to send Policemen out to combat men possessed with revolvers, without any other arm
than a short club. If the law will not protect the Police by heavy penalties from armed
resistance, they should at least have weapons to enable them to defend their lives. In no
other country in the world are the guardians of the peace handed over defenceless to the
mercy of armed criminals.'

On the same day the *St. James's Gazette* began its editorial by stating
the obvious, 'Burglars now commonly carry revolvers, and policemen
not being provided with these weapons are entirely at their mercy.'
Having examined the situation the *Gazette* finally came to the conclusion
'. . . but then arming of the Police would be an un-English proceeding,
and would perhaps still further brutalize the burglar'. Over and above
shooting on sight and cold-blooded murder it is difficult to visualize
what further brutalities the writer had in mind.

An impressive list of recent London burglaries took pride of place
in *The Chronicle* dated 31 August, followed by an appropriate article.

THE BURGLARY SEASON

'The startling burglarious affairs of Holloway and Wimbledon have again brought under the consideration of the authorities the question of arming Police who perform night duty in suburban London. At the beginning of the present month, when the evenings were rapidly shortening, representations were made by several Constables stationed in the suburbs to their superior officers, to the effect that whatever might be the courage and physical strength of a Policeman, both are powerless against a burglar armed with a revolver, when the Constable had only in his possession for defence against offensive purposes the lignum-vitae baton. These representations were duly transmitted to the proper quarter, but the occurrences referred to have hastened the serious consideration of a question which two years ago, when burglary was rife in the metropolitan suburbs, would have been solved, at any rate to the satisfaction of the Police, but for the disinclination of the Government to arm the civil force of the country. In the course of the ensuing week it is stated that the question will be discussed by Sir W. Vernon-Harcourt [the Home Secretary] . . . and the heads of the various divisions, with the assistance of the Chief Commissioner.'

Such a meeting did take place and, once again, the Home Secretary was assured that the constables did not wish to be armed. Sir William, however, was unconvinced and asked for further reports. The Director of Criminal Investigations, Howard Vincent, was also directed to prepare a memorandum giving his opinion on the subject together with details of the occasions when firearms had been used against police. This memorandum is dated 6 September 1883 and lists ten cases since October 1878 where the use of revolvers by burglars resulted in one constable shot dead, one who later died of his injuries and six who were wounded. In the other two cases the bullet 'passed through his clothes without inflicting injury'. He gives his opinion that in only two of the ten cases 'the possession of a revolver would probably have prevented the attack by the assailant or secured his arrest; in the remaining eight cases the circumstances of the struggle or attack preventing even the use of a truncheon would have probably hindered the use of a revolver'. He goes on to say: 'The issue of revolvers is not so far as can be ascertained generally desired by the Police, and many Officers are of opinion that it would be dangerous to the public. But, as I find that sticks are frequently carried by Police in country districts, who conceal them from their Inspectors as being contrary to regulations, I share the opinion of many Officers that the issue of an approved pattern to exterior Divisions would be advantageous to the service.' The last paragraph states, 'I think also that legislative means should be taken, if not to hinder the present enormous sale of foreign revolvers for a few shillings, at least to punish more severely burglars and housebreakers found with them in their possession.'

The memorandum, either intentionally or otherwise, is rather misleading. In the original draft, Vincent's paragraph, dealing with the wishes of police about arms, has been heavily amended and in the memorandum as presented it is much more emphatic that the police themselves do not wish to be armed. However, in the same paragraph he appears to agree that officers in outer Divisions should be armed although it can be read that he refers to an approved pattern of stick (whatever that may be) rather than a revolver. The last paragraph implies that cheap foreign weapons are an important factor and ignores the availability of cheap British revolvers. His final point overlooks the fact that a burglar was usually only found with a gun in his possession when he had used it to shoot some unfortunate constable.

Vincent's report was accompanied by a covering letter from Labalmondiere, by now one of the two Assistant Commissioners, which read: 'In submitting the accompanying reports I have to point out that the occasions on which Police have been attacked are very rare, and I cannot think that it can be requisite to arm them any further. I agree with the final paragraph in Mr Vincent's report, as the number of revolvers imported from Germany at a cost of 4s 9d each is very large. I am of the opinion that a Police Order should be issued directing P.C.s when visiting any house where there is reason to believe burglars may be engaged to, before entering, loosen and take in hand their truncheons.' Not for the first time, nor the last, there was obviously a wide gulf between the views of the chairborne constabulary and those of their colleagues who were at the sharp end. This was even apparent to the Home Secretary, or Secretary of State for Home Affairs to give him his correct title, whose reply was received four days later.

'Confidential. The recent murderous attacks on a policeman by a man armed with a revolver has again fixed the attention of the Secretary of State on the question of the sufficiency of the means of protection at present afforded to the Police, and on the expediency of arming them with revolvers or some other more efficient weapon than they at present possess . . . When this question has been previously raised by the Secretary of State he has been assured by the Commissioners that there was no discontent on the part of the Force with the present armament or any desire for further protection. This impression seems to have been derived from the reports of the Superintendents though the Secretary of State was always inclined to doubt whether this really represented the feeling of the Constables. In consequence of the recent attack on a Constable by a man armed with a revolver the Secretary of State has called for fuller reports which embrace the opinion of the Inspectors who are more likely to be aquainted with the real sentiments of the men. A summary of their reports has been furnished to the Secretary of State and has convinced him that the view previously reported to him by the Commissioners was erroneous and that there is a wide spread and general dissatisfaction in the Police with the present means furnished them for self defence. This feeling appears . . . to be perfectly natural and entirely well founded. Though the majority of the Superintendents are adverse to the use of revolvers by the Police it is remarkable that on this subject the opinion of the Inspectors is as nearly as possible equally divided. This reveals a state of feeling in the force entirely different from that which has been formerly reported to the Secretary of State. He is quite convinced that the Police as a body are not satisfied that their protection should be left on its present footing. There are differences of opinion as to the proper remedy to be adopted but all are of the same mind that the truncheon and the rattle as at present employed are not adequate to their safety. Mr Vincent has informed the Secretary of State that he is surprised at the amount of discontent in the Force on this subject and that he was before unaware of the extent to which it existed.

It is impossible that this condition of things and this state of sentiment in the Police Force should be allowed to continue for a moment longer than is necessary in order properly to consider and deal with the matter which if allowed to remain as it is, may demoralise the whole spirit and courage of the Police. The Secretary of State, with these reports before him disclosing a most serious danger in the Police, finds himself unfortunately without the means of consulting the Chief Commissioner or Col. Pearson [the other Assistant Commissioner]. It is impossible of course that the Secretary of State can come to so grave a decision affecting the Force as that of arming the Police without the advantage of their counsel. The Secretary of State cannot at all accept the suggestions of Col. Labalmondiere in his letter of Sept. 6 as affording in any respect an adequate solution of the matter.'

Having fired a salvo in the direction of the Commissioners generally and Colonel Labalmondiere in particular, the Home Secretary expressed his opinion that in view of the present situation there ought to be at least two of the Commissioners (i.e., the Commissioner and an Assistant Commissioner, or both Assistant Commissioners) available in the Metropolis at the same time. He felt that making such an arrangement about leave would not be difficult and 'which he is confident therefore will be hereafter observed'. Owing to the urgency in the matter of arms for the Metropolitan Police he wished to consult with all the Commissioners together 'and unwilling as the Secretary of State is to encroach upon the much needed holiday of the Commissioners he feels that in a matter so vital to the interests of the Police they will at once take the matter in hand . . .' A copy of this letter was delivered by hand to the absent Commissioners at their holiday addresses; they returned to London forthwith.

3
Arming the Police

Henderson held a series of meetings with his assistant commissioners and ordered every sergeant and constable serving on outer Divisions to submit a report indicating whether they wished to be armed when performing night duty. The result was quite frightening; 4,430 out of a total of 6,325 asked to be issued with a revolver. The next step was to examine the advice given by the police legal adviser, Mr James Edward Davis, a barrister, which had been prepared on 27 December 1882. This note, written in a barely legible hand, was presented at a meeting of the Commissioners on 20 September 1883.

'POLICE CONSTABLES MAY LAWFULLY USE REVOLVERS IN THE FOLLOWING EMERGENCIES

1. In self defence where there is necessity for resorting to the use, as when the Constable is attacked by a person with firearms or other deadly weapon and cannot otherwise reasonably protect himself. A Constable (as a private person also) may resort to a revolver as a means of defence.
2. If a Constable finds a person committing, or attempting to commit, a murder, he is justified in shooting him, if reasonably necessary to prevent the completion of the offence.
3. In the case of committing burglary, or robbery with violence, if the offender, after the Constable has told him he will fire, does not at once desist, the Constable may use his revolver. If the offender is himself armed and offers violence, the justification of the Constable may be as before stated under (1) without notice.
4. If immediately after the complete offence under (2) or (3), the offender flies, the use of the revolver, after notice, to disable him in continued flight, is lawful, if no other means to effect his capture are reasonably open to the Constable. If death ensues it is misadventure. The Constable would not be criminally responsible.
5. If while watching or surprising a supposed offender, and the case is not ripe for arrest, and the reality of the offence is unknown, and the supposed offender fires, or manifests an intention to use a deadly weapon towards the Constable, the Constable is justified in using a revolver.
6. In attempting to effect an arrest under warrant, or without a warrant after a lapse of time after the commission of the crime justifying such an arrest, the use of the revolver is not justifiable. If resistance is offered by the use of firearms or deadly weapons so as to bring the case within (1) and the rules there laid down, a revolver may be used.'

Davis mentions that the constables murdered at Kingston and Dalston might have lawfully used revolvers under rules 1 and 5 and adds, 'It is obvious that in all cases of death or wounding resulting from the use of a revolver by a Constable his complete justification depends on facts, which upon trial or inquest, would be the province of a jury to determine; but the Constable should always act as if the jury, if it came before a jury, would find and express the truth and act firmly and fearlessly, but not rashly.'

There are several interesting points in these notes. A 'deadly weapon' which is mentioned in 1, 5 and 6 has never been defined in a court of law, for almost anything may become an instrument of offence, and deadly, if used with that intent. As far as the first half of rule 3 is concerned, it would be remarkable if a burglar or robber did not desist in these circumstances, if only to escape. In rule 4 (shooting a fleeing felon after challenging him to stop) it is difficult to visualize what other method of capture is 'reasonably open' to a constable other than physical pursuit and arrest.

Since arming the Metropolitan Police was now a real possibility, the Commissioner was anxious to take advice on anything to do with the subject, including the action to be taken by armed constables who were guarding prisons since the Clerkenwell outrage. This was triggered by a call for additional guards on Millbank Prison, which held Fenian convicts, and again Davis was instructed to report on the legal position. His reply is dated 20 September 1883.

'FELONIOUS ATTEMPTS FOR THE RELEASE
OF ONE OF MORE PRISONERS

If a Constable, so on duty, sees any person attempting to enter the prison forcibly by scaling the walls or otherwise under circumstances reasonably leading to the belief that the person has for his object the rescue or release of another confined in the prison, or the injury of any officer of the prison, or any injury to the fabric of the prison (including in the word prison, the prison walls) he should call upon the offender to desist and to surrender, failing either he may and ought to fire. If the attempt witnessed does not admit of a moment's delay, as for example if the Constable is reasonably assured that an explosive substance is being applied, or about to be applied to the prison, or any personal violence with deadly weapons is about to be used towards another, he may and ought to fire. If the Constable, in the discharge of his particular duty above referred to, is himself engaged in deadly conflict whether by the use by the felon of firearms or other weapon, he may fire to protect his own life. In the service of the above instructions the Constable should not use his revolver rashly or in any way of retaliation or on mere suspicion, but on full reasonable assurance of the felonious purpose of the offender.'

As soon as Henderson received this reply from his legal adviser he applied to the Home Office for authority to arm all the police on duty at Millbank Prison. This was granted on 22 September 1883 with the proviso that it did not extend to those officers 'employed in the public thoroughfare'. As armed police were only on duty at the main gate, or patrolled outside the prison walls (warders inside already carried carbines) it is difficult to understand the Home Office embargo on public thoroughfares; unless it meant those streets not in the immediate vicinity of the walls. Possibly this was the subject of a local instruction which, together with the briefing for armed constables, has not survived.

On 21 September 1883 the Commissioner wrote to the Home Office on the question of arming the rest of the Force in the outer districts. After the usual preamble that the views of the Home Secretary had been carefully considered the letter continues: 'The Commissioners are not prepared to take the responsibility of recommending the Secretary of State to issue an order that the Police are in future to carry revolvers when employed on night duty in the exterior districts. At the same time looking to the feeling which appears to have been evoked among the Police the Commissioners would submit for the consideration of the Secretary of State whether it might not be desirable to issue revolvers to such men as desire to have them when employed on night duty in the exterior districts and who can, in the opinion of the divisional officers, be trusted to use them with discretion.' Henderson also complained that armed policemen would run a grave risk if they shot anyone and a copy of Mr Davis's advice was enclosed with the letter. The Commissioner also mentioned again the alternative of pairing men on isolated beats. Although 300 beats had been double-manned, the Force was still under strength and any further doubling would have seriously weakened police cover in inner parts of the Metropolis.

Godfrey Lushington, the Permanent Under-Secretary at the Home Office, replied on 24 September to the Commissioner's memorandum stating that the Home Secretary agreed on the danger inherent in an armed police force. However, 'Under the circumstances stated, Sir William Harcourt is prepared to sanction the experiment to the extent proposed, i.e., he sanctions the issue of revolvers to such men as desire to have them when employed on night duty in the exterior divisions. In the case of men supplied with revolvers the Secretary of State has to instruct you that the men are to be strictly enjoined that the revolver is only to be employed in self defence under the circumstances stated in

Mr Davis's minute of December 27 under Head 1 and not for any of the other purposes set forth under the other Heads of the same minute. The Secretary of State desires special attention to be paid to this instruction as it will greatly obviate the risks apprehended and he does not think it safe to entrust the Police Constables with the discretion involved in the other Heads of Mr Davis's minute.'

In other words, an armed constable now had the same rights in this matter as the rest of the populace. He could officially use force against like force and defend himself, where necessary, with a firearm. Henderson instructed his superintendents to ascertain how many of their men wished to be armed and submit the numbers, together with any other recommendations they might have.

A side issue, which came to light as a result of arms for the constables at Millbank, concerned the three sergeants and 24 constables from 'A' Division who had guarded Newgate Gaol round the clock since the Fenian explosions. Each man was armed with a loaded Adams revolver, but only four of them had ever been instructed in the revolver's mechanism and none of the twenty-seven had ever fired a round in practice! Henderson immediately gave orders that a sergeant from 'A' Division and one from each of the ten outer divisions should be nominated and trained as instructors. The chosen eleven duly attended the Haymarket premises of Lang & Son, gunsmiths, for a one-day course which cost the Police Fund a guinea per man, plus the cost of any expended ammunition. There is nothing in the records to indicate how the sergeants were selected; they may have been ex-soldiers, pressed men, volunteers or probably a combination of all three.

Among the recommendations from superintendents were those from 'N' and 'S' Divisions who still did not want their men to be armed, whatever the Home Office might decide, and the superintendents generally had obviously tried to persuade the rank and file to reject firearms. However, a total of 931 constables felt strongly enough about the matter to resist such pressure and still wished to carry firearms on night duty. Other recommendations included shortening the truncheon, substituting a whistle for the rattle and replacing the old-fashioned Adams with a Webley revolver, similar to the model carried by the Royal Irish Constabulary.

These reports were sent to the Secretary of State on 8 October 1883 with a covering letter from Labalmondiere who made a last-ditch stand on the question of firearms. 'I have read the Superintendents' memorandum and concur with its recommendations, and I further think that cutlasses should be issued to those Constables who have applied for revolvers and the issue of these latter should be refused. I do not see that many of the Superintendents in their recommendations refer to the indiscretion of their men, but I believe that the feeling of Superintendents N and S is shared in by others. I do not think the responsibility can be entirely removed from these superior officers.'

This last sentence probably gives the true reason, for the first time in this mass of correspondence, why the superintendents had always been so adamant that their men should not be armed. If anything went wrong, irrespective of what happened to the erring constable, some of the blame would certainly fall on his superintendent for failing to ensure that he was properly instructed and supervised. In any case, confrontation with an armed burglar, in a dark lane late at night, always looks less dangerous when read about the next morning.

Very little of this information was made public at the time with the inevitable result that rumours flew in all directions. One of the most persistent, even believed by many policemen, concerned the adoption of a new and improved truncheon which incorporated a whistle in one end. This caused one constable to write an anonymous letter (signed 'one of the crowd') to *The Times* ridiculing the idea. On 22 September the *Saturday Review* published a long article which poured scorn on the proposal to give policemen whistles, pointing out '. . . it is as absurd to arm the police with whistles as to arm a regiment of cavalry with bugles', and '. . . as to the proposed combination of whistle and truncheon, even if the burglar did not use the simple expedient of knocking the whole apparatus down the constable's throat, he would have plenty of time, before the music ended, of getting out of harm's way'.

Even so the pendulum was starting to swing the other way, and the Press cooled to the idea of actually arming the police. The thought had provided good copy for a number of years, but now that the reality was in sight much of the appeal had disappeared. The *Daily Telegraph*, in an editorial on 27 September thundered, 'To arm our Police Force in what are called "dangerous neighbourhoods" with six-shooters is a kind of desperate resource which does not recommend itself to an impartial judgement, even though the majority of the Police themselves . . . seem favourably disposed to the innovation. The risks of inconsiderate shooting are far too great to allow for this particular remedy against murderous depredators – at all events, until other less objectionable methods have been tried.' The article went on to suggest that householders arm themselves with a gun or buy a bulldog, and proposed the reintroduction of the lash for imitators of Mr Peace.

Two days later the same newspaper revealed to startled readers that, 'London Policemen are in future to be armed. This is the grave decision which has been arrived at by the Scotland Yard authorities, in conjunction with the Home Office; and it is generally surmised that those responsible for the safety of the Metropolis have considered well the many and serious objections which can be urged against the innovation.' The article went on to question what would be thought of the capital of England when it was necessary to safeguard the lives of its citizens by arming the Police. It also queried whether police cartridges should not be loaded with lead shot, instead of a bullet, as the former would cause less damage in the event of an accidental shooting. However, the writer continues quite fairly, 'the question then arises whether a shotted cartridge would be efficacious in disabling the burglar . . .'

In any event the die was cast and the Commissioner had written to his superintendents instructing them to arrange training for those officers who wished to be armed. The superintendent of 'S' Division was still most unhappy about all these revolvers. On 13 October 1883 he replied to Scotland Yard: 'I beg to report that the only arrangements I have to propose respecting the instruction of men desirous of being armed is that PS Concannon should attend at the several stations and explain the mechanism of the revolver, how to clean it and carry it, and the method of taking aim, but I presume it is not intended that there should be any target practice. The quieter the thing is done the better. I hope I may be pardoned if I say again how sorry I shall be to see firearms placed in the hands of Policemen. I am quite sure there is no need for it and the public will soon look with great disfavour upon the practice.' It is difficult to understand how arming the police, an exercise conceived in a blaze of publicity, could be done quietly. It is even more difficult to understand the mentality which allowed a policeman onto the streets with a loaded firearm, although he had never handled or fired it in practice.

On 16 October 1883 the Commissioner received formal authorization from the Home Office for the issue of revolvers 'to the 931 Constables employed on night duty on the exterior sub-divisions of the exterior Divisions, the revolvers to be of the new and lighter sort, and the old ones issued in 1867 to be disposed of in exchange; also of 7175 whistles . . . being issued, and of certain alterations being made in the length and mode of carrying the truncheon . . .' The Receiver duly placed an order with Philip Webley & Son, Birmingham, for 931 centre-fire .450 calibre revolvers (later known as the Metropolitan Police model).

Adams Patent Small Arms Manufacturing Company tried to retain the Metropolitan Police custom and on 20 October offered to supply their New Model No. 5 at a cost of £2 1s 3d each. Chequering the stock, after the style of Model No. 4, would increase the price by sixpence per weapon. The company also sent six different revolvers as samples. In the competitive world of weapons manufacture the Metropolitan Police had figured among the prestigious clients in the Adams advertising material for many years. No doubt the loss of such a name was worse than the actual loss of sales, for on 29 October their samples were returned and the company were informed that an Adams had not been selected.

The question of whether the cartridge should contain lead shot or bullets [first mooted in the *Daily Telegraph* on 29 September] was also raised by the Receiver in October. He sent a memorandum to the Commissioner, asking that all Adams revolvers issued to Divisions be returned to store, and also asking how many cartridges should be purchased, and whether they should be loaded with bullets or buckshot. He was advised that the ammunition would be bulletted and ten rounds issued with each weapon.

On 5 January 1884 the first nineteen Webley revolvers were delivered to Scotland Yard and a few days later the Receiver asked to which Divisions they should be sent. At the same time he suggested that the weapons be numbered consecutively from 1 to 931, marked 'M.P.', and a record kept of each officer to whom a revolver was allocated. His most important point is made in the last sentence of his letter – 'There appears to be at present no General Order respecting revolvers.' In other words, the Metropolitan Police was preparing to issue nearly 1,000 unmarked revolvers, without instructions to the recipients and without any record of distribution. A committee of four superintendents was assembled to report on the matter and pass their findings to Labalmondiere, but the gallant colonel washed his hands of the affair and delegated the task to the other Assistant Commissioner.

The committee reported on 23 May 1884 and, with one exception, its findings were later reproduced word for word. The exception was a recommendation that the legal adviser's memorandum of 27 December 1882 should be published in its entirety as part of the regulations. Committee members obviously had not seen the letter from the Home Office dated 24 September 1883 (stating that a constable could only fire in self defence) despite the fact that the Home Secretary 'desires special attention to be paid to this instruction'. A final draft of the proposed regulations governing firearms was approved and published as a police order on 30 June 1884.

'THE FOLLOWING REGULATIONS RELATING TO THE ISSUE TO, AND USE BY POLICE OF REVOLVERS, HAVING BEEN APPROVED, THE SUPERINTENDENTS ARE TO SEE THAT THEY ARE STRICTLY ADHERED TO.

1. Revolvers are only to be issued to men who desire to have them when employed on night duty, and who can, in the opinion of the Divisional Officer, be trusted to use them with discretion.
2. Revolvers are to be kept at the Stations to which men who are to use them are attached, the Officers on duty thereat being held responsible for their safe custody and efficient condition.
3. A revolver is to be issued to a Constable on parading for duty, on his own application only, at the time of parading. It is to be loaded by the Officer parading the relief, and placed in a holster. An entry is then to be made in the Occurrence Book showing the number and name of the Constable to whom a revolver has been issued, also the number of the revolver.
4. The revolver is to be carried in a holster on the belt on the right side in front of the truncheon, and is not to be taken out of the holster for any purpose whatsoever, except in self defence.
5. Officers carrying revolvers are to be strictly enjoined that they are only to be used in self defence where there is necessity for resorting to their use, as when a Constable is attacked by a person with firearms or other deadly weapon and cannot otherwise reasonably protect himself, a Constable (as a private person also) may resort to a revolver as a means of defence.
6. On going off duty, the Officer in charge of the Station is to receive the revolvers from the Police, and in their presence extract the cartridges, carefully examine both weapon and cartridges and make an entry in the Occurrence Book of the condition in which they are delivered to him.
7. The Officer having the use of a revolver is to report, on going off duty, every instance in which he has had occasion to remove it from the holster during his tour of duty, whether it was used or not. Such reports are to be dealt with as "Urgent" and submitted at once to the Commissioner through District Superintendent.
8. Before a revolver is issued to an Officer, he is to be properly instructed in its use, and a report of his competency submitted through District Superintendent, to Commissioner for his approval.'

It will be seen that only Rule 1 from Davis's memorandum had survived to be incorporated in paragraph 5 of the new regulations. However, this survivor was of paramount importance. Despite many alterations to the rules that would be made in the years to come, paragraph 5 remained the foundation-stone for all future instructions to armed Metropolitan Police officers. It stayed virtually unchanged for nearly a century, until 2 August 1983, when it was rewritten as the result of Home Office Circular No. 47.

In paragraph 3 it appears that a constable could carry a revolver, and fire it if necessary, but was not permitted to load or unload the weapon. Rule 4, if rigidly applied (which it probably was) must have made life difficult for left-handed officers. Presumably the regulations were also meant to apply to armed police guarding prisons or protecting Royalty and Ministers of the Crown; despite the words 'night duty' in paragraph 1. Another omission was rectified on 9 December in a police order directing that members of the Criminal Investigation Department were bound by the same regulations.

The effect of the June police order was to allow a trained Metropolitan constable to carry a revolver on night duty in outer districts if he so wished. However, despite the fears of senior police officers, there was little reaction from the public. Suburban streets of the Metropolis were not littered with shot burglars (or shot policemen for that matter) and the Press lost interest. Within a decade the numbers of men carrying a firearm on night duty had dwindled from a few hundred to a few dozen, although the authority remained in force for another 52 years.

Between divisions there was an enormous difference in the number of men who wished to be armed. 'N' Division, with a strength of 826, had only two applicants, and one of those was a mounted officer who already carried a sabre. 'R' Division, on the other hand, with 519 constables, submitted 311 applications. However, Superintendent 'N' was one of the senior officers vehemently opposed to arms for police and his attitude was certainly responsible for the lack of response from his men. Jobs were scarce, even if poorly paid, and indirect pressure could easily be applied to a constable to make him agree with his superintendent. The two applicants from 'N' Division must have been strong-minded men, or rebels, or both.

Training now began in earnest, but obviously differed throughout the Force as each superintendent made his own arrangements.

Superintendent Worels of 'Y' Division, for example, sent one inspector and 110 constables to be instructed by the 3rd Middlesex Rifle Volunteers at the unit's range in Tottenham. The overall fee of £10 was presumably paid from the Police Fund. Superintendent Firmett of 'X', on the other hand, hired Wormwood Scrubs range for a day and asked Webley & Son if his men could be supervised by a representative from the firm. Webley replied that they would be delighted to send their Mr H. Webley to assist in any way he could, but asked that the other superintendents might be told of the date so that their men could also attend. The initial training class was therefore cancelled and Colonel Pearson was asked if the offer should be accepted on behalf of other divisions. As a result, Mr Webley met Pearson at Scotland Yard and undertook to train sergeants as divisional instructors on a range at Nunhead, near Peckham. The class was duly arranged and the selected sergeants were instructed to attend in plain clothes (on Pearson's personal order). Paper targets were supplied by Webley & Company, but the trainees used police Webley revolvers and ammunition.

This last point caused a certain amount of embarrassment later on as Mr Webley had requested that each man be supplied with 'a fair amount of ammunition'. Unfortunately nobody at Scotland Yard had any idea what constituted a 'fair amount' and no one thought to inquire. As a result, most of the sergeants arrived at the range clutching ten rounds, although some had twenty. Three days later Webley wrote to Pearson stating that the men had been instructed and had proved themselves fairly efficient marksmen at nine and fifteen yards – 'many of them able to command a 5-inch bull at the first distance'. The letter adds, 'There are two points that Mr Webley would like to draw attention to. Firstly that before a man <u>could be expected</u> to make a fairly reliable shot with a revolver he should be permitted at least <u>200 rounds</u> of ammunition to practice with. Secondly that when a man has practiced with, and become accustomed to a pistol of a certain number, he should always have the same revolver served out to him. By doing this a man gains complete confidence in his weapon, a matter of vital importance in an emergency. Whereas if he first has one pistol then another served out to him, with neither of which he may have practiced, it is needless to point out that bad shooting would be the result in the majority of cases, even if the man were a good shot with a pistol he had practiced with.'

The underlining is from the original letter, but it would be many decades before revolutionary ideas about the amount of training ammunition and one man wedded to one gun were accepted. Nothing more was heard from Webley & Company except a letter dated 18 June 1884 in which the firm asked the Commissioner for a testimonial as to the manner in which the contract had been executed and, as an afterthought, 'perhaps mentioning the training at Nunhead?' The Roumanian Government was about to order 6,000 revolvers and was looking for a supplier; Webley wished to back their tender with a letter from the Metropolitan Police.

By 26 July 1884 all the constables who wished to carry a revolver had been trained and their names and competency reports were forwarded to the Commissioner for his approval; but not all the men who applied were successful. Superintendent 'T' for example, would not certify any of his 37 applicants as competent, while Superintendent 'N', stubborn to the last, suggested that as his mounted officer carried a sword he should not have a revolver as well. Pearson forwarded the papers to the Commissioner and agreed that a firearm was unnecessary in this case, but the Commissioner overruled him. On 29 July 1884 Pearson sent a memorandum to all the superintendents directing that the men reported as competent were to be issued with a revolver on application, including mounted branch officers. He added that the police order regarding issue and use of revolvers was 'to be strictly complied with'.

4

Whistles, Truncheons and Cutlasses

Whistles and improved truncheons had been approved by the Home Secretary and a contract for 7,175 whistles, costing 11d each, had been awarded to J. Hudson & Company of Birmingham. Before completing the order the firm suggested that whistles supplied to inspectors and above should be of superior quality to those issued to sergeants and constables. The idea of a 'superior whistle' was abandoned, but only after the matter had been seriously considered and passed to the Commissioner for a decision. By now all police clothing, accoutrements, saddlery and weapons were inspected by War Office examiners, who rejected 641 of the new whistles as defective. In a note to the Home Office dated 3 May 1884 the Receiver used this fact to justify the inspection fees of £15 14s 10d and also mentioned that 'as regards revolvers the proportion of rejections is far higher'.

By 26 June 1884 all suburban officers had abandoned their rattles and the Receiver noted that 'the whistles are greatly appreciated and I fancy that soon they will have to be supplied to the whole force'. His prediction was correct and early in 1885 Henderson directed that the remaining rattles be withdrawn and replaced by 5,680 whistles.

Coincidently another Birmingham firm, Bent & Parker, were also manufacturing whistles, which were stamped 'Metropolitan Police'. A Mr Crosbie bought one of these from a shop in Wandsworth, after reading an advertisement in the *Illustrated London News*, and fearing that they might be used 'by unscrupulous persons as an emblem of office' wrote to the Receiver on 23 January 1885 to condemn the practice. Mr Parker was invited to Scotland Yard and agreed to recall all the 'police' whistles and replace them with an unmarked type. Since he could not sell them elsewhere he successfully offered his remaining stock of 2,000 marked whistles to the Receiver for 10½d each.

Truncheons were even more troublesome. Tenders were invited from four firms for a supply of lignum vitae truncheons, and the contract was awarded to Ross & Company who had quoted a price of 1s 3d per truncheon. The new type was known as the no. 2 while the old model

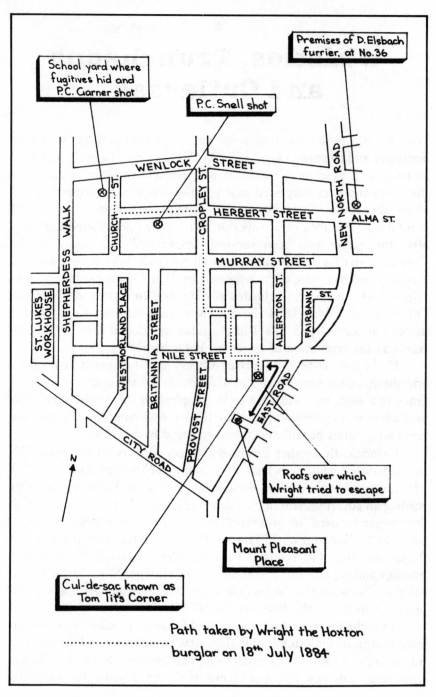

School yard where fugitives hid and P.C. Garner shot

Premises of D. Elsbach furrier, at No.36

P.C. Snell shot

WENLOCK STREET

CHURCH ST.

CROPLEY ST.

HERBERT STREET

NEW NORTH ROAD

ALMA ST.

MURRAY STREET

SHEPHERDESS WALK

ST. LUKES WORKHOUSE

WESTMORLAND PLACE

BRITANNIA STREET

ALLERTON ST.

FAIRBANK ST.

NILE STREET

PROVOST STREET

EAST ROAD

CITY ROAD

N

Roofs over which Wright tried to escape

Mount Pleasant Place

Cul-de-sac known as Tom Tit's Corner

Path taken by Wright the Hoxton burglar on 18th July 1884

was called the no. 1. When a quantity of no. 2 truncheons were tested by the Royal Army Clothing Depot staff in Grosvenor Road, several of them broke during trials. Six no. 1 models were then supplied by Ross & Company and one of these also broke when tested. Despite breakages, the no. 2 model was issued to the Force although the Receiver later noted that they not only broke during trials but also at other, and more critical, moments. Unfortunately the 'critical moments' which occasioned his comments are not on record, but presumably a certain number of malefactors' heads and shoulders were stronger than the truncheons.

Unlike their suburban colleagues, officers on night duty in inner divisions were still unarmed. At about 1 a.m. on 18 July 1884, James Wright a 38-year-old tailor, and William Wheatley a labourer aged 25, broke into a furriers at 36, New North Road, Hoxton. Each man wore a false beard and carried the tools needed for their crime, i.e., chisel, jemmy and skeleton keys on a leather belt under his coat, and a revolver. They were also equipped with a dark lantern. While smashing open a case of silver plate the two men were disturbed by the householder and escaped through the front door, still carrying some stolen loot in sealskin bags. P.C. 429G David Garner was called from the next street and, assisted by other officers, began to search the locality for the two burglars, who had gone to ground. Four hours later Garner found Wheatley hiding in a nearby school yard at the back of Holy Trinity Church. He climbed over the railings and tried to arrest his man, but during the struggle Wheatley drew his revolver and fired three shots; two of them missed but the third went through Garner's thigh. Although he was fast losing blood, the constable was still struggling with the gunman when help arrived in the form of Frederick Thomas, a fireman, and Police Inspector Maynard. Both men lived nearby and had run half-dressed from their lodgings after hearing the shots.

Meanwhile Wright, who had also been hiding, tried to slip away unnoticed, but walked into Acting Sergeant 373G Clifford and P.C. 462G Snell who were running towards the church. Wright shot Snell in the stomach and made off closely pursued by Clifford. By now the neighbourhood was roused and several people who came to their doors and windows were threatened by Wright that they too would be shot if they interfered. The chase continued through several streets until the gunman made the mistake of running into a cul-de-sac, then known as Tom Tit's Corner, with about twenty citizens and policemen raising the hue and cry at his heels. There was a convenient ladder to hand which he climbed, followed by Clifford and several of the pursuers, onto the tiled roofs of the surrounding houses in Nile Street.

Wright now began to jump from roof to roof as the crowd below shouted encouragement to the hunters and kept them informed of his progress. Undoubtedly there would have been further casualties had the loaded chamber not fallen from the burglar's revolver (the result of a loose retaining screw) which rendered the weapon useless. Moving from roof to roof, Wright held out for an hour, hurling abuse, threats and tiles at his would-be captors and the gathering crowds below. He was eventually arrested by Police Sergeant 9G Walsh who had anticipated Wright's next change of direction and managed to get ahead of him and hide behind a chimney stack. Walsh was assisted by a Mr Forster who earlier had been one of the recipients of a flying roof tile. When Wright was secured the crowd demanded that he be thrown down to them to be dealt with, which caused the intrepid gunman to seek assurance from the police that they would protect him. He was taken to Kingsland Road Police Station, followed by a large crowd of people, several of whom managed to get in a number of blows before he was safely incarcerated. While in custody both men confessed to the shooting of P.C. Chamberlain of 'N' Division, in Park Street, Islington, a few weeks earlier.

That morning's edition of the *Daily Telegraph* compared the 'pursuit and capture of Wright, the Hoxton burglar, along the tiles of the Nile Street houses' to Dickens' 'Bill Sykes, the murderer of Nancy, pursued from cellar to roof by a raging mob'. Strangely enough the editorial did not advocate that police in inner divisions should also be armed at night, but instead resurrected a previous theme – the flogging of armed burglars. 'Can the Police be expected, nobly as their duty has been performed in the present instance, to feel any confidence in the truncheon as a match for a revolver? If so, is it not absolutely necessary, in the interests of public safety, to make examples of burglars caught with a pistol or other firearm in their possession as shall effectively deter similar scoundrels as flogging terrified the garotters?' However, flogging was unlikely to deter a criminal who already faced a maximum sentence of life imprisonment for burglary and the death penalty for murder, whether committed with or without a firearm.

Two attempts had already been made, in 1881 and again in 1883, to legislate against the carrying of loaded revolvers in a public place, but both foundered on the fundamental right of an Englishman to carry a firearm for his own defence. Howard Vincent, the former Director of Criminal Investigations, who had resigned from the police service in 1884 and entered politics, attempted to introduce a Bill in 1887 which would have imposed a statutory minimum sentence of 10 years' penal servitude for anyone committing a burglary while armed. But as the original offence of burglary still carried a life sentence, Vincent's Bill was rather a fruitless exercise and it was withdrawn when he was opposed by the Home Secretary. Restrictions on firearms and their use would have to wait until well after the turn of the century.

A side-issue arising from the 'Bill Sykes' shootings concerned cutlasses. Superintendent Sherlock of Islington queried why his station was still holding 605 cutlasses which had not been issued for years and were in any case useless against revolvers. Doubtless Sherlock had in mind the recent shooting of one of his men, P.C. Chamberlain. A check with other divisions, completed on 19 March 1885, revealed that the Metropolitan Police still held 5,427 cutlasses at various stations and dockyards; a later count increased this figure to 5,441. Samples were sent to the Surveyor General of Ordnance who gave his opinion that the weapons were useless and only worth the scrap value of the brass on the hilt and scabbard. Horncastle & Pember, a firm of auctioneers at 314, Regent Street, whose professional services were used by the Receiver, disagreed and believed that the cutlasses would easily sell on the open market because of their police association. The matter was referred to the Home Office which decided it would be contrary to policy to allow the public to buy police weaponry and directed that unwanted cutlasses be broken up at the Royal Arsenal.

The Commissioner decided that ten cutlasses were to be retained in each of the 20 Divisions, including Thames, plus 107 at Woolwich and 421 by police in the dockyards – Portsmouth 151, Devonport 131, Chatham 111 and Pembroke 28. Henry Roads, a carman of 398, Caledonian Road, was given a contract for collecting 4,713 cutlasses from various police stations and taking them to Woolwich. In due course the scrap value of the brass, £90 12s 3d, was sent to the Receiver who in turn paid Mr Roads the rather paltry sum of £7 10s for all his labour. The remaining 728 cutlasses were never officially withdrawn and some, at least, continued to be carried. In 1900 for example, a superintendent sent in eleven cutlasses and 37 scabbards for exchange or repair. When it was pointed out that they were no longer an official issue, and hence would not be repaired, he asked for them to be returned as 'they are actually used by the men at Purfleet and elsewhere'. Certainly Thames officers continued to take them out until just before the Great War 'just in case', as one retired veteran put it, although they were stowed in the well of the launch, rather than worn. The directive did not apply to Mounted Branch officers who retained their swords until 1925.

In the main however, the truncheon and revolver were the chief arms of police and on 29 April 1885 the Commissioner agreed to the provision of an annual practice for those constables authorized to carry a revolver. This was quite an historic step and although the amount of ammunition fell rather short of the 200 suggested by Mr Webley, in fact it was only six rounds per man per annum, at least it was a start.

Events in the coming year however, were to divert the attention of police and Press away from firearms and back to public order. On Monday 8 February 1886, the London United Workmen's Committee held a meeting, of which they had given notice, in Trafalgar Square at the same time as an opposing faction, the Social Democratic Federation. Only a small number of police were posted to the square although a reserve of 563 men was in the immediate vicinity. Colonel Henderson, the Commissioner, delegated command of the operation to the 74-year-old Robert Walker, one of the two surviving district superintendents. Walker, who was not known by sight to many of the police on duty, arrived at the meeting in plain clothes, a psychological error which would be repeated by a number of senior officers in the years to come. He was badly jostled in the crowd and to add insult to injury had his pockets picked.

After the obligatory speeches the London mob, about 5,000 strong and full of original sin, went on the rampage through Pall Mall and into Oxford Street, via Hyde Park. Walker was still trapped by the crowd milling about in Trafalgar Square, Henderson was absent from his office, the reserve was mistakenly directed to the Mall instead of Pall Mall and police administration, together with the shopkeepers whose premises were looted, had a very bad day. Not for nothing was the day to be known as 'Bloody Monday'. The mob was finally dispersed at about 5 p.m. when the leading ranks were repeatedly baton charged by the late turn relief, seventeen men in all, from Marylebone Police Station. A new and weak Home Secretary appointed a committee (chaired by himself) to inquire into the riots 'and the conduct of the Police Authorities in relation thereto'.

Henderson gave his evidence and promptly resigned before he could be thrown to the wolves. He had been well liked by his men and by the time of his resignation, on 26 March 1886, the strength of the Force had grown to 13,115. The new Commissioner, General Sir Charles Warren, was a professional soldier who detested civil servants, disliked politicians and was not over-fond of policemen, although he did succeed in improving the quality of police boots.

The February riots had been responsible for more shattered truncheons and it was decided to examine all the truncheons from an entire division, selected at random. The choice fell on 'M' Division whose truncheons were duly tested by a master artificer and his assistant from the Royal Army Clothing Department at a cost of 16 shillings per day. So many truncheons were broken during the trials that a different wood was selected for the next batch. The no. 2 had been made from lancewood (which was cheap), but the replacements were turned from cocus wood. At this time uniform sergeants and constables, both foot and mounted, still carried the no. 1 truncheon which was 15½ inches long and weighed 14 ounces. The no. 2 model was issued to officers and all ranks of the CID and Thames Division. It was only 12½ inches in length and weighed 12½ ounces. £900 worth of cocus wood truncheons were purchased in October 1886 and by June 1887 all the old no. 2 truncheons had been withdrawn from service and handed to Thames Division to use as firewood in their new steam-powered launch.

Attempts to find the best type of wood continued for some years but with indifferent results. In the last experimental batch, made of partridge wood, 61 of the 211 truncheons broke at the first test. In 1886 the truncheon scabbard was finally abolished in favour of a specially sewn pocket in the trousers since '. . . the carrying of a truncheon in a case imperils the safety of the Police Constable at times, as it can be used as a lever to nip him around the stomach by means of the belt, take away the breath, and thus leave him at a disadvantage'. It appears that 'Bloody Monday' had seen a few disadvantaged constables suffering from nipped stomachs.

Warren's short period in office was marked by the first verifiable case of a Metropolitan policeman firing his revolver on duty. On 18 February 1887, Police Constable 161P Henry Owen was able to put his training into practice and also had the opportunity to use his new whistle. In the officer's own words, 'I beg to report that at about 5 a.m., while on duty at Keston Common I noticed a quantity of smoke in the direction of Keston Village. I made all possible haste to the spot and discovered a large general shop belonging to Thomas Cyrus Haslett was on fire and well alight and knowing that inmates were sleeping in the upper part of the dwelling-house situate at the rear of the shop and adjoining to it I blew my whistle, lustily called out fire, and hammered the shutters. Failing to get any response and fearing that the lives of the inmates would be placed in jeopardy if there were any further delay, I drew my revolver No. 236 and fired six cartridges over the roof of the dwelling-house. I then scaled the side fence and made my way to the rear of the house just as Thomas Cyrus Haslett, aged 87 and [three other named adults] issued from the back door of the premises, Mr Haslett stating that he was awoke by hearing a rumbling noise, evidently the shots from the revolver, and found the room was full of smoke.' Owen adds that he then helped the occupants to remove books and property before the fire gutted both the shop and dwelling quarters. Inspector Eastwood minuted the report that the constable had acted wisely, but Superintendent Butt disagreed and felt that firing a revolver was 'an unusual method to adopt' and not justified. The report was forwarded to Colonel Pearson who remarked that he did not attach much blame to the officer and, after the Commissioner had been informed, the matter was allowed to rest.

A few months later, on 13 October 1887, the secretary of the South London Rifle Club wrote to the Commissioner stating that he had seen police officers at Nunhead range firing their annual practice [of six rounds]. He was so appalled at the poor standard of marksmanship that he offered a challenge cup, plus a number of cash prizes, to be competed for by all ranks of the Metropolitan Police. There may have been an element of self-preservation in this offer for a number of the constables shooting so badly were the same men who patrolled the area in which he lived. The offer was refused although the Commissioner added that he was prepared to allow police to practise privately, in their own time and at their own expense, if they wished.

The autumn of 1887 and the 'Battle of Trafalgar Square' saw the biggest confrontation yet experienced by the Metropolitan Police. Trouble had been brewing since the summer when many of London's vagrants took up residence in the square and refused to move. Political agitators had turned the squatters into a volatile and potentially dangerous mob. Matters finally came to a head at a mass rally, which had been banned, in Trafalgar Square on Sunday 13 November 1887.

About 1,700 police were deployed four deep along the south side of the square and two deep on the other sides, with another 2,000 held in reserve at key points. At 4 p.m. there was an organized attack against every part of the police cordon and despite assistance from mounted men [the first time that the Mounted Branch had been used in this role] the thin blue line was in danger of being overwhelmed. A squadron of Life Guards supported the police in Waterloo Place, two companies of Foot Guards from St. George's Barracks reinforced the north side of the square and a troop of cavalry, escorting a magistrate armed with a copy of the Riot Act, forced their way along Whitehall.

It was the first time since 1866 that soldiers had been called out in aid of the civil power and by 6 p.m. the situation was under control, although sporadic rioting continued for another three weeks. Although no one had been killed, so many injured had been taken to Charing Cross Hospital that the wards and receiving-rooms were full and rows of casualties were lying in the courtyard and on the pavement outside.

A year later, following the inevitable inquiry and a series of clashes with the Home Office, Warren departed. James Munro, the new Commissioner, held the reins of office from 3 December 1888 until 21 June 1890 when he too, disenchanted with the Home Office, suddenly resigned. During his eighteen months he had efficiently handled a major dock strike and a minor police strike. The strength of the Force had risen to 14,995.

The Battle of Trafalgar Square was probably responsible for a small hollow granite tower which was erected in the south-east corner of the square towards the end of the nineteenth century. Many Londoners vaguely thought that it was something to do with the sewers, but it was in fact a secret observation post with a reinforced door. The interior was just large enough to hold three police officers who monitored demonstrations through the ten vertical slits let into the sides of the tower. A hand-cranked telephone with a direct line to Scotland Yard enabled the observers to call up reinforcements.

5
Firearms Training

Munro was succeeded by Colonel Sir Edward Bradford, a distinguished cavalry officer and a veteran of the Indian Mutiny. His missing left arm was the result of a close encounter with a tiger and not, as many supposed, with a mutineer.

On 20 January 1892 a police sergeant, Joseph Joyce, was shot by an armed burglar named Wenzell in Charing Cross Road. Despite his severe injuries Joyce managed to hold his struggling prisoner until help arrived. The sergeant died of his injuries and his murderer was hanged at Newgate Prison on 16 August. For some reason the death of P.S. Joyce did not rouse the clamour associated with the murder of a policeman, despite the fact that he was the first officer for eight years to die of gunshot wounds.

In November 1893 the Receiver asked if all the weapons issued to divisions were still required and, if so, should more be purchased. As a result, superintendents were directed to submit reports stating the exact number of revolvers carried by police during the winter of 1892/3. The returns showed that although a number of weapons had been occasionally issued for such reasons as 'guarding the van in which the Dynamite Prisoners were conveyed' only a few revolvers were still being drawn on night duty in outer sub-divisons. Many stations therefore now held guns surplus to requirements and in 'P' Division, for example, only six revolvers from a stock of 165 had been regularly issued. A memorandum dated 14 November 1893 altered the scale of issue to ten revolvers for an inner division and 50 to each outer division; surplus weapons to be returned to the Receiver's store.

By 1901 most of the sergeant instructors had been retired or promoted and the annual range practice was often supervised by any rank with army experience. In compliance with the original police order, the revolver (a Webley gateload model) was still loaded by the officer in charge and passed to the next firer. He in turn stepped forward, fired his six rounds and handed back the weapon to be unloaded and reloaded. But firearms and untrained men are a lethal combination and so it proved for 'R' Division on 31 October 1901. A group of constables at the Ammunition Works, East Greenwich, were being coached by P.C. 577 Walton who had served seven years with the colours before joining the Force in 1894. Walton showed the class how to aim and fire, but miscounted the rounds and fired five instead of six. He stepped back from the firing-point and as he began to unload, the sixth round fired. The bullet passed through the left thigh of one of his colleagues, P.C. Farley, and struck the left knee of a second officer, P.C. Reed.

On the same afternoon another group of sergeants and constables from the same division, supervised by Sub-Divisional Inspector Lee, were assembled at the Gravel Pits, Bexley Road, Eltham. Police Sergeant 16 Macdougall completed his practice but also made the fatal mistake, literally, of firing only five rounds instead of six. He handed the weapon to another sergeant who began to unload; two empty cases had been ejected when the sixth round was fired. The bullet struck Macdougall under the jaw and shattered his spine; he died two days later in the Cottage Hospital at Egham.

With a gateload revolver, as the name implies, it was necessary to operate a small gate at the rear of the cylinder before the gun could be loaded. Pushing the loading gate to one side exposed one of the six chambers in the cylinder, but it was still essential to thumb the hammer back halfway. This last action locked the hammer in the half-cock position and disengaged a stop, thus allowing the cylinder to be manually rotated. Each chamber could then be loaded, one at a time, through the loading-gate aperture. In order to unload, the hammer was again drawn back to half-cock position and the gate opened. Empty cases were then ejected singly through the gate aperture by means of the ejector rod; this swing-out rod was housed in the cylinder spindle when not in use. Apparently no one had realized that if a particular component in the mechanism was worn, it could allow the hammer to disengage from the half-cock position and fall forward. If this happened when a chambered live round was in line with the firing-pin the revolver would fire, without any pressure on the trigger. This may well have been the cause of the two accidents to 'R' Division personnel, although there is nothing in the records to suggest that the two revolvers in question were ever stripped and examined.

Superintendent Wakeford of 'R' reported the two shootings to Assistant Commissioner Howard who roundly blamed the range officers for lack of supervision and Wakeford for appointing them in the first place. On 2 November 1901 Howard sent a memorandum to all divisional superintendents asking for their suggestions on future safety precautions at the annual firing practices. Their replies, with few exceptions, were generally useless and included one from the super-intendent at Vine Street that blanks be used instead of live ammunition! One of the exceptions, of course, was from Wakeford who questioned every aspect of police firearms training and particularly the instruction that obliged untrained sergeants to load, issue and unload revolvers when parading reliefs. He also suggested that all live firing be conducted on a properly constructed range, the person in charge to be qualified and a scoring system instituted to ensure that each man fired all six rounds in the weapon. Finally, all divisional revolvers should be used in rotation, in case any were defective.

The end-product of these deliberations was a two-page police order headed 'Revolver Target Practice' which was published on 18 July 1902. A firer was now permitted to load and unload his own revolver on the range, provided that he was personally supervised by a chief inspector or inspector in charge. Furthermore, 'A careful count is to be kept of the shots fired by each individual' and any defective round should be withdrawn 'with great care at the firing-point, while holding the revolver facing the target'. There were also seven commonsense safety rules, as for example, '(e) No man will handle his weapon on the range except when standing in position at the firing point.' In addition, each recruit [or candidate as he was then known] before being posted to a division was to be instructed 'as to the manner of using and handling a revolver'. A supply of revolvers and a quantity of drill rounds was to be supplied to the Preparatory Class for that purpose.

As the prospective range officers were as inexperienced as the men being supervised, the police order also included a complete drill sequence for handling a gateload revolver. These instructions were reasonably explicit as is shown by the section on loading, although the word 'pouch' is used both for the revolver holster (first paragraph) and the ammunition pouch. The breech is in fact the loading-gate.

'On the word "Ready": Seize the pistol with the right hand, unbutton the pouch with the left, draw the pistol from the belt and pass it to the left hand, holding it nearly upright with the forefinger outside the trigger guard, and half cock with the right hand. Open the breech with the forefinger and thumb of the right hand, take the cartridges from the pouch (holding them by the rim) with the forefinger and thumb of the right hand, place one in each chamber, pressing them well home with the thumb, revolving the cylinder at

Range training was suspended during the conversion period, but by the end of 1905 a total of 345 converted Webleys had been issued and divisions resumed the annual firing practice. Another 25 weapons were later each fitted with a rebounding hammer, but the fate of the 304 unconverted gateload revolvers is not known. Regulations concerning training and the issue of revolvers remained unchanged and in fact were again published in a police order dated 27 April 1906. This P.O. also belatedly informed the Force about a new Pistols Act which had been law since 1903. Although the Act only provided a few minor controls, at least it was made an offence to sell firearms to the mentally disordered or to anyone under 18 years of age.

In the following year, on the other side of the English Channel, a bungled assassination attempt would lead, eighteen months later, to the murder of a London policeman and a small boy.

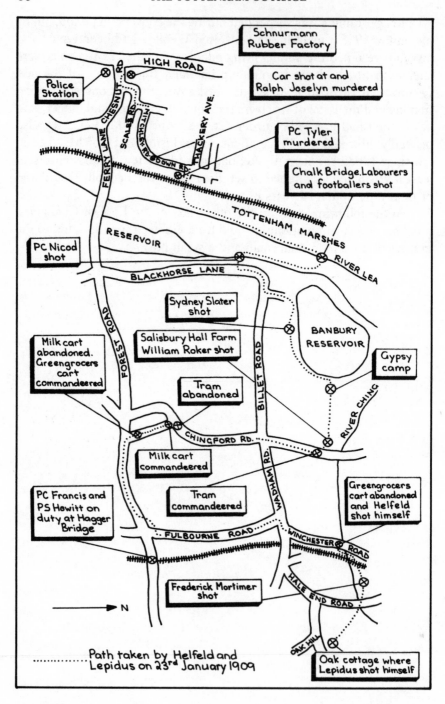

Schnurmann Rubber Factory

Police Station

HIGH ROAD

Car shot at and Ralph Joselyn murdered

PC Tyler murdered

Chalk Bridge. Labourers and footballers shot

FERRY LANE

CHESNUT. RD.

SCALE RD.

HITCHEN RD.

DOWN RD.

THACKERY AVE.

TOTTENHAM MARSHES

RESERVOIR

PC Nicod shot

RIVER LEA

BLACKHORSE LANE

Sydney Slater shot

BANBURY RESERVOIR

FOREST ROAD

Salisbury Hall Farm William Roker shot

Milk cart abandoned. Greengrocers cart commandeered

Gypsy camp

BILLET ROAD

Tram abandoned

RIVER CHING

CHINGFORD RD.

Milk cart commandeered

WADHAM RD.

Greengrocers cart abandoned and Helfeld shot himself

PC Francis and PS Hewitt on duty at Hagger Bridge

Tram commandeered

FULBOURNE ROAD

WINCHESTER ROAD

HALE END ROAD

N

Frederick Mortimer shot

OAK HILL

Path taken by Helfeld and Lepidus on 23rd January 1909

Oak cottage where Lepidus shot himself

6

The Tottenham Outrage

On 1 May 1907 an anarchist plot in Paris to kill the President of France aborted when the assassin's bomb exploded in his pocket and blew him to pieces. His companions crossed the Channel and two of them, Paul Helfeld aged 21 and Jacob Lepidus [both surnames were false], the 35-year-old brother of the dead man, fled to Scotland and went into hiding for more than a year. Eventually, desperately short of money, they made their way to London where Helfeld went to work at the Schnurmann Rubber Factory in Chestnut Road, Tottenham. He left after a few weeks complaining that the job was too hard, but he had, in the meantime, taken a keen interest in the collection of the weekly wages. Every Saturday the wages clerk, Albert Keyworth, aged 17, was taken in the factory owner's car, driven by Joseph Wilson, to a bank in South Hackney where he drew £80 in gold, silver and copper for the wage bill. On his return, carrying a canvas money-bag, he walked through the factory gates to the cashier's office; Wilson remained in the car.

At 10.30 a.m. on Saturday 23 January 1909, Helfeld and Lepidus, armed respectively with a .32 Browning and a 6.5mm 1894 model Bergmann pistol, were lounging one on each side of the factory entrance. Both weapons were magazine fed and self-loading although commonly, but inaccurately, called automatics. The car arrived a few minutes later. Keyworth got out and as he walked across the pavement he was seized from behind by Lepidus who tried to snatch the bag. During the struggle both of them rolled into the gutter where the chauffeur joined in, held Lepidus in a headlock, and pulled him off the clerk. At this point Helfeld fired a number of shots at Wilson which riddled his heavy leather driving coat and one slanting shot actually passed through each layer of his clothing, including his vest. However, in the words of the police report 'in a miraculous and unaccountable way he escaped injury'. Meanwhile Lepidus managed to snatch the canvas bag and fired at Keyworth as he regained his feet; the bullet missed.

Two 'N' Division constables, 403 Tyler and 510 Newman, clearly heard the shots in Tottenham Police Station which was on the corner of

Tottenham High Road and Chestnut Road, and ran out down the station steps. They turned the corner in time to see George Smith, a burly gas stoker, tackle Lepidus and bring him down. As the two men wrestled on the ground Helfeld straddled their bodies and fired four times at his moving target, which was Smith's head. Two bullets creased Smith's scalp, one missed and the other hit him in the chest below the collar-bone. His 'escape from death was equally remarkable' stated the official report and he survived to be photographed proudly wearing his bullet-holed coat. The two gunmen ran along Chestnut Road, followed by P.C. Tyler on foot and P.C. Newman in the motor car which was still being driven by Wilson. A number of unmarried constables lived above the police station and two of these, 406 Bond and 637 Fraiser, jumped through the open window of the locker-room and joined the chase. They were followed by several night duty officers who, roused by the commotion, hastily donned clothing and ran out of the front entrance.

The fugitives, occasionally turning and firing at the crowd which had joined the hue and cry, ran through Scales Road and into Mitchley Road where Helfeld stopped to reload. The car accelerated towards them and both men opened fire. A fusillade of bullets smashed the windscreen and several pierced the vehicle's radiator; both the driver and P.C. Newman were injured by flying glass. Ralph Joselyne, aged 10 running towards the car, possibly for protection and crouching as he ran, suddenly tumbled into the kerb with blood flowing from his mouth. One of the bullets had passed at an angle through his body. Cradled in the arms of a leatherworker's wife, the little boy died before he could be taken to hospital.

By this time those on foot had caught up and P.C. Bond borrowed a small revolver from someone in the crowd and fired four shots – they all missed. The gunmen now headed towards a railway foot-bridge at the end of Down Road which would enable them to cross on to Tottenham Marshes. P.C.s Tyler and Newman tried to head them off by cutting across some waste ground where they were protected by a five-foot-high wall which surrounded a Council depot. Tyler, aged 31, an ex-soldier and the more active of the two, was in the lead as the fugitives ran out from behind the other end of the wall. He shouted at them to surrender; Helfeld stopped, took careful aim and shot Tyler through the head. Newman remained with his fallen comrade who was carried to Oak Villa, a house in nearby Thackery Avenue. A doctor was summoned and the Constable was taken by ambulance to Tottenham Hospital where he died five minutes after admission. Tyler had been a policeman for six years and married for twelve months.

Meanwhile a message had been sent to the station for firearms but they were safely locked in a cupboard and the key could not be found. Eventually the lock was smashed and armed officers on bicycles, their own or borrowed, made their way towards the footbridge. Another message to the Divisional station at Stoke Newington requested armed reinforcements, and policemen from surrounding stations were told to converge on Tottenham Marshes.

Lepidus and Helfeld had now been forced to turn north-east and were running between a canal and the west bank of the River Lea, looking for a crossing place. A number of footballers and some labourers working on the marsh joined the chase and three of them were wounded by the gunmen as they crossed the river over Chalk Bridge. They jogged on until they came to Mill Stream Bridge which spanned a reservoir tributary and here they rested, firing continually and wounding two more of their pursuers. P.C. 313 Nicod borrowed a revolver and crawled forward to get a better shot, but the weapon was defective; before he could move back out of range he was hit in the left thigh and left leg. The chase continued along the south side of Banbury Reservoir where Sidney Slater, a horse keeper who had outdistanced the rest of the pack, was fired at six or seven times and disabled. P.C. 267 Spedding managed to get within forty yards and fired several shots from a borrowed revolver, all of which missed. Both fugitives were tiring and most of the shooting was left to Helfeld, who used his left arm as a support, while Lepidus reloaded.

Crossing a gypsy encampment the two men fired at anything moving, scattering gypsies and stampeding ponies, but fortunately there were no casualties, human or equine. At Salisbury Hall Farm the gunmen stopped and rested behind a haystack while Helfeld took pot-shots at the posse to keep them at bay. The pursuers went to ground but even so William Roker, a 32-year-old labourer, was hit in both legs and seriously wounded.

The farmyard abutted Chingford Road which carried a single-track tramline with loops at various points to enable trams to pass. Both fugitives broke cover, dashed into the road and hijacked tramcar no. 9 which was en route to Lea Bridge Road, Leyton. After stopping his vehicle the driver fled to the top deck so Lepidus put a pistol to the conductor's head and made him drive instead. As the tram pulled away the three passengers, an elderly man and a woman with her child, flung themselves on the floor as the windows were shattered by bullets and shotgun pellets fired by the crowd. Approaching a loop line near St. John's Road, the conductor slowed down to allow another tram, going in the opposite direction, to pass and the woman and child scrambled off unseen. The male passenger, Edward Loveday aged 63, was shot in the throat when he attempted to follow them. Meanwhile the tram which had just passed was stopped by Police Sergeant 7 Hale, emptied of its passengers, boarded by about forty policemen, and reversed in pursuit of tramcar no. 9.

Further along the road the captured tram was in danger of being overtaken by a pony-drawn cart commandeered by P.C. 50 Hawkins who was carrying a service pistol. However, as Hawkins was about to fire, Helfeld brought down the pony with one carefully aimed shot and the cart crashed, spilling the P.C. and his driver onto the road. As the tram reached the next major bend the conductor told Helfeld that there was a police station round the next corner; the two men jumped from the tram and ran to an unattended milk-cart. The driver, George Conyard, hurried from a nearby shop and was shot in the chest and right arm when he tried to stop the two gunmen.

The milk-cart was driven along Farnham Avenue towards Forest Road where it crashed while taking a bend. Abandoning the wreckage Lepidus and Helfeld stopped a greengrocer's horse and cart by pointing a gun at the young driver's head and the lad hastily leapt from the driving seat. Lepidus took the reins and Helfeld sat on the tailboard with a pistol in each hand firing at their pursuers. By now the pack consisted of a large number of policemen and civilians, some with pistols and revolvers and the remainder unarmed. There was also one constable who was seen pedalling a bicycle furiously, a cutlass balanced across the handlebars. Virtually everyone in the chase was mounted or carried on anything with wheels or hooves and the posse was led by motor car, L.N. 1662. This vehicle, driven by chauffeur Frederick Williams, had been boarded at 11.30 a.m. in Forest Road by P.C.s 747 Shakespeare and 558 Gibbs. They were accompanied by a civilian, Mr Thomas Brown, armed with a double-barrelled shotgun, who was exchanging shots with the gunmen. Mr Brown later claimed 12s 6d damages for a bullet hole through his trousers.

Police Sergeant Howitt and P.C. 616 Francis were on duty at Hagger Bridge when they heard shots and the sound of police whistles.

Both officers attempted to stop the horse and cart, but jumped aside when several shots were fired at them. However, their action caused the horse to swerve off the road and across some waste land into Fulborne Road, and thence into Wadham Road. From there the fugitives turned into Winchester Road, where the horse and cart were abandoned, and Lepidus and Helfeld ran to the River Ching. Lepidus succeeded in climbing the six-foot boundary fence on the river bank, but his companion tried and failed. The leading pursuers were almost at his heels and he shouted to Lepidus, 'Go on, save yourself. I've only two left,' and shot himself above the right eye. He was still alive and before he could fire again he was disarmed. Struggling violently he was overpowered and taken to the Prince of Wales Hospital.

Now the posse concentrated on Lepidus, and P.C. 789 Zeithing was within a few yards of him when the gunman turned and fired three shots. All the bullets missed Zeithing although two passed through his greatcoat lapels and the third passed over his left shoulder. This last bullet went through the chest and out the back of a civilian in the chase, Frederick Mortimer, who had just thrown a brick at the gunman. Lepidus ran across Hale End Road, through a field, and disappeared from sight behind Oak Cottages, Hale End. The end cottage had four rooms and a lean-to which served as a scullery. It was occupied by Charles Rolstone a coal porter, who was at work, but his wife and three children were in the house.

Shortly after noon Mrs Rolstone heard police whistles and went to the front gate with her son, but was told to go back inside as there was a murderer in the vicinity. She went indoors and saw Lepidus, his face covered in blood, presumably caused by birdshot from the fowling pieces which had been fired at him, peering through a small window in the lean-to. Mrs Rolstone ran from the cottage screaming 'Oh, my children,' and fell sobbing into the arms of a neighbour. Charles Schaffer, a baker who had stayed with the chase throughout, and P.C. 36 Dewhurst burst open the lean-to door and brought the other two children safely out from the kitchen. Fortunately for them the gunman had meanwhile moved upstairs after trying to hide in the front room chimney.

Lepidus now appeared at the front bedroom window but was driven back by a hail of fire from the posse. P.C. 636 Eagles, one of the 'J' Division officers at the scene, had borrowed a self-loading pistol from someone in the crowd. He climbed a borrowed ladder placed against the rear of the cottage and opened a back bedroom window. At the same time, two 'N' Division men, P.C. 714 Cater and P.C. (CID) Dixon, both armed with service revolvers, broke into the house through a ground floor window. A mongrel dog tied up outside was released and sent up the stairs in the hope that it would flush out the gunman or divert his attention. Eagles, from his vantage-point on the ladder, saw the dog appear on the landing, but at the same instant Lepidus pointed a pistol through the partly opened bedroom door. The constable tried to shoot, but was unable to operate the safety catch on his borrowed weapon; his life was probably saved by the fact that Lepidus was nearly out of ammunition. Eagles slid down the ladder and was joined by Dixon, Cater and Inspector Gould, also armed.

P.C. Eagles exchanged his defective pistol for Dixon's service revolver and the three officers, Eagles, Dixon and Cater in that order, mounted the narrow staircase and onto the tiny landing. The front bedroom door was now shut and Dixon called on Lepidus to surrender. There was no response so Eagles fired twice and Cater once through the door panels and this was followed by a shot from inside the room. The party burst through the door and saw their quarry, his face covered in blood, lying on a small bed in the corner of the room. Eagles snatched the gunman's pistol from his hand but Lepidus was apparently dead. His body was taken down into the yard where death was certified by two doctors before it was removed to Walthamstow Mortuary. Eagles believed, until the inquest, that he had fired the fatal shot, but a comparison of the bullets proved otherwise. The bullet taken from the dead man's head matched one fired from the Bergmann pistol and not Eagles's service revolver. It was clear that the police had missed and Lepidus had shot himself.

The chase had lasted more than two hours and covered a distance of more than six miles. Approximately 400 rounds had been fired by the two murderers and there were 25 casualties, two of them fatal and several serious. It provided a field-day for the newspapers and the *Daily Mirror* devoted the whole front page on Monday 25 January to photographs of thirteen of the dead and injured. These appeared under a double headline, 'Murderous Outbreak of Russian Anarchists in London: Three killed, Many Injured. Heroic Policemen among the Slain'. Many papers also carried articles blaming lax administration of the Aliens Act, and several queried the efficiency of police firearms training and out-of-date weaponry. A special report was prepared for

King Edward VII and the Commissioner was advised that His Majesty found it 'almost inconceivable that such a thing could have occurred in these days on the very outskirts of London'.

Among the wreaths laid on P.C. Tyler's grave after the service [he was given a public funeral on 29 January] was one from the Imperial Russian Consul-General. An accompanying letter to the Commissioner expressed admiration for the London Metropolitan Police and deep sympathy for the bereaved but added, 'The murderer who is said to be a Russian subject was not a Russian speaking ethnographically'. Both Helfeld and Lepidus were born in Latvia, at that time part of the Russian Empire. Helfeld lingered on in hospital until he died on 12 February, following an operation. While he was alive the Home Office feared a 'Fenian'-type rescue and the constables in the ward and those patrolling the hospital grounds were all armed. The local Super-intendent noted that this caused 'a good deal of nervous tension to the authorities including doctors and nurses'.

In the aftermath of the outrage came the inevitable claims for compensation, thirty-one of them, for damage or injury. Mrs Lizzie Green claimed for her cap which had been snatched from her head [probably with a view to disguise] by one of the gunmen. Arthur Rowntree's bicycle needed 3s 9d worth of repairs after being used, with permission, by P.C. 50 Hawkins – a determined man who had borrowed the machine after his pony and cart episode. The owners of the injured pony made a claim [false] for vet's fees and exaggerated depreciation in the value of the animal. An original approach was made by the employers of George Dawkins on his behalf. He had been driving a horse-drawn brick cart about half a mile from the incident when he heard shots and saw part of the chase. As a result he was obliged to soothe his ruffled nerves with half a pint of ale in the 'Victory' public house and since that date had become mentally disordered. Claim disallowed. Mr Thorogood, who lived in Oak Villa, claimed £1 10s for three pieces of carpet, a tablecloth and an overcoat which had been spoiled by blood from P.C. Tyler's wound as he lay dying on the floor.

Police Orders of 23 March stated that P.C.s Eagles, Cater, Dixon, Dewhurst and Nicod were to be promoted to sergeant, without examination, in recognition of their courage, and P.C.s Newman and Zeithing were to be advanced to the highest rate of pay for their rank. Inspector Gould, Sergeant Hale and Constables Spedding, Bond and three others, all of whom had been active during the pursuit, received awards from the Bow Street Court Reward Fund for their courage. Eagles, Cater and Dixon also received the retrospective award of the King's Police Medal when that decoration was instituted on 7 July 1909.

Ralph Joscelyne's mother never forgot her little son and she kept the shoes he had been wearing on the day he was killed. Following her last wish they were buried with her, when she herself died, nearly fifty years later.

7

The Siege of Sidney Street

On 4 February 1909 a Board consisting of three senior officers, convened by the Commissioner to evaluate acts of gallantry by police and civilians during the Tottenham outrage, was charged with a further task: 'Whether the service revolver is suitable or should be replaced by some other type and whether the number allotted to each station is adequate.' This second issue appears to have originated with Superintendent Jenkins of 'N' Division who, not unnaturally, suggested that instead of two revolvers at each station there should be six, of a modern design.

While the Board deliberated, Superintendent Quinn of Special Branch was increasingly uneasy about the ten .45 Webley Bulldog revolvers which were the only weapons available for his officers 'when engaged on protection or other dangerous duties'. These were all that remained of twelve such weapons which had been purchased for the C.I.D. back in 1882 during the Fenian troubles. Quinn sought the advice of Mr Churchill, a gunmaker of 8 Agar Street, who told him that his revolvers were out of date and quite worthless. In Mr Churchill's opinion, 'they would be a positive danger in a mêlée as, except at very close quarters, their shooting could not be depended upon'. He did however offer to buy them for 4s each, provided he supplied the replacements. By the end of the month Quinn had spoken to the Commissioner who authorized the purchase of two Colt 'automatic pocket pistols' at a cost of £3 3s each.

In March 1909 the Board recommended that the Webley revolvers supplied to the Force should be withdrawn and replaced by the Colt No. 3 automatic pistol. Nothing happened until 1910 when the subject was again raised and the Commissioner consulted the War Office about a suitable firearm for police use. Trials of various weapons were conducted at the Army Inspection Department, Enfield, and in due course the Chief Inspector of Small Arms reported his findings. First, the .32 calibre Webley & Scott automatic pistol should be adopted as a handgun for the Force and the same model, but in .22 calibre, used for training purposes. Secondly, a few officers from each division should receive instruction on these pistols at Enfield to enable them, in turn, to instruct their colleagues. By the end of 1910 none of these suggestions had been implemented, but the subject was to be revitalized following a siege in an East London street.

On Friday, 16 December 1910 at about 11.30 p.m., five City of London policemen were shot by armed burglars at the rear of a jeweller's shop in Houndsditch. Sergeants Bentley and Tucker, together with P.C. Choats, died from their wounds while Sergeant Bryant and P.C. Woodhams were seriously injured. The men responsible for the crime, all Russian nationals, were armed with self-loading pistols and during the fight one of them had been shot in the back by one of his own side. Nevertheless, the gang, which included a woman, escaped taking with them the wounded man.

At 12.30 p.m. the next day, as the result of belated information from a doctor, detectives entered 59 Grove Street in the East End and found the body of Poloski Morountzeff, alias George Gardstein. He was fully dressed, lying on a bloodstained bed, and had died from a gunshot wound in the back. A loaded 7.65mm Dreyse pistol and a quantity of ammunition, in several different calibres, was found in the room.

As the original crime had been committed in the City of London and the criminals had gone to ground in the Metropolitan Police district both Forces liaised in the subsequent investigation. Several arrests were made, but police still searched for the last three men involved in the City killings. These were believed to be Fritz Svaars, Joseph Solokoff and Peter, nicknamed 'Peter the Painter', later identified as Peter Piaktow. Eventually the trail led to 100, Sidney Street, Stepney, a three-storey tenement building let off into rooms and occupied by a number of Russian immigrants.

According to an informant, Fritz Svaars and a friend known only as Josef or Yoshka were being sheltered by a Mrs Gershon in a room on the second floor. Svaars was wanted for murder and robbery in Latvia in 1905. In the early hours of 3 January 1911, the City and Metropolitan forces each deployed 100 men into the area. Surrounding streets were cordoned off and armed police occupied vantage-points covering the front and back of no. 100, whence the occupants had been evacuated by 4.45 a.m. Mrs Gershon had already been lured out by a subterfuge, quietly detained and questioned, but it was some time before she admitted to the presence of the two men in her room. The last policeman to leave the house left the front door propped open and the gas lamp was left alight in the passage. Snow, which had been falling intermittently all night, was now turning to sleet and dawn was still three hours away.

At 7.30 a.m. as the sky lightened senior police officers at their command post, in an archway entrance opposite no. 100, decided to give the wanted men an opportunity to surrender. Detective Inspector Wensley left the group and threw a handful of pebbles up at the top floor window. There was no response and he turned back into the archway entrance to find more pebbles. Suddenly six shots were fired in rapid succession through the first floor window at the command group in their archway. All the shots missed except for one bullet which struck Detective Sergeant Leeson in the chest and came out through his back.

City police, in another yard entrance nearby, returned fire and the battle had begun. Leeson staggered into a yard behind the archway and the gates were slammed behind him. Poor Leeson thought he was dying and asked Wensley to 'Give my love to the children. Bury me at Putney.' Despite his wound Leeson declined to be treated by Dr Solomon Krestin who practised at 98, Sidney Street, as he doubted his medical qualifications, and he was examined by Dr Johnstone who had run all the way from his surgery in Mile End Road. With great diffficulty the wounded man was manhandled through the falling sleet, over a 10-foot-high boundary wall, onto an outhouse roof and thence down into a brewery yard. While crossing the wall the stretcher-party came under heavy fire from the attic window of no. 100, about 40 yards away, and a detective constable was wounded in the hand. Leeson was eventually admitted to London Hospital at 8.30 a.m., an hour after he had been shot.

Some of the volunteer stretcher-bearers were unable to move for about half an hour because of the continuous and accurate fire directed at them, and the command group discussed the situation. In the words of Superintendent Mulvaney, 'It was palpable that these men dominated the situation, there was no approach to the house but by the front door, the roofs were of the kind known as gable and unapproachable. It was equally plain that any attack by the front door would have resulted in a great sacrifice of life. Their weapons were far superior to our revolvers, of which at this time we only had a few. It was therefore decided that Military Aid be sought as more effective weapons were required.'

Following priority telephone calls to the Deputy Commissioner and the Home Secretary, authority was given to call in the army.

Meanwhile the two gunmen, continually shifting from window to window on different storeys, from the attic to the ground floor, fired at anything that moved with weapons which had now been identified as Mauser pistols. Further police reinforcements arrived and by 9 a.m. about 500 men, some of them mounted, were needed to control the ever-increasing crowds of spectators. Superintendent Mulvaney rode to the Tower of London and returned at about 10.15 a.m. with a subaltern, two colour-sergeants and 17 men, all volunteers, of the 1st Battalion, Scots Guards.

Three of the guardsmen were taken to a bottling store on the top floor of Mann & Crossman's brewery. The store had three large slatted windows set at right angles to Sidney Street and the marksmen could just see the attic and second floor windows of no. 100. Aimed shots from the guardsmen's new short Lee-Enfield rifles soon drove the two gunmen down from their commanding attic and second floor windows onto the first and ground floors. Here they were exposed to equally accurate fire from soldiers in the houses opposite, in positions formerly manned by police. The other Scots Guards were placed across the road in front of the police cordon at each end of Sidney Street.

Between 11 a.m. and 12 noon another 65 policemen armed with service revolvers arrived from surrounding divisions. Other officers who had been sent out to scour local gunsmiths arrived in taxi-cabs piled with shotguns and rook rifles which were issued to men with military or shooting experience. Mr Churchill, the Home Secretary, arrived just before midday accompanied by catcalls from some of the crowd who recalled his strenuous opposition to Bills that would have restricted alien immigration.

From 12 until 12.30 p.m. the volume of fire from both sides reached a crescendo and thereafter died away to scattered shots. Just before 1 p.m. smoke began to trickle from the chimney and broken windows and in Mulvaney's opinion the fugitives had deliberately fired the building to try and escape in the smoke and confusion. As the smoke thickened one of the gunmen leaned out too far through a window in order to shoot and immediately became the target of concentrated rifle fire. He fell back, almost certainly killed by a bullet through the head. By 1.30 p.m. the first flames were clearly visible and although the Fire Brigade appliances were at the scene, called at 1.3 p.m., the firemen were dissuaded from tackling the flames. Churchill's orders were to let the house burn. At about this time a second detachment of Scots Guards, three officers and 51 other ranks, arrived with a Maxim machine-gun drawn on a cart. A section of Royal Engineers had arrived from Chatham and the last and most impressive military unit, a troop of the Royal Horse Artillery, trotted up at 2.40 p.m.

The last shots from inside the house may have been fired at 1.50 p.m., although by that time the building was a raging inferno and the supposed shots may have been ammunition exploding in the heat. Just after 2.10 p.m., when the roof had caved in, firemen began to play their hoses on the gutted shell of the house from the front and back. However, the siege was to claim one more victim when the upper floor and part of one side wall collapsed and buried five firemen in the rubble. They were dragged out and taken to London Hospital, but District Officer Pearson later died of his injuries. The remains of two charred bodies, together with a 7.65mm Browning and two 7.63mm Mauser pistols, were later recovered from the debris inside the house.

The entire episode had been an incredible affair from start to finish. English detectives hunting the killers made their inquiries among a close knit community many of whom only understood, or only admitted to understanding, Russian or Yiddish. The investigation was further complicated by the number of aliases used by most of the suspects. Morountzeff for example, in addition to Gardstein, was also known as Garstin, Poolka Milowitz, Morintz, Morin, but held a passport in the name of Schafshi Khan. The City police were convinced that the group responsible were Anarchists, but the Metropolitan Police was equally sure that they were criminals, albeit with Anarchist associations. Certainly the number of alleged refugees from Tsarist oppression who were wanted in Europe for criminal, rather than political, offences lent support to the latter theory.

Police positioned around 100, Sidney Street carried revolvers that were thirty years old, and the arms of some of their City colleagues were even more ancient, and included obsolete Adams revolvers. The few rifles available were elderly Martinis, or Lee-Metfords fitted with a .22 tube for target shooting at 25 yards on an indoor range. Obviously none of the senior police officers present were aware of the destructive power of a Mauser self-loading pistol, the backsight of which was calibrated to 1,000 metres. The 7.63 millimetre cartridge, breech-loaded in a clip of ten, fired a nickel-covered bullet with a muzzle energy of 385ft lb. Four years later, during the First World War, it was found that this bullet could penetrate both front and back of two steel helmets placed side by side from 100 metres. Neither did they appreciate the mentality of gunmen prepared to fire at an injured man on a stretcher and his helpers. Another factor, although not known at the time, was the amount of ammunition available to the besieged. During the course of the battle they are estimated to have fired between 400 and 600 shots, answered by about 1,000 rounds from the assorted weapons used by police and 500 rounds by the military.

Despite heavy gunfire for more than five hours, only two policemen, a guardsman and four onlookers were slightly injured, mostly by spent bullets. A postman insisted on completing his delivery, and was allowed to do so with a police escort, and several neighbours, including children, came to their front doors or looked out of windows from time to time to watch the proceedings. The nearest police cordon was only 90 yards away from the house, although at an angle, and officers sheltering in Sidney Street doorways were all well within range of the opposing Mausers. Only the fire of the Scots Guards made it impossible for the two gunmen to take accurate aim, otherwise there must have been a heavy casualty list.

Starting the next morning much of England's Press lambasted everyone in sight including immigrants, police and Mr Churchill. The *Daily Telegraph* complained of the 'Foreign riff-raff introduced into England' and according to the *Pall Mall Gazette* the Continent's 'most abandoned ruffians' had been invited to call themselves political refugees and come to live in Britain. Many of the editorials censured police handling of the affair and the call for military aid. Several questioned why it had not been possible, as police were in the house at one time, to contain the gunmen in their room or quietly enter it and arrest them. *The Times* also felt that the police should have been able to cope without the army and completely disapproved of the Home Secretary's presence. Furthermore, it could not understand 'how the ruffians were to have been captured by the procedure adopted'. Moral issues were ignored by the *Daily Mirror* whose readers were treated to two dozen photographs and diagrams, plus dramatic side headings such as 'Death amid flames', 'Rescue under Fire' and many others. The immaculate Superintendent Mulvaney, driven in a pony and trap to brief the guardsmen who were waiting to march, was totally transformed by a piece of descriptive journalism. 'Get the Guards! The Houndsditch assassins are firing on the police! The Military are wanted.' 'These words, gasped out by a breathless and dishevelled police-sergeant to the Beefeater at the main entrance gate of the Tower of London, gave the men of the Scots Guards stationed there the first warning that their services were needed.' All good stuff and splendid value for a halfpenny (real money – not decimal currency).

Reaction in foreign newspapers varied and ranged from the French who generally approved to the Germans who strongly disapproved and referred to 'shooting sparrows with cannon'. In the USA the Press took the opportunity to score a few game points after the numerous occasions in the past when American use of firearms had drawn adverse comment in the British Press. According to the *New York Sun*, 'John Bull seems to be beginning to fear that his martial anti-burglar campaign in Stepney has made him look ridiculous. Many of his newspapers tell him so . . .'

The last detachment of Guards, a machine-gun and two quick-firing field guns, all arriving when the siege was over, had reduced tragedy to farce and allowed the world to snigger; but what were the options open to senior police officers on that bleak Tuesday morning? There were six adults, two of them old people, and eight children, whose ages ranged from 1½ to sixteen years, who had to be evacuated from the building. To leave them in a situation where they might be caught in a gun battle or even worse, used as hostages, was unthinkable. In the event the noise made by moving all these occupants must have alerted the gunmen in their back room. The options were five in number – starting with the arrest of the fugitives.

1. Opening the door from their room exposed a tiny landing and the head of a narrow staircase from the first floor. There was no cover from fire and the gunmen were armed, desperate murderers. Who would be the first suicidal man to approach the door – certainly not one of the journalists who advocated such a move.

2. Contain the fugitives in the back room by posting armed officers – but where? Two fairly slim policemen [unheard of in 1911] might have been able to lie side by side on the staircase and rest their antiquated revolvers on the landing. If the gunmen burst out of their room, Mausers blazing, the two policemen immobile on the stairs would have been trapped. Police below them dare not fire for fear of hitting their colleagues and the staircase becomes a killing ground – still with no guarantee that one or both of the murderers will be disabled.

3. Clear the building and use an interpreter with a speaking-trumpet to call on the fugitives to surrender, telling them that they have nothing to fear [only the gallows]. In fact police threw pebbles to attract their attention, but stupidly within range of the Mausers.

4. Sterilize the immediate area by evacuating residents from nearby buildings, undoubtedly causing great inconvenience and some hardship, and establish a sit-out siege for as long as necessary. Unfortunately this type of operation requires a containment-party with weapons and training at least equal, and preferably superior, to those contained. This requirement was present at Spaghetti House, Balcombe Street and other sieges in the 1980s – it was conspicuously absent at Sidney Street in 1911.

The unpalatable fact that police were out-gunned, out-ranged and not equipped to handle the situation led inevitably to the last option. There was only one type of trained man armed with a weapon which could compete with a Mauser fired from behind cover, and he was readily available. The army, not for the first nor the last time, was called in to aid the civil power.

A King's Police Medal was awarded to each of the five City policemen and, in addition, the two who survived were promoted. Sergeant Leeson was also promoted, which allowed him a better pension, before he was invalided from the Force as the result of his injuries. 'Peter the Painter', variously described as an arch-criminal, the anarchist mastermind, or one of Stalin's agents, should have been nicknamed 'Peter the Red Herring'. Although doubtless aware of the Houndsditch enterprise he had not participated in the project and, had he been found, there was insufficient evidence to charge him even with being an accessory after the fact. As far as anarchism was concerned he was an academic anarchist who preferred books to bombs. He was never traced, although sightings continued for the next three years from cities as far apart as Naples, New York and Melbourne.

As the recriminations died away eager hands reached out to the compensation committee with claims which totalled £2,196 6s. Mr and Mrs Clemens, for example, were the old couple who occupied a ground floor room at no. 100 for a weekly rent of 2s 9d. They claimed £122 15s which included £65 for a large quantity of underwear and linen, allegedly Mrs Clemen's stock-in-trade, which had never existed. Her husband's claim for books valued at £12 had been prepared by his grandson who obviously copied the titles from a trade list, including the catalogue numbers and prices! The size of Charles Martin's claim [Martin owned 100, Sidney Street] caused the committee to comment that it had no intention of rebuilding his house on the lines of Buckingham Palace. Neither would the committee be responsible for neighbours' spoiled bread, miscarriages and the loss of a valuable sheep-dog.

Only one person was ever actually convicted of an offence connected with the City killings. Nina Vassilleva, Morountzeff's mistress and the woman who had been with the gang at Houndsditch, was found guilty of the comparatively minor offence of conspiracy with intent to break and enter. She was sentenced to two years' imprisonment, but five weeks later the conviction was quashed on the grounds of misdirection by the trial judge! As far as police were concerned it was a dismal end to a dismal episode.

8

The 'Evilly Disposed'

Sidney Street brought matters to a head and a decision on police firearms was now urgently needed. On 12 January 1911 fourteen modern pistols and revolvers were tested on the .22 rifle range of the 24th (County of London) Territorial Battalion at Kennington. The Home Secretary, the Commissioner and a gunmaker were among those present, and when Mr Churchill was asked if he would like to start the tests there was some slight confusion. The Churchills, Winston the politician and Robert the gunsmith, both reached for the first weapon. However, Winston Churchill later fired several of the guns and showed great interest in the Mauser, a pistol which he had carried in the Sudan campaign and again in the Second Boer War.

The final choice for a police handgun was the .32 Webley & Scott self-loading pistol. A detachable magazine with an 8-round capacity was housed in the butt, and the bullet developed a muzzle velocity of 1,050 feet per second. Home Office authority was sought to buy 1,000 of these pistols and, implementing the 1910 training recommendation, 100 single-shot models in .22 calibre. On 26 August an impatient Home Secretary wrote on the Home Office file, 'This has dragged interminably. Please report when the police are actually to be armed with the pistol.' Even so, it would be the end of the year before the first consignment was delivered.

Since 1908, correspondence had passed between the Royal Navy and the Metropolitan Police on the question of guarding HM ships refitting in Royal dockyards. It had been suggested that the armed Royal Marine pickets should be replaced by constables (also to be armed). As police, especially the Superintendent at Portsmouth dockyard, refused to be held responsible for fittings and stores on board, or for the safety of the ship, the Admiralty finally shelved the idea in June 1911. This question of armed police in dockyards may have prompted a Police Order dated 3 November 1911.

'Police armed with revolvers are, when they detect the approach of any person or persons whose actions are suspicious, to challenge such person or persons by calling out "Halt, who goes there?" If the person or persons fail to reply to the challenge or to give a satisfactory explanation and continue to advance, the Constable should, if circumstances permit, repeat the challenge and warn them that unless they stop he will fire, at the same time, if possible, blowing his whistle. If they still advance, and he has reason to infer from their actions or from the surrounding circumstances, that they are evilly disposed, it will be necessary for him to fire with the object of disabling them.

On hearing the sound of the police whistle, or the discharge of firearms, Police on adjoining beats are to hasten in the direction of the alarm and render assistance. A communication stating the cause of the disturbance and exact locality is to be sent as early as possible to the Officer in charge of the Establishment.

The officer in charge, on receipt of the alarm, will instantly call out all resident Police, and after issuing the available revolvers, direct them to proceed forthwith to the place indicated, where they will act as directed by the officer in charge.

It must be borne in mind that in any such emergency the Superintendent should be informed at the earliest possible opportunity, in order that he may take over the direction of further police enquiries.

The foregoing instructions apply especially to Magazine Stations, but are to be observed in all cases where Police are specially armed for the purpose of protecting property.'

Apart from introducing the standard challenge, which would have been a familiar warning to anyone in a naval or military station, the order states that the suspect should be disabled. This word can be interpreted in several ways, even when facing the 'evilly disposed', but it implies that the officer should fire to incapacitate rather than to kill. Although it must have been accepted that a person might die as the result of being shot, whatever the firer's intention, the object was not deliberately to cause death. This doctrine has survived to this day, and police still shoot to stop rather than to kill.

During the last two months of 1911 a total of 920 Webley & Scott .32 pistols, complete with two magazines and sixteen rounds for each weapon, were delivered and issued to Divisions. Another six pistols were provided for the Preparatory Class and a number of divisional officers were selected to be instructed at Enfield on the new weapon. All .45 revolvers were returned to store for the Receiver to sell, thus recouping part of the cost of the pistols. In March 1912 the 100 .22 pistols were issued to stations for the use of Divisional Shooting Clubs which formed part of the Metropolitan Police Shooting League. The League was made responsible for producing printed safety regulations and the Commissioner, in a memorandum to his Superintendents dated 25 June 1912, outlined the conditions of use for the training pistols. They were only to be used 'under the guidance of officers who have been trained at

Enfield or elsewhere' and a special grant of 10,000 rounds of .22 ammunition would be made 'so as to afford as many as possible an opportunity of a preliminary practice'. Obviously the chance to allow men to practise in their own time with a weapon similar in weight and type to an operational pistol was too good to miss.

These facilities were not made available to dockyard police who later exchanged their naval Webley Mark IV revolvers for the .455 self-loading pistol when it was adopted by the Royal Navy in 1913.

By 1914 war clouds were beginning to gather and on 4 March the Comptroller of the Royal Mint requested that police on duty at the building should be armed. It was feared that foreign agents would enter the printing room and disrupt production of the new £1 and 10s banknotes which were to replace the gold coinage. The Commissioner agreed and the guards, who were drawn from 'H' Division, henceforth carried .32 pistols. An extra charge of 3d per weapon, per day, was promptly added to the Royal Mint's private service agreement.

On 4 August 1914, when war was declared, the strength of the force had risen to 22,048. This impressive figure was to be whittled away as 1,019 naval and army reservists were recalled to the colours and another 1,000 men were withdrawn to guard military establishments and strengthen the dockyard contingents. The ghosts of the policemen, who in 1864 had been told they needed military discipline, must have chuckled when 350 Metropolitan policemen were seconded for duty as drill instructors for the recruits of Kitchener's new army. Police pensioners and the enrolment of special constables helped to fill the numerous gaps. On 7 August, 281 old .450 Webley revolvers were issued from store and sent to police stations for defence against enemy attack. Fortunately the Kaiser's troops never crossed the English Channel and the elderly weapons remained silent.

The accidental shooting of a constable was responsible for a memorandum dated 1 September 1914 which called attention to the safety regulations, especially when handling automatic pistols. Later in the year, Police Orders of 15 December up-dated the old revolver drills to accommodate self-loading weapons. The actual regulations were unchanged except for a proviso that men selected for annual firing practice must first have received instruction on a .22 pistol. An attempt was also made to raise the standard of police shooting by introducing a minimum pass mark and the annual ammunition allotment was raised from six to 24 rounds.

Yearly practice now consisted of sixteen rounds fired in two groups of eight followed by another eight rounds to qualify. All firing took place at a distance of twenty yards from the target and the 'standard of efficiency' was four shots out of eight within a 15-inch ring. In the event, few officers fired the course because annual practice was suspended in January 1915. This was intended as a temporary measure, but munitions for war had priority and practice ammunition would not be available to the police for another six years.

The year 1915 saw the death of three policemen, two killed in an air raid and the third, Detective Constable Young, was shot in the chest by a retired army officer who was wanted for fraud. At his trial the accused claimed he had been drinking (he was in fact an alcoholic) and his revolver fired when the D.C. tried to arrest him. Although charged with murder he was only found guilty of manslaughter and sentenced to twelve years' imprisonment. Captain Gorges was the first man to shoot and kill a Metropolitan police officer and escape the hangman's noose.

In 1916, during the Easter uprising in Ireland, the Royal Irish Constabulary borrowed 143 Webley & Scott pistols and 3,000 rounds of ammunition from the Metropolitan Police. There were no other firearms incidents during the war.

On the outbreak of war a constable's weekly wage was 30s to 42s, depending on his length of service. During the next four years there was no increase in police pay although the cost of living had more than doubled; in fact it had spiralled by a staggering 151 per cent. Consequently by 1918 many policemen and their families were living in poverty and some, especially those on the lower pay scales, were actually undernourished. This had been recognized by almost everyone except the Government – even *The Times* was sympathetic.

On Friday, 30 August 1918, as the German armies fell back towards the Hindenburg Line, 6,000 Metropolitan policemen refused duty. Both the Home Secretary and the Commissioner were out of London, and Lloyd George, the Prime Minister, appears to have panicked. Armed troops were posted to main government buildings and the special constabulary was called out *en masse*. By the next morning virtually all uniform constables in the Metropolitan and City forces were on strike. Just after 1.30 p.m. that same afternoon, the strikers' delegation left 10, Downing Street having been granted an immediate increase in pay, pensions for widows and an establishment to represent the men's interests. At 6 a.m. on Sunday 1 September, the police were back on the streets of London – the shortest and most effective police strike in history was over. The Commissioner's head rolled and a new incumbent, General Sir Nevil Macready, son of a famous Victorian actor, took office on 3 September 1918.

Macready cannot have relished his task, especially after the Armistice on 11 November 1918. The end of the war brought civil disorder, another and unwarranted police strike, a resumption of Irish terrorism and an increasing use of motor cars and firearms by criminals. Nearly five years of wholesale slaughter on the Western Front had apparently cheapened the value of human life.

However, there were still domestic problems within the Force and one of these was the decision that inspectors and above would no longer carry swords, which were accordingly returned to store on 29 January 1919. This meant that officers were left with a patent leather belt complete with sword-slings but without the accompanying sword, so a further direction also withdrew the slings. This was the start of a lengthy affair which continued for the next two years and involved the Home Office, the Commissioner and all his superintendents and inspectors.

In March 1919, the Superintendents Representative Committee asked that the superintendents' sword-belt might be withdrawn and replaced by a sash or girdle. But they also considered 'that in order to distinguish Police Inspectors from Municipal employees, Theatre and Music Hall attendants and others, the slings should be retained'. The inevitable clothing board was constituted and on 1 April the members recommended a black leather shoulder-belt with pouch for superintendents and a black mohair belt for inspectors. These suggestions were approved by the prospective wearers and the Receiver duly wrote to the Home Office seeking approval for the change.

Either the Receiver's letter was badly worded or completely misunderstood for on 11 October the Home Office wrote to the Commissioner asking why the inspectors wished to wear mohair girdles of a military pattern instead of black belts. The Commissioner replied on 20 October that 'there seems to be some little misunderstanding' and explained that when swords were abolished the sword-belt and sling was inappropriate without the sword, and the slings were therefore also withdrawn. He continued, '. . . and then it was brought to my notice that the patent-leather belts, which are of a military character, together with the uniform worn by an Inspector give the impression that the Inspectors might be mistaken for cinema or restaurant door-keepers,

and they were exercised in their minds on the subject'. The letter concludes that the proposed mohair girdle has no connection with any
article of military uniform and the Receiver must have been mistaken if
he suggested it.

On 19 November, the Home Office refused to sanction the change
on the grounds of cost. As the mohair belt had been discarded the
inspectors asked if the sword-sling could be restored to the belt and the
Commissioner agreed. As officers were once again wearing both sword-
belt and sling the superintendents were consulted about having their
swords returned. Eleven were in favour, six against and five were non-
committal. Finally, on 3 December 1920, superintendents were given
back their swords, but only to be carried in no. 1 or full dress. Sword-
belts and slings for officers would be worn for another fifty years.

Amid the problems of inspectors being mistaken for door-keepers
the Metropolitan Police found time to issue a small 45-page booklet
entitled *Drill Instruction*. Five thousand copies were printed in June 1919
and part of the introduction by the new Commissioner read, 'It is
necessary that Officers of all ranks should keep up their knowledge of
drill, and it must be understood that if at any time they show themselves
deficient in this respect, it may be necessary to direct their attendance at
the drill ground for further instruction, which under such circumstances
will have to be done in their own time.' What the ex-servicemen thought
about this is known, but not suitable for publication. Many years later at
the Police College, an institution devoted to widening the students'
outlook, a group of Metropolitan officers would debate the motion that
'Foot drill broadens the feet and not the mind!'

9
The Turbulent Twenties

During the post war period P.C. Kelly of 'T' Division became the first London policeman to die at the hands of an armed criminal since 1915. On 11 February 1920 at 3.30 a.m. the constable saw a man in a khaki overcoat standing against the front gates of Acton Town District Railway Station. As Kelly approached, the suspect drew a pistol and shot him in the chest, stomach and leg. James Cleaver, a private night-watch-man, who ran to the officer's aid, was shot in the shoulder and although his terrier dog bit the gunman several times the man escaped and was never traced. It was subsequently found that the gates had been forced and the booking office rifled. The constable was given medical aid and later transferred to St. Thomas's Hospital for an operation to remove the three bullets.

There were some interesting news items about policemen on page 11 of *The Times* newspaper dated 23 February 1920. Eight Chinamen had been arrested in a suspected opium den in Limehouse; two 'W' Division officers received awards for tackling a lunatic armed with a loaded rifle, and P.C. Kelly died in hospital at 11.45 p.m. the previous night. Kelly was 34 years old, an ex-serviceman, and had been married for two weeks when he was shot.

Following an outcry in the Press, similar to the editorials of the 1880s, questions were asked in Parliament '. . . as to whether, in view of the numerous crimes of violence recently committed, steps would be taken to provide the police with something more effective than wooden truncheons'. The Home Secretary, to whom the question was addressed, smartly bounced it across to the Home Office to clarify the position in regard to arms and the Metropolitan Police. As nobody in the Home Office knew the answer [not an unusual state of affairs] the file was passed to the Commissioner for his observations, '. . . whether the Metropolitan Police should in any cases or under any conditions carry revolvers'. Macready minuted the papers as follows:

'The Metropolitan Police are already supplied with automatic pistols (.32) to the number of 1006, which are distributed throughout Divisions. These pistols are given to Police

Officers who desire to have them when employed on night duty and who can, in the opinion of the Station Officers, be trusted to use them with discretion.

I think the number of pistols might, with advantage, be suitably increased, providing it is possible to give the men sufficient practical instruction. The present course of instruction is, in my opinion, quite useless, and should be increased to ensure that the men who are trusted with pistols are able to make effective use of them without danger to the general public.

I have been considering this matter for some time and have come to the conclusion that it would be inadvisable to make pistol practice too public, as we might lay ourselves open to the accusation of training the police to shoot down their fellow creatures in case of labour troubles.

As an alternative I have arranged for pistol competitions to be held in various Divisional Shooting Clubs this summer, with a view to encouraging the use of the service pistol by the men, and I hope this will increase the numbers of those who are adepts in its use.

I think the Regulations in force for the carrying of pistols are sufficient, although, as I have said before, the numbers might with advantage be increased, together with the amount of ammunition allowed for practice.'

Obviously Macready, like Henry before him, preferred his men to practise in their own time, thereby saving public money and avoiding public comment. There were also some points in his minute which were not strictly accurate. The number of pistols on Divisions was less than stated and the course of instruction was not only 'quite useless' it was also non-existent. It had been suspended since the beginning of 1915 and never reinstated.

On 14 April 1920, General Macready relinquished his appointment as Commissioner in order to take command of the British troops in Ireland. He was succeeded by Brigadier-General Horwood who had served as one of the Assistant Commissioners since 1 November 1918.

Post-war street disturbances had shown that the 1912-pattern 21-inch truncheon carried by mounted police was too short. In 1920 it was replaced by a 36-inch baton with a leather-covered grip. When not in use it was sheathed in a leather scabbard which was usually strapped to the nearside of the saddle. Its 1912 predecessor had been carried in a spring-loaded case.

On 11 May 1920 Police Orders announced that .32 pistol ammunition was available and Superintendents were to requisition a sufficient quantity for the annual practice, as soon as possible. In June of that year, in response to further questions in Parliament on the subject of arming the police, the Home Secretary stated, 'No new departure is being made with regard to the arming of the Metropolitan Police or their instruction in the use of firearms. For nearly forty years officers on night duty have been permitted, if they wish, to carry revolvers for their own protection . . .' Meanwhile a new Act, designed to restrict the traffic in firearms, was passing through Parliament.

The Firearms Act 1920 repealed the Pistols Act of 1903 and introduced compulsory registration for anyone manufacturing, selling or using a firearm. However, smooth bore shotguns and air weapons were exempt and a very liberal interpretation was applied to 'war trophies' which did not need a firearms certificate provided they were registered and ammunition did not form part of the trophy. An exemption was always given, for example, to a war-widow in respect of her dead husband's revolver [but not a rifle] and invariably to an ex-serviceman who had captured an enemy weapon [other than a rifle or a field gun]. Thus the first arms amnesty in the 1950s produced gallant old veterans with weapons ranging from a Maxim machine-gun taken from the Turks at Gallipoli to a German anti-tank gun captured on the Western Front.

In November 1920, Superintendent 'W' Division asked if the time had come to return the 281 aged .45 revolvers first issued in 1884 and reissued in 1914. He was told that they would have to remain in Divisions as there were only two spare .32 pistols left in the Receiver's store. It was possibly due to this correspondence that the Receiver asked if he should buy more pistols, and authority was given on 1 December to purchase another 300.

As a result of the number of armed criminals who had fired on police in recent months, the question of firearms for police was again raised in the House of Commons on 1 December. The Home Secretary replied, 'In the Metropolitan Police any constable engaged on dangerous duty is supplied with a revolver if he desires, subject to proper precautions as to his training in handling and instructions as to when it may be used . . .'

By this time a number of defects, possibly due to age and wear, had been discovered in the .32 Webley & Scott pistols purchased in 1911. The most serious weakness was that in some cases the weapon could be fired even when the safety catch was set at 'safe'. During December 1920 and January 1921 the pistols were sent in batches of 50 to be examined by the Army Inspection Department at Enfield Lock. In addition to other faults the inspection revealed that magazines supplied with the last consignment of pistols differed slightly from the 1911 type and were not interchangeable. This led to yet another police internal memorandum.

On 14 March 1921 a Police Order rectified the dangerous practice, identified by Superintendent Wakeford twenty years earlier, of weapons being loaded by untrained station officers. The regulation now read, 'A pistol is to be issued to a Constable on his own application when parading for duty; it is to be loaded by the officer parading the relief *if he has a knowledge of firearms*, if not, then by the officer to whom issued, and placed in a holster.'

Fear of renewed Irish terrorism was responsible for an additional issue of pistols throughout the Force; twenty to each outer and ten each to inner divisions. This reduced the reserve supply to a handful and another 300 pistols were purchased in June 1921. In the same month information was received that the Sinn Fein proposed to raid gunsmiths' establishments in England to collect arms for the cause. Special motor patrols operated in central London, constant surveillance was given to firearms dealers' premises in outer London and random road-blocks were mounted in the suburbs. All the officers engaged in these operations were armed, and the Receiver's store was again denuded of reserve weapons. Another 500 .32 pistols were purchased in July.

Meanwhile, men in the dockyard divisions found themselves at a disadvantage with their naval pistols and they put their case to the Commissioner through the new Police Federation. The Constables' Branch Board meeting held on 22 June 1921 forwarded a resolution (no. 78) which read, 'That this Board respectfully ask the Commissioner to favourably consider the advisability of substituting the .32 Webley & Scott Automatic Pistol for the .455 Webley Scott Automatic Pistols with which the men at Dockyards are at present armed. The former pistol is much lighter and more effective. The men at some Dockyards are carrying .455 Webley Scott Pistols and 21 rounds of ammunition which, together with the holster and pouch weigh 5¾ lb. and which is suspended from the left shoulder by means of a strap.' From the description it is almost certain that these were ex-Royal Naval Air Service holsters of a semi shoulder holster type, but worn outside the tunic. Unfortunately naval dockyards were restricted areas and there are no photographs showing a constable wearing this rather cumbersome equipment.

The cost of supplying hundreds of .32 pistols to the dockyards would have been borne by the Police Fund, whereas the .455 weapons were on loan, free, from the Royal Navy. The Commissioner saw no reason to change this happy state of affairs and he noted, 'Under the present financial conditions this extra charge cannot be favourably received.' This reply was sent to the Constables' Branch Board on 4 August together with the observation that 'in view of the informative nature of the Resolution, the Commissioner considers it inadvisable to publish it in Police Orders'. Presumably, although Metropolitan police officers had carried arms in the dockyard divisions for some years, this was regarded as a delicate matter which should not receive publicity, even in Police Orders.

It was now the turn of the Sergeants' Branch Board and at a meeting held on 9 December 1921 the committee approved resolution no. 3 on the agenda: 'That the Commissioner be respectfully asked to increase, where necessary, the number of pistols kept at stations, as information has reached this committee that, on occasions all the pistols at certain stations have been issued, leaving none available for use in an emergency.'

Eight days later, as the result of this request, confidential memorandum C.33 was sent to all divisions.

'PISTOLS

Superintendents are to submit reports by 1st despatch 21st December, giving information on the following points:

(a) The name and number of all Stations where all pistols have been issued at one time.
(b) The number of times no pistols have been available.
(c) Whether this arose, if at any time, only on the occasions when special motor patrols were operating.
(d) Whether the present supply is adequate to meet normal demands.
(e) Whether any increase is recommended, and, if so, to what extent.'

There was an enormous variation in the figures submitted by Divisions in reply to the memorandum. Although 'E', 'H', 'M', 'T' and 'Y' had nil returns, 'C' reported that the Division had often been stripped of pistols and this was only remedied when an extra 70 weapons were issued to Vine Street Station. 'D', 'F', 'G' and 'W' had all supplied armed men to 'C' Division, or for patrols and road-blocks in their own areas and, at times, were also short of pistols. 'N' Division reported that revolvers had been borrowed direct from the Royal Small Arms Factory at Enfield to cover the shortfall, and 'R' Division had been lent a supply of revolvers from Woolwich Arsenal. [These two entries must have raised a few eyebrows at Scotland Yard].

'V' Division had coped well except on 15 January 1921 when armed Sinn Feiners attempted to dynamite the Vacuum Oil Works in York Road, Wandsworth, and again the next night when a similar attack was made on Barnes signal-box (which controlled an important junction on the London and South-Western Railway). As for the remaining areas the number of occasions when a Division's stock of pistols had all been issued, and there were none left for an emergency, varied from 'L' and 'X', twenty and 45 times respectively, to 'J' and 'S' recording 223 and 171 occasions. As a result of the inquiry, additional pistols were issued from store to those stations where an increase was thought to be necessary. During this period it appears that nearly 2,000 policemen carried arms each night throughout the Metropolis.

During the scare certain Government buildings were again guarded by armed officers, one of whom made it his career. In 1939 an inspector visiting the Home Office stumbled across a tiny room containing a uniformed 'A' Division constable, the morning newspaper, and tea-making equipment. Not unnaturally the inspector asked the constable what he was doing and was told that he was a protection officer. 'Protection?' 'Yes sir, the Sinn Feiners.' As the IRA had just launched another series of bomb attacks in the capital the inspector thought that the posting must be a recent innovation. However, the duty state at Cannon Row Police Station revealed that the P.C. had been temporarily posted to the Home Office, not in 1939, but in 1921! For the past eighteen years the forgotten man had quietly drawn his pay every Wednesday and returned to his cubby-hole. Stranger things have happened in the army of course – but only just.

A running chase after the style of the Tottenham outrage began at about 2.35 p.m. on Thursday, 22 June 1922 when Field Marshal Sir Henry Wilson alighted from a taxi-cab outside his home at 36 Eaton Place, Chelsea. He was wearing full uniform having just unveiled a plaque at Liverpool Street Railway Station commemorating employees of the Great Eastern Railway who had died in the war. A former military adviser to the Ulster Government and, since his retirement, MP for Ulster, his home province, he was a prime Sinn Fein target.

As he crossed the pavement to his front door he was shot several times (nine bullets struck him according to one report) by two men who had been lying in wait. Sir Henry drew his sword in an attempt to defend himself; the only field marshal in history who was fated to die sword in hand. The assassins were Reginald Dunn and Joseph O'Sullivan, both

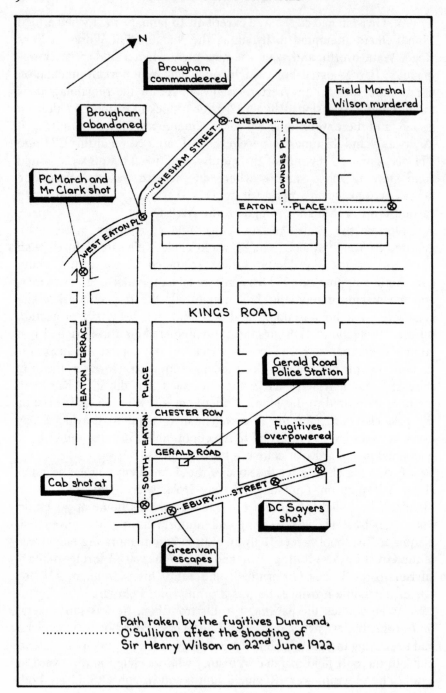

N

Brougham commandeered

Field Marshal Wilson murdered

Brougham abandoned

CHESHAM STREET

CHESHAM ... PLACE

LOWNDES PL.

PC March and Mr Clark shot

EATON ... PLACE

WEST EATON PL.

EATON TERRACE

KINGS ROAD

SOUTH ... EATON ... PLACE

Gerald Road Police Station

CHESTER ROW

Fugitives overpowered

GERALD ROAD

Cab shot at

EBURY ... STREET

DC Sayers shot

Green van escapes

Path taken by the fugitives Dunn and O'Sullivan after the shooting of Sir Henry Wilson on 22nd June 1922 aged 24 and each armed with a Webley .380 calibre revolver. The cab man, who had witnessed the shooting, was obviously a practising non-interventionist, for he immediately drove away and was not interviewed by police until 24 hours later. Both ambushers made off, reloading as they went, shouting to some roadmenders who gave chase to 'keep back'. Dunn had a wooden leg and was not able to run in the accepted sense of the word. At this point they attempted to board a passing van, but were foiled by the driver who was struck in the face by a revolver butt during the struggle. The two murderers then turned right into Lowndes Place where they tried to engage a taxi, but a passing lorrydriver, who was also an eyewitness, shouted a warning to the cabby who slammed the passenger door and escaped.

After turning into Chesham Place and thence into Chesham Street, Dunn and O'Sullivan commandeered a one-horse open brougham, driven by a coachman in full livery, and standing on the carriage steps fired several shots at their pursuers. The two men left the brougham at the end of Chesham Street and entered West Eaton Place on foot. Here the chauffeur of a private motor car swerved his vehicle towards the fugitives but one of them fired and punctured the offside rear tyre; the car hit a kerb and stopped. Meanwhile several policemen had joined the hue and cry and the sound of police whistles and gunfire had attracted others. One of these was P.C. 411B Walter March who ran along Eaton Terrace and confronted the two gunmen as they came towards him. Despite the fact that they were armed March immediately tackled O'Sullivan, but was then shot in the groin at point-blank range by Dunn. As O'Sullivan and March both fell to the pavement Alexander Clark, the chauffeur of the damaged car, jumped out of his vehicle to help and was shot in the right thigh, the bullet passing through his leg.

Leaving March on the ground in a pool of blood, O'Sullivan got to his feet and he and Dunn turned into Chester Row and then turned right into South Eaton Place. This was a mistake, as their route took them past the mouth of Gerald Road which housed a police station with single mens' accommodation. All the available duty men who could be spared, plus eleven off-duty constables, who were mostly in shirt sleeves, turned out and some had the foresight to draw a pistol and ammunition. The gunmen hurried towards Ebury Street firing more shots to deter their pursuers and although no one was hit, a bullet passed through the rolled-up left sleeve of one of the off-duty men, P.C. 202B Duff. Since the armed officers were at the back of the crowd and unable to shoot, the murderers' fire was answered with successive volleys of truncheons and the odd milk bottle. These all missed, but the truncheons were retrieved for future use as the posse moved forward. Another off-duty man, P.C. 519B Skilton, stopped a cab and asked the driver to pass as close as possible to the two fugitives so that he could lean out and hit one with his truncheon. Unfortunately, as the taxi drew abreast of the two men they both opened fire and Skilton was obliged to duck; he threw his truncheon, which missed. As there were now several bullet holes in the cab Skilton decided to return to Gerald Road Police Station for a pistol, a decision of which the taxi-driver undoubtedly approved.

Turning left into Ebury Street the gunmen tried to climb onto a small green van, but the driver accelerated and they fell off. They now walked backwards threatening with their weapons the hostile crowd pressing towards them. More shots were fired, one of which hit Detective Constable Sayers in the right leg from a distance of about ten yards. The shots drew more flying truncheons and on this occasion one struck O'Sullivan on the head. P.C. 510B Walter Bush took advantage of the distraction to rush O'Sullivan and knock him to the ground. As they wrestled he tore a revolver (later found to contain four live and two expended rounds) from the Irishman's hand. During this encounter, Dunn took deliberate aim at the policeman's head, but his gun misfired and before he could again squeeze the trigger he in turn was overpowered by P.C. Duff (still in his bullet-holed shirt sleeves).

The prisoners were taken to Gerald Road Police Station where Dunn gave his name as O'Brien and O'Sullivan identified himself as James Connelly. Their true names were only established after police notices had been circulated to other forces and the Press. Both men were sentenced to death at the Old Bailey on 18 July and their appeals were dismissed on 3 August. The *Daily Herald* had taken a keen interest in the prisoners, urging clemency, and on 5 August under a by-line 'Rushing an Execution' the paper stated, '. . . the petition forms for the treatment as prisoners of war of O'Sullivan and Dunn may be signed at the office of the Finsbury Labour Party . . . and also at the 'Worker's Dreadnought' office at . . .' The execution date was fixed for 10 August, but the place was kept secret for fear of an armed rescue attempt and police with pistols were on stand-by at both Wandsworth and Pentonville prisons. Large crowds gathered outside both buildings on the day. Some prayed, some sang the Irish rebel song 'Wrap the green flag round me boys' and others were just curious. The prison bell at Wandsworth tolled at 8 a.m. and the death notices were posted half an hour later.

P.C.s March, Duff, Bush and D.C. Sayer were given rewards from the Bow Street Reward Fund, March having arrived there with the aid of crutches. All four were later awarded the King's Police Medal. Another sixteen officers received small sums of money from the Fund. Mr Clark, the chauffeur, was presented with £25 and a gold watch valued at £50, but later complained that he had not been given a King's Police Medal!

A week after the assassination of Sir Henry Wilson, the Right Honourable Winston Churchill, MP, Secretary of State for the Colonies, was given an armed escort from 'A' Division to follow his official car. One of the officers selected was P.C. 711A Smith who was not only an authorized shot (i.e., authorized to use a police handgun), but equally importantly, owned a motor-cycle combination. P.C. 682A Brook, described as 'an expert rifle shot' was chosen to ride in the sidecar; both officers were to wear plain clothes and carry a .32 pistol. On 3 July Mr Churchill's Special Branch bodyguard reported that the motor-cycle was no longer required as his principal had been 'given the use of an armoured Rolls-Royce motor'. Six days later, however, the two 'A' Division men resumed duty as escorts – presumably the armoured Rolls was no longer available.

On 22 July at 11.10 a.m on the London road between Guildford and Ripley, Mr Churchill's driver overtook a heavy lorry, but as Smith attempted to follow the official car he collided with a vehicle coming in the opposite direction. Both the motor-cycle and sidecar were badly damaged and the unfortunate P.C. Brook sustained compound fractures to both legs and his left arm. The bodyguard later reported that when he noticed the escorts' absence it was assumed that they had either missed the way or sustained a punctured tyre. On 24 July two officers from 'W' Division took over escort duty, but were provided with an unmarked car. The discussion between Smith's insurance company and the Receiver continued for some weeks as the insurers maintained that combination XZ 7567 was only insured for private use and not for racing round the countryside on police duty. Eventually the two parties agreed to share the repair bill between them.

By August 1922 the terrorist threat was receding and the Press returned to the perennial favourite of armed criminals and unarmed police. An editorial in *The Times* that month drew attention to weaknesses in the Firearms Act and called for more stringent control of firearms.

'A disquieting feature of the last few weeks has been the growing abuse of firearms. Nowhere has this abuse been more apparent than in London itself. Hornsey, Lewisham, Kensington, Camden Town, Gray's Inn Road and Belgravia have all heard within recent times the echoes of revolver shots . . . The question might be asked: For what purpose does anyone in London, outside the Military and the Police, want a revolver? Many shopkeepers and bankers wish them for the protection of their premises. Others wish them for target shooting, others for self protection. A very large number, ex-members of the Services, wish to preserve them as mementoes of the War. Many people accustomed to travel in foreign countries, also possess them. The authorities admit that there are a large number of people in possession of firearms who do not hold certificates . . . The weakness of the Firearms Act, it is stated, is that the only people who register are those who are the least likely to make criminal use of the weapons. Criminals do not apply for certificates. The fact that they are able to secure both arms and ammunition indicates there are leakages in the present system.

The most dangerous side of the increased circulation of revolvers which followed demobilisation is, of course, the number of criminals who now carry arms and their readiness to use them to avoid capture. Before the war it was extremely rare for the burglar to carry a firearm, the ordinary thief never did so, and so-called "hold-ups" or daylight raids on shops were rarely accompanied by the production of revolvers. So far the authorities have set their faces against the arming of the police. But it is imperative to make the criminal realize that it does not pay to carry firearms. The handicap of an unarmed constable against an armed man is so great, and it says much for the devotion to duty of the present Metropolitan Police Officer that he rarely hesitates to tackle a wanted man, whatever the danger.'

In the same month a number of questions were again asked in Parliament about the amount of time spent in revolver training for police. As a result the Home Secretary suggested that all officers liable to carry a firearm on duty should undergo a short course of firing practice, at least once a quarter, the Police Fund to defray the cost of ammunition. The Commissioner replied that an annual firing course appeared to suffice.

Later that year a police constable committed suicide with a service revolver which apparently he had abstracted during the annual practice. This nasty incident led to directions, given in memorandum no. 361 dated 17 November 1922, that in any future firing practice a sergeant would be detailed for duty, in addition to an instructor. The sergeant was to be responsible for the safe custody of guns and ammunition before, during, and after the practice.

Following the cuts in public expenditure proposed by the Geddes Committee in 1922, known to all and sundry as 'The Geddes Axe', police recruitment was suspended. In 1925 the manpower shortage was eased when the Admiralty and the War Department accepted responsibility for policing their own establishments. Over a period of eight months this released 1,326 Metropolitan policemen who returned to duty in the Metropolis in time for the General Strike. The trouble began in the coalfields, spread to the railways and at midnight on 3 May 1926 the TUC leaders called a mass strike. In London nearly 60,000 special constables, wearing civilian clothes but equipped with a steel helmet, police armlet and a truncheon, or a chair leg or copper stick (wash-tub variety), assisted the regular force. Thousands of volunteers moved food supplies and by 12 May the General Strike was over.

As life returned to normal the Receiver returned to his ledgers. On 22 October he wrote to the Commissioner enclosing a list of pistols issued on loan to Divisions during the Sinn Fein crisis and not yet returned to store. 'The Auditor having called attention to the fact that these loans are still outstanding, the Receiver would be glad to learn whether the Commissioner is of opinion that the pistols can now be returned to Store or whether they should be permanently allotted to the Divisions.' The accompanying list showed a total of 296 pistols which had been lent to five Divisions over and above their issued allocation.

Horwood sought the advice of Major-General Sir Wyndham Childs, Assistant Commissioner (Crime), whose reply dated 1 November indicates a certain degree of nonchalance on the question of police firearms. 'I think that Divisions ought always to have in their possession a supply of pistols or revolvers. One never knows what may happen. There are plenty of Irish gunmen still knocking about London. I notice in today's paper an Irishman has been arrested with a revolver.'

In answer to a further query from the Commissioner asking how many pistols should be kept in Divisions, Childs replied, 'I cannot discover that there has been any method under which pistols have been issued. My opinion is that every Division in the Metropolitan Police District should have a supply of pistols. It appears that only 'A', 'C', 'S', 'Y' and 'Z' Divisions have pistols. I cannot understand why.' As Childs had held his appointment since 5 December 1921 it seems reasonable to say that he could have bestirred himself to ascertain the facts. The Receiver's report showed only the 296 extra weapons which had been lent on a temporary basis to 'A', 'C', 'S', 'Y' and 'Z' Divisions in the

1920s; Childs obviously thought that this figure represented the entire stock of pistols held by the Force.

Eventually Superintendents were instructed to submit detailed returns showing the number and types of weapons held at each station. These reports were summarized on 22 November and showed a total of 2,065 handguns throughout the Divisions. However, 111 were .22 single-shot training pistols, and aged .45 Webley revolvers accounted for another 270. Thus only the remaining 1,684 were operational .32 Webley & Scott pistols. In fact the figure should have been 1,683 for buried deep in one of the returns is a brief note by Superintendent 'R' Division that one of the .32 pistols issued to Lee Road Police Station could not be found. The Metropolitan Police had lost another pistol!

As a result of the audit, 209 pistols were returned to store and on 1 December 1926 the Commissioner agreed that the obsolete .45 Webleys which had seen 42 years' service should be withdrawn. The Receiver was asked to sell them, but they were so old that only scrap-metal value remained. Their final fate is unknown.

In 1926, *The Times* lauded the 'tact, patience, impartiality and impeccable conduct' of the Metropolitan Police; 1928, however, saw the pendulum swing the other way, with allegations of police brutality (unfounded) and corruption (well founded). The Commissioner took a smart pace to the rear and retired on 7 November 1928. He was described by a contemporary as a man who mistook arrogance for leadership and was known to his subordinates as 'the chocolate soldier'.

His place was taken by General Viscount Byng of Vimy whose appointment was warmly welcomed by the *Telegraph*, but not by the *Daily News*. 'We regard with the utmost misgiving the appointment of another soldier . . . at a very critical juncture in the affairs of the Metropolitan Police.' Byng of Vimy, a former 10th Hussar, was a veteran of two wars in which he had served with distinction. He took his title from the capture of Vimy Ridge on the Western Front, stormed by Canadian troops under his command on 9 April 1917.

In 1929 the Metropolitan Police celebrated its centenary, in common with the Boat Race, the London omnibus and the London Zoo. Fortunately any supposed analogy went unheeded, even by *Punch*. On Saturday 25 May the occasion was marked with an inspection in Hyde Park by the Prince of Wales, followed by a march past at Buckingham Palace, with 39 Superintendents, 304 Inspectors, 929 Sergeants and 6,932 Constables. A total of 4,224 officers and men of the Special

Right: The predecessor. Charles Rouse, born 1785, complete with lantern, rattle, cutlass and truncheon – the latter appears to be fitted with a swivelling knuckle guard. Rouse, last of the old style watch, photographed outside his box in Brixton Road. (Met)

Right: One of the 'Graveyard' patrols, October 1829.

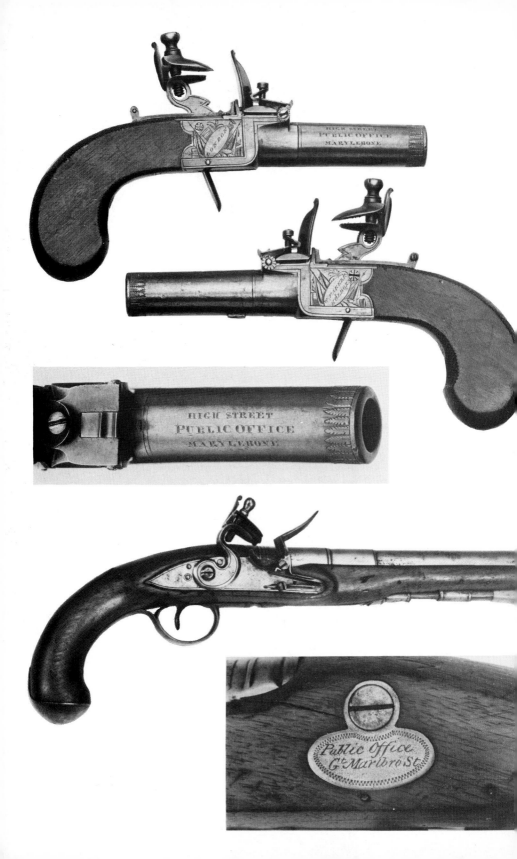

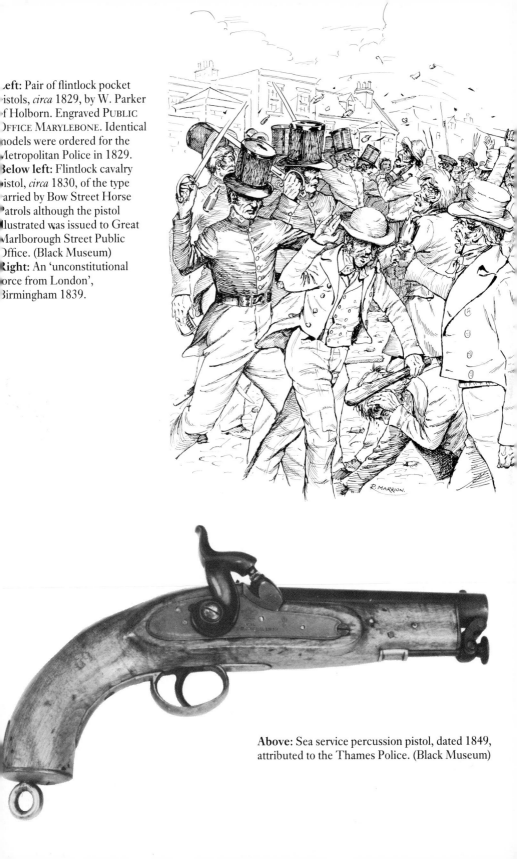

Left: Pair of flintlock pocket pistols, *circa* 1829, by W. Parker of Holborn. Engraved PUBLIC OFFICE MARYLEBONE. Identical models were ordered for the Metropolitan Police in 1829.
Below left: Flintlock cavalry pistol, *circa* 1830, of the type carried by Bow Street Horse Patrols although the pistol illustrated was issued to Great Marlborough Street Public Office. (Black Museum)
Right: An 'unconstitutional force from London', Birmingham 1839.

R. MARRION.

Above: Sea service percussion pistol, dated 1849, attributed to the Thames Police. (Black Museum)

METROPOLITAN POLICE OFFICE,

4, *Whitehall Place.*

PISTOLS, SWORDS, TRUNCHEONS, RATTLES, &c.

TERMS AND CONDITIONS

OF THE

CONTRACT

FOR THE

Supply of Pistols, Swords, Truncheons, Rattles, Handcuffs, &c.,

FOR THE USE OF THE METROPOLITAN POLICE.

For the Service of the Three Years ending the 31st December, 1859.

1st.—That the Contractor enter into a Bond, with one Surety, in the Sum of One Hundred Pounds, for the due fulfilment of his engagement.

2nd.—That the Articles required are to be delivered by the Contractor, free of all charges, at the Police Office, Great Scotland Yard, on Monday in each Week, to be there examined by Officers appointed for that purpose.

3rd. That such articles as shall be pronounced by the Examiners as being unequal to the patterns exhibited be rejected, and the Contractor be bound to remove them at his own cost, and the Receiver of Police shall be at liberty to purchase or procure the same articles of other persons, charging the difference between the price of such articles and the contract rate, to the Contractor, if others are not immediately supplied by him in lieu of the rejected articles.

4th.—That a breach of any of the Covenants of the Contract, as expressed in this document, shall empower the Receiver of the Police of the Metropolis forthwith to terminate and make void the Contract absolutely, by giving a written notice to that effect to the Contractor; and such Contractor and his Surety shall be liable to be sued upon the Bond for the recovery of the Penalty therein expressed.

5th.—That the Contractor shall transmit his Accounts to the Receiver's Office for payment every quarter.

N.B.—The sealed Patterns are exhibited at the Metropolitan Police Office, No. 4, Whitehall Place.

TENDER.

To the Receiver for the Metropolitan Police District.

SIR,

I hereby undertake to enter into a Contract for the supply of Pistols, Swords, Truncheons, Rattles, Handcuffs, &c., as specified in the following List, equal in quality and in conformity to the sealed Patterns, at the several prices stated opposite to each Article, agreeably to the foregoing Conditions of Contract; and I propose the following party as Surety for the due performance of the Contract.

Signature *Parker Field & Sons*

Residence *233 High Holborn London*

Date *Aug 19th 1856*

Dublin Metropolitan Police.
Superintendents Office
G. Division
11 Dec. 1867

I have to report that I have just received information from a reliable source to the effect that the rescue of Richard Burke from prison in London, is contemplated. — The plan is to blow up the Exercise walls by means of Gunpowder, — the hour between 3 & 4 P.M. and the Signal for all right, a white ball thrown up outside when he is at Exercise —

(Signed) Daniel Ryan —
Superintendent

Comm' of Police

Opposite page, top left: Printed contract for Metropolitan Police arms and accoutrements, 1857. (PRO)

Opposite page, top centre: Short truncheon, probably carried by inspectors until the 1860s.

Opposite page, right: 1864 truncheon case with spring-loaded base and fold-over top flap.

Opposite page, bottom left: Mounted police constable, *circa* 1867. He wears the new comb helmet with a brim, but still carries his sabre (withdrawn in 1868).

Top left: Letter from Dublin giving advance information, which the Commissioner largely ignored, of the Clerkenwell Prison explosion. (PRO)

Top right: The aftermath.

Above: Metropolitan policemen learning cutlass drill at Wellington Barracks, 1867. (*Illustrated News*)

Above: New-style uniforms and truncheon cases. Wimbledon Common rifle meeting in 1870.
Top right: Metropolitan Police edged weapons 1871. Top to bottom 1. Sabre for mounted superintendents and inspectors, 2. Sword, foot superintendents and inspectors, 3. Cutlass, foot sergeants and constables. (Enfield)
Centre: .450 Adams breech-loading centre-fire revolver issued to the Metropolitan Police. (Black Museum)
Bottom: Webley .45 gateload revolver stamped with a crowned M.P. Issued 1882. (Black Museum)

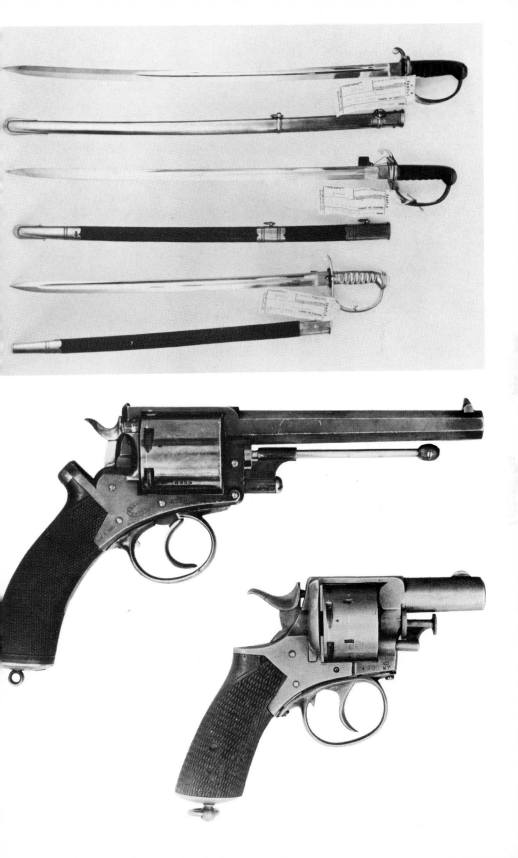

Left: 'An Unequal Match'. *Punch* cartoon following the murder of P.C. Atkins on 22 September 1881.
Below: Drawn sabres escort Fenian prisoners from Bow Street Police Station to Millbank Prison in April 1883. The three guards on the prison van also hold Adams revolvers including the driver! (Graphic)

Right: The Tottenham Outrage 1909; an artist's impression of the tram chase. Lepidus holds a pistol to Wyatt's head (the conductor who was forced to drive) while Helfeld fires at police from the rear platform. (*Illustrated News*)

Below: Memorial card for the two dead victims. (Met HM)

In Loving Memory

OF

Police Constable, **TYLER**, aged, 30 years,

AND

RALPH JOSCELYNE, aged 10 years,

who were murdered by two aliens, in Tottenham

SATURDAY, JANUARY 23.

Buried Jan. 29th, 1909, at Abney Park Cemetery

Top left: Siege of Sidney Street, 1911. Cartridges being issued to H Division officers armed with borrowed shotguns. (*Illustrated News*)

Bottom left: Finishing touches to a dummy policeman for drawing fire. (*Illustrated News*)

Above: Mr Winston Churchill, the Home Secretary, backed by City and Metropolitan police in Sidney Street. The Metropolitan officer holding a shotgun, P.C. Albert Knight, was the last survivor of the siege and died in 1967 at the age of 88. (Press Association)

Below: The house ablaze in the closing stages of the siege. Hundreds of bullets have marked the bricks and frames around the windows. (*Illustrated News*)

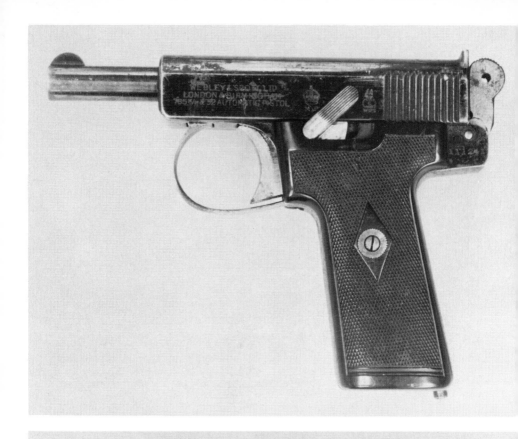

Metropolitan Police Office.

SPECIAL MEMORANDUM.

JAMES CONNOLLY, age 24, height 6ft., complexion fresh, full face, clean shaven, eyes blue, hair dark brown, well built ; dress, Scotch fawn sports jacket, blue serge trousers, blue and white striped shirt, light brown trilby hat, no waistcoat, black shoes.—JOHN O'BRIEN, age 24, height 5ft. 7½, complexion fresh, rather thin face, high cheek-bones, high forehead, blue eyes, clean shaven, hair very dark brown, large ears, right wooden leg ; dress, black jacket and trousers, no vest, blue striped shirt, brown trilby hat ; occupations and addresses refused.

JAMES CONNOLLY.   JOHN O'BRIEN.

The above described two men, whose portraits are herewith, will be charged concerned together with the murder of Sir Henry Wilson, and the attempted murder of Police Constables March and Sayer, and civilian, Alexander Clark, by shooting with revolvers at and in the vicinity of Eaton Place, S.W. Both men have declined to give any information concerning themselves or where they reside. Any information respecting them will be gladly received by Police of New Scotland Yard or Superintendent Bacchus, Walton Street Police Station.

It is also desired to trace driver of taxi-cab who was engaged by Sir Henry Wilson, who left the cab to enter his house, 36, Eaton Place, when he was shot.

Top left: .32 Webley & Scott pistol issued in 1911. (Black Museum)
Bottom left: .22 single-shot model for target practice. (Black Museum)

Above: Memorandum released to the Press and posted at all police stations asking for information about the killers of Sir Henry Wilson. (Met)

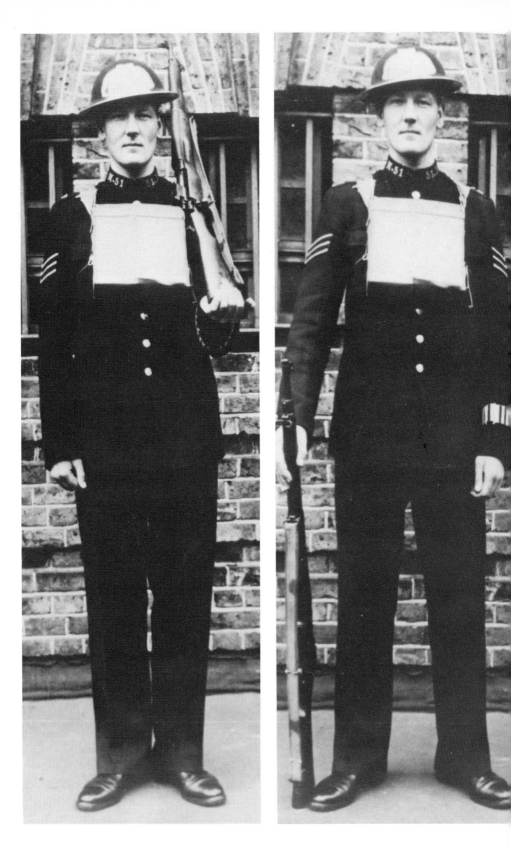

Opposite page: P. S. Young, M Division, with one of the first rifles issued to the Metropolitan Police in 1940. (Met HM)
Above: .38 Enfield revolver on loan in 1968. Similar in appearance to the .380 Webley & Scott revolver issued in 1956. (Black Museum)
Right: Walther 9mm PP (Polizei Pistole) pistol being drawn from a shoulder holster, 1968. (Met)

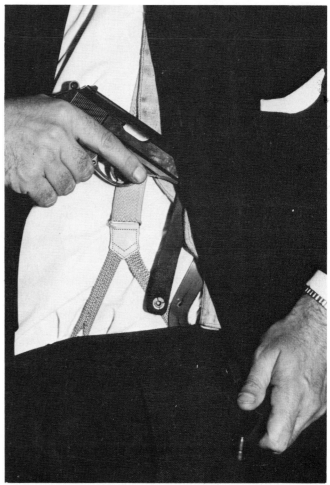

Above left: Early gas gun training in 1968.
Above right: Gas gun training film; police

photographer working under difficulties!
Below: Instructors training at Woolwich Arsenal.

Constabulary held the parade area and lined the route. As one participant was heard to remark, 'Look at this lot, I wonder who's minding the shop?'

Byng successfully resisted an attempt to abolish the Mounted Branch, started the police-box system and was responsible for the first Information Room. Above all, he believed in personal contact with his men and leading from the front. When, because of ill health, he was forced to retire on 9 September 1931, he left a legacy of restored professional pride to the 20,000 men of his Force. He had been an outstanding Commissioner; he was well liked and sorely missed.

10

The Thirties

Marshal of the Royal Air Force, Viscount Trenchard assumed his duties as Commissioner on 2 November 1931. In the previous July a Government committee had recommended wage cuts of 12½ per cent for police; reduced a month later to 10 per cent, to be taken in two annual stages of 5 per cent. Three million men were out of work, 500 naval ratings had mutinied at Invergordon and there were 42,000 applications to join the Metropolitan Police.

In October 1932, after several cases of armed criminals taking pot-shots at policemen, a question was asked in the House of Commons if the Home Secretary would consider arming police on night duty in London. The same questioner also wanted to know whether members of the Flying Squad were armed. In contrast to the open, if sometimes inaccurate, answers given in the past, Lord Trenchard did not see fit to divulge this information. 'The Commissioner has the discretion to arm police officers when he considers it necessary, but it would not be in the public interest to state how that discretion is exercised.'

The subject of truncheons again came to the fore on 24 October 1932 when a motor tyre manufacturer wrote to the Commissioner asking if he would consider adopting a rubber truncheon for the Metropolitan Police and enclosing two samples. Opinions among senior officers were divided. One felt that this type of truncheon would be 'un-English' although another wrote that it would be at least as English as sticks studded with nails 'as provided for demonstrators'. Someone else was concerned with the cost of replacing approximately 20,000 truncheons throughout the Force, while another minute suggested that only the CID should have rubber truncheons. Finally, it was decided to seek expert medical opinion and on 2 November Sir Bernard Spilsbury of University College Hospital was shown the samples and asked for his comments.

Rather to the surprise of the 'un-English' lobby, Sir Bernard stated that the rubber truncheon would cause far less injury than the wooden rigid type used at present. He also queried whether a rubber truncheon was heavy enough to 'stop people' but intimated that this was a matter for the police. It was finally decided that a hardwood truncheon was more effective than rubber and the matter was dropped – at least in Britain. The German Press had already reported that London policemen were using *Gummiknüppeln* (blackjacks) against demonstrators. In consequence Scotland Yard received a letter from the Fatherland asking if this were true, as the blackjack 'to the German mind is synonomous with tyranny and oppression'. On 21 November the Yard assured the uneasy gentleman in Pforzheim (who may shortly have gathered evidence at first hand in his own country) that there was no truth in the reports.

During this period, motor patrol officers of the Surrey Constabulary had been issued with a short, flexible leather-covered truncheon, weighted at one end, and it was suggested that Metropolitan Police traffic patrols should carry something similar. Although the Surrey truncheon was also regarded as 'un-English', and was a third dearer than its partridge-wood counterpart, the discussion continued for some months. The matter was finally shelved in February 1933 when it was accepted that very few of London's traffic patrols carried a truncheon. This was a personal decision by the men owing to the risk of injury caused by the truncheon if the wearer were involved in a motor accident.

On 24 July 1933 confidential memorandum no. 13 gave details of a revised system for pistol training. Until that date any man who so desired was allowed to attend annual firearms practice, but this had meant that the number of trained men varied from division to division. Henceforth 24 men from each Division would attend a yearly firing practice and proficiency test. About six men of each inner Division and eight from each outer Division were to be CID officers. A record would be kept in each Division of all the men selected, together with the dates and results of their tests. A number of central officers, including sixteen from Flying Squad, ten Special Branch, ten motor drivers and eight wireless operators were also to attend a similar course.

It was also decided to standardize the number of weapons held in Divisions and on 13 April 1934 senior officers were required to give their comments on the proposal. Two of them considered that the .32 pistol was unsuitable, although they did not give a reason, and suggested that the 'new .45 bore Webley revolver with a 3-inch barrel or the .45 bore Colt with a 2-inch barrel would be infinitely preferable'. On 3 May the Commissioner minuted the papers, 'It is not considered that any change of the type of weapon issued to Police is necessary.' On 12 June the issue of arms was finalized in confidential memorandum no. 9 as follows: (a) 10 pistols and 320 rounds of ammunition to be held in reserve at each Divisional Station; (b) 6 pistols with 192 rounds for each Sub-Divisional Station and (c) 3 pistols with 96 rounds in each Sectional Station. Because of his additional protection responsibilities Superintendent 'A' was informed that the memorandum did not apply to his Division.

The revised system phased out .22 training pistols and 132 of these and 69,000 cartridges were returned to the Receiver's store. Almost immediately, 'C' Division Shooting Section asked to be allowed to buy some of these weapons for the use of club members. On 16 August the Receiver noted, '. . . there is no market for these pistols except for sale as scrap-metal. If the Commissioner considers it desirable, the athletic clubs of other divisions might be informed of the fact that these weapons are available for distribution, free of charge, for use in the shooting sections'. In the event 100 .22 pistols were given to the various shooting clubs, although the members still had to buy their own ammunition. Cartridges were supplied at cost price of 18s per 1,000 rounds plus 11 per cent for departmental charges (whatever they may have been). However, the Receiver also undertook to continue to supply .22 ammunition at that rate, plus the 11 per cent, so presumably the cartridges were still cheaper than paying the full retail price. In order to comply with the Firearms Act each club was given a free firearms certificate.

Lord Trenchard retired on Armistice Day 1935 and the Police Federation lit bonfires to celebrate his departure. His successor, Air Vice-Marshal Sir Philip Game, had served with Trenchard as his senior staff officer at the Air Ministry.

One of the new Commissioner's first proposals concerned police weapons. Regulations governing the issue of firearms to police, which had been in force since 1884, were changed as the result of a Police Order published on 28 July 1936. A gun could no longer be drawn by a night duty constable at his own request, and the order read: 'Automatic pistols (.32) and cartridges are kept at C.O. (Scotland Yard) and all Stations for issue in cases of necessity. Pistols will only be issued to officers who have been properly instructed in their use, and can give a satisfactory reason for issue.'

The same P.O. also gave details of the revised pistol course which would be fired at a 12-inch target from a distance of twenty yards. In addition, the number of rounds was increased from 24 to 32. The practice part of the course consisted of four rounds fired right-handed and a further four left-handed, all slow fire, followed by two similar sequences, rapid fire. These sixteen rounds were followed by a proficiency test of eight rounds fired with the right hand, slow fire, and another eight also right-handed, rapid fire. Presumably natural left-handers were allowed to use the strong hand. As a time limit was not imposed it is difficult to estimate just how fast the 'rapid' sequences were fired or for that matter how slow was slow. Obviously every shot was aimed, using the sights, and there was probably little real difference between the rapid and slow rates of fire.

An acceptable standard of proficiency was a total of 50 per cent hits, but, 'It is not absolutely essential for all the selected officers to pass the proficiency test, so long as each proves clearly that he is capable of handling a pistol'. This last addition to the regulations is quite astonishing. Either the man was a safe, competent shot capable of hitting a target or he was not. If the latter, it was wrong to allow him to carry a loaded firearm on the streets of London (or anywhere else).

In conjunction with revised training a small eight-page booklet on the .32 pistol was produced in 1936 and thirty copies were sent to each Division for issue to instructors and men under training. The cover is marked 'Confidential. For use of Police only' but this may have been intended for the police user rather than as a reference to the contents, as the information was readily available from any gunsmith. According to the handbook all shots were fired in the duelling stance with the body half-turned sideways and the firing arm extended and slightly bent (known in the trade as 'the stand and deliver' position). The rules governing range discipline followed those formulated in 1902, but were still sound common sense. Unfortunately the guidance on firing the weapon and investigating a fault left much to be desired, but was no worse than similar military instruction of the period.

The carrying of a truncheon on motor-cycle patrol was again raised in 1936, this time by Superintendent 'Y' Division who asked for a truncheon pocket to be added to motor-cyclists' breeches, for use when they patrolled on foot. He also suggested some form of holder should be attached to the motor cycle to hold the truncheon when the machine was being ridden. After experiments with various types of clips and pockets, the shorter (No. 2) truncheon was issued with each motor cycle and carried in a special holder.

The Firearms (Amendment) Act 1936, which came into operation on 1 May 1937, merely scratched the surface of the firearms and crime problem. It was now an offence to shorten the barrel of a smooth bore gun to less than twenty inches and to convert any imitation firearm to a firearm proper. In addition, the dispensation for war trophies, granted under the 1920 Act, ceased to have effect. The holder of such a trophy was now required to obtain a firearms certificate.

In August 1936 Captain Fawcett, HM Inspector of Explosives at the Home Office, asked whether police would consider using the new army revolver in place of an automatic. He was apparently swayed by the fact that the German police had recently changed their self-loading pistols for revolvers. Three days later the captain forwarded an extract from the 1929 Text Book of Small Arms which indicated that the pistol was not as reliable as a revolver. This correspondence continued until, in 1938, the Commissioner decided that every weapon in the Metropolitan Police should be checked and test fired. On 7 February 1939 the results showed that more than 15 per cent of the 1,225 pistols held in Divisions were defective.

Instructions were given the next day to replace all 188 suspect handguns from the Receiver's store and the question was mooted whether, in the event of war, revolvers should be issued in place of pistols. By March 1939 it was decided that in view of the large stock of pistols held by the Force, plus the cost of any exchange, there 'is no real cause for changing the type of weapon'.

During this period, as war clouds gathered, the IRA returned to London and there were seventeen bomb incidents in the West End and at main line terminals. The campaign was just as ineffective as those which had been mounted in the 1880s and 1921.

11
The Second World War

When Great Britain went to war on 3 September 1939 the strength of the Metropolitan Police stood at 18,428 – 930 men short of its full establishment. Two days later all three reserve groups were mobilized. The first reserve consisted of 2,737 police pensioners who re-engaged, a second reserve of 5,380 special constables who now served on a full-time basis and the third consisted of 18,868 police war reserves recruited for the duration of the war.

On 24 May 1940 the British Expeditionary Force in France had begun to withdraw towards the Channel ports and the 'miracle of Dunkirk'. On the same day Scotland Yard issued confidential memorandum 20/40.

'PROTECTION OF POLICE PERSONNEL AND POLICE BUILDINGS.
ISSUE OF FIREARMS
1. In view of prevailing conditions, it is necessary to take precautions against the possibility of the enemy or his agents obtaining control of, or causing damage to, certain vulnerable points [these included power-stations, generating plants, telephone exchanges, etc.] and buildings of public importance including Police Stations. Attempts to seize or destroy could be made either by direct force or subterfuge, and, while no hard and fast rules can be laid down to meet all possible contingencies, the following will serve for guidance as to the line of action to be taken . . .'

Paragraph 2 dealt with police stations and advocated distributing pistols in various parts of the building in case part of the station was captured or damaged. It was accepted that unqualified men might have to use the weapons and it would be sufficient 'if an officer who is thoroughly conversant with the use of pistols explains the mechanism . . .' The third paragraph covered public buildings and vulnerable points and laid down that only qualified shots or those known to be capable should be selected when detailing men for armed posts. It included the sensible precaution that an officer should not be required to carry a pistol on these duties unless he felt confident of his ability to use it if necessary. Paragraph 4 is interesting in that it mentions firing a warning shot. 'As to the actual use to be made of a pistol by an officer for self-defence or protective purposes, obviously much must be left to the discretion of the individual concerned, but it should be pointed out that the firing of a shot, not necessarily at the intruder, and even after an entry has been effected, may be the best means of giving the essential warning to those inside.'

In order to meet the possible demand for firearm users, arrangements were made for a short course of instruction to be given to as many officers as possible. The regular force was to be trained first, followed by the auxiliaries, and any firing would be restricted to .22 shooting. Generally instruction was confined to safe handling, loading and unloading, the sight picture [correct alignment of the sights on the target] and trigger pressure.

By 29 May German forces had occupied most of the French Channel ports and the invasion of England was a real possibility. The Commissioner issued secret memorandum 6/40 for distribution to all officers above the rank of inspector.

'In connection with the arming of police engaged on certain duties, the Secretary of State has considered the question in the light of the existing situation and in particular of the possibility of parachute landings. The following is an extract of a letter which has been received from the Home Office on this subject, and it is reproduced for the general guidance of Senior Officers who may at any time be called upon to issue instructions:

"It must be borne in mind that the police are not a combatant force, and that, even in the existing situation, the main body of the police must remain available for the performance of normal police duties, for which the carrying of arms may be unnecessary or even undesirable; and that in the case of enemy landings by parachute the functions of the police would be in the main confined to observing and reporting their presence to the Military Authorities and preventing attempts at sabotage and other acts of violence by isolated individuals and overpowering and arresting the individuals where possible. Subject to the observance of this fundamental principle there are, however, certain purposes for which it would, in the existing circumstances, be proper and desirable for the police, whether regular or auxiliary personnel, to carry arms, namely:

(a) Guarding vulnerable points against sabotage, so far as this is undertaken by police.

(b) Protecting important police stations against attempts to seize them by enemy raiding-parties, whether parachutists or not. For this purpose, selected members of the staffs of the stations should be armed.

(c) Armed motor patrols employed in parties of from two to four men, especially in the rural districts . . ."

The Commissioner's memorandum added, 'To enable the conditions envisaged above to be met, the number of pistols in Divisions will be increased. In addition a supply of rifles and ammunition will be issued to all Divisions as soon as they are available.'

Both memoranda remained in force for more than five years until they were cancelled on 31 July 1945. This cancellation failed to reach at least one station where the secret memorandum, sealed in a packet strengthened by two generations of sticky tape, was religiously handed over, three times a day as the reliefs changed, for the next fifteen years. In 1959 a young and curious duty officer opened it in front of the horrified eyes of an elderly station officer who clearly regarded the packet as sacrosanct.

On 1 June 1940, 3,500 Canadian Ross rifles, which had last seen service in 1916, and 72,384 rounds of .303 ammunition were received from the military and distributed to divisions. Thames Division had the smallest allocation – 61 rifles and 'S' Division the highest with 190. Fifty rifles were also issued to the London Fire Brigade and 100 to the Port of London Authority Police. As training ammunition was not available a liberal interpretation was placed on the words 'rifle instruction'. This usually consisted of explaining the mechanism and sights with some elementary coaching in holding and aiming. Fortunately Hitler's airborne troops failed to make an appearance and the matter was never put to the test.

The threat of invasion, coupled with a shortage of full-bore ammunition, caused many more policemen to participate in .22 pistol and rifle shooting. On 5 July Superintendent 'X' Division reported that all his .22 allocation had been fired and 'The majority of the men are anxious to have the opportunity of firing practice, and I received applications from most Stations in this division for additional ammunition.' Similar requests were received from other divisions and the file was minuted, '. . . it would appear that the enthusiasm in Divisions has outstripped the available supplies of ammunition'. It was then decided to issue the remaining 20,000 small bore rounds together with an intimation that this would exhaust available stocks. By this date full-time auxiliaries were also receiving non-firing instruction in the use of handguns. On 28 October the War Office was asked to supply 50,000 rounds of .22 ammunition and after some confusion about the type required (long or short) the military finally delivered the first 10,000.

Although London had already been bombed, the first concentrated air raids began on Saturday 7 September 1940. More than 350 tons of bombs were dropped on the Metropolis leaving the dock areas ablaze, with 'H', 'J', 'K', 'M' and 'R' Divisions bearing the brunt. GHQ Home Forces sent the code word 'Cromwell' (invasion imminent) to Southern and Eastern Commands and the London area and the military and civilian forces were placed on full alert. However the raid signalled not invasion but the start of the 'Blitz' which lasted nine months. Civilian casualties in London alone totalled more than 23,000 dead and many more thousands injured.

Once again the Metropolitan Police started to lose guns, but this time the deficiencies were due to German bombers. A typical example occurred at 3.30 a.m. on 9 September when P.C. 585E Simpson was guarding a vulnerable point (in this case Holborn telephone exchange). After the building had been bombed Simpson was dug out of the rubble leaving under the debris his helmet, tunic, one trouser leg and a .32 pistol with two loaded magazines. Happily he recovered from his injuries, but the weapon and ammunition were never found. Simpson may have had the gun in one of his pockets because by September there were still many handguns issued without holsters. Owing to a shortage of 727 holsters presumably the same number of armed officers carried loaded firearms in their pockets or thrust into waistbands.

The large number of loaded weapons, coupled with very elementary instruction, led to the inevitable accidents. Bullet holes appeared in such diverse places as the police room in the House of Commons, the front doors of various police stations and a desk in Broadcasting House. Even worse was the tally of shooting accidents to police personnel, some of them serious, including the death of a special constable in October 1941 – the result of a defective firing-pin in a .22 pistol.

Until 1941 the police service had been a reserved occupation but in that year, in order to meet the demand for aircrew, regular police were allowed to volunteer for the RAF or Fleet Air Arm as pilots or observers. Of 1,696 policemen who volunteered, 383 were killed in action and 116 decorated for gallantry. Early in 1942 recruiting for the regular police force was suspended, but regulars and auxiliaries under the age of 25 and 30 respectively were permitted to join the other armed services. More than a hundred regulars were to lose their lives while serving in the Royal Navy and the Army.

By 1941 nearly 2,000 pistols had been issued to the Metropolitan Police, but this figure included one lent to the Duke of Kent and twelve with the detention camp detachment on duty in the Isle of Man. One had been lost when a 'C' Division wireless car was wrecked in January 1941 and two were destroyed when Holloway police station was bombed on 20 March 1941. On 22 January 1941 about 21,000 lease-lend USA revolvers had also been issued to Divisions although it was noted that 'the revolvers are, however, of doubtful quality'. In March 1942 all officers above the rank of inspector were issued with .45 revolvers plus twelve rounds of ammunition; their .32 pistols were withdrawn and placed in reserve. On 29 September 1942 the Duke of Kent's pistol was reported lost when his aircraft crashed, but the weapon was subsequently found by his chauffeur in the back of the royal car.

On a number of occasions Timber Control had licensed the import of Maracaibo ebony from South America to make truncheons for some police forces. On 7 January 1943 the Ministry of Home Security inquired whether English beech could be used for the same purpose, owing to the high cost of importing wood in wartime. The Receiver replied that Metropolitan Police staffs were made of partridge-wood from the West Indies and sufficient stocks were in store. In the case of exceptional demand the Force would resort to the 'chair leg' variety.

Yet another query about truncheons was raised in 1944 when it was discovered that there were still 229 police motor-cycles without truncheon clips or holders. The Receiver stated that these could not be supplied, due to shortage of labour and material, and felt that the truncheon could be safely carried in the pocket of the rider's breeches. However, motor-cyclists feared an abdominal injury in the event of an accident (this implies that the no. 2 truncheon was carried in a front fob pocket below the waist) and zip-fastened leather containers were eventually fitted to all the machines.

More important matters were to occupy the Metropolitan Police as the first V1 missile, known to Londoners as the 'flying bomb' or 'doodlebug' landed on 12 June 1944. Nine months later the 2,341st, and last, V1 fell at Waltham Cross on 28 March 1945. Flying bombs were responsible for 5,376 civilians killed and another 15,169 seriously injured. The first of an even more terrible weapon, the V2 rocket, fell at Chiswick on 8 September 1944. Between then and 30 March 1945, 513 ⸱⸱ ⸱ ⸱ts fell in the Metropolitan Police district killing 1,612 people and leaving 5,614 injured. London air raid sirens sounded for the last time on 10 April 1945; German forces in Europe surrendered on 4 May.

During six years of war, nearly 1,900 cases of damage to police buildings had been reported and 124 of these were serious. Ten police stations had been so badly damaged that they were partially or totally evacuated and the old adage about lightning not striking twice in the same place did not apply to bombs. Putney section house was hit on 8 September 1940 by a bomb which penetrated a side wall and followed a diagonal path into the basement, where it exploded. The next night another bomb took exactly the same course and exploded in the same place. This added another sixteen casualties to the fifteen suffered the previous night. 'Lightning' also struck twice at East Greenwich police station which was badly damaged by a bomb in May 1941 and even more seriously damaged by a flying bomb three years later. A total of 96 regulars, 86 war reserves and 26 specials had been killed on duty and another 1,942 regulars and auxiliaries injured. In view of the constant involvement of the Force on the streets of London during air raids, these casualty figures could easily have been trebled. Gallantry during air raids earned members of the Metropolitan Police 276 honours and awards.

Sir Philip Game retired on 31 May 1945 and most of the pensioners and auxiliaries followed him into civilian life. It had been a long, hard six years for all of them. After the exodus the regular strength of the Metropolitan Police stood at 12,231, the lowest figure since 1885.

12
Post-War Violence

On 31 July 1945, rifles and revolvers were withdrawn from stations which then reverted to the pre-war allotment of pistols. Thousands of chair-leg truncheons, which had been issued to auxiliaries in 1939, were taken from store and sold to the Dutch Government to replace their own police truncheons which had been confiscated by the Germans.

The new Commissioner, Sir Harold Scott, who had spent 36 years in the civil service, took up his appointment on 1 June 1945. Before Scott was offered the post he was asked by the Home Secretary if he could ride a horse. Herbert Morrison might have done better to have picked a juggler, rather than an equestrian, to head post-war Britain's largest police force. Recruiting for the regular force was resumed on 1 January 1946, but this coincided with the departure of 2,682 men who were beyond pensionable age. In addition, an unexpectedly large number of regulars who had joined the armed forces elected not to return to the low pay and petty restrictions of police service. Figures for both crime and the manpower situation steadily worsened throughout 1946.

Yet another pistol had gone astray for on 21 February 1946 the incoming Sub-Divisional Inspector at Stoke Newington police station reported that he had checked the firearms and found that Webley & Scott .32 pistol no. 134431 was missing and had been replaced by a Mauser 7.65 pistol (obviously a war souvenir). The former SD Inspector, who was joining the Control Commission in Germany, was unable to shed any light on the substitution of these weapons. As neither pistol had been used in the commission of crime the matter was quietly shelved.

An inquiry from the Receiver, who wished to replace some of the .32 pistols, brought a reply from Webley & Scott on 1 October 1946 that this model was no longer produced. The firm offered a choice of the Webley Mark IV .38 revolver with a 3-, 4- or 5-inch barrel, or a Mark III .32 revolver with a 3-inch barrel. The file was minuted that the matter should be examined again in twelve months' time.

P.C. Nathaniel Edgar, a uniform officer working in plain clothes while temporarily attached to the CID, became the first Metropolitan policeman to be killed after the war. On the evening of 13 February 1948, in the course of questioning a suspected housebreaker outside 112, Wades Hill, Southgate, he was shot three times in the right groin and thigh. However, Edgar had already noted the suspect's name and identity-card number in his pocket-book. Accordingly the net was spread for Donald George Thomas who had deserted from the army in January 1945. Edgar, a married man with two sons, who had rejoined the police after three years in the Royal Navy, died in hospital an hour after he was found lying in the street.

Five days later Thomas was arrested by armed police in a boarding-house at Clapham. He was overpowered before he could use the 9mm Luger pistol which he grabbed from under a pillow. After being cautioned he was asked if the weapon was loaded and admitted, 'That gun's full up and they were all for you.' The Luger was in fact fully loaded with eight rounds in the magazine and one in the breech. Forensic examination confirmed that the bullets in Edgar's body had been fired from the same pistol. Thomas was found guilty of murder, but as the death penalty had been suspended his sentence was commuted to penal servitude for life.

By 1948 a constable's weekly pay was more than 20 per cent below the national average; ten years previously it had been 12 per cent above. The end of general demobilization in 1948 also marked the end of a ready-made supply of candidates and for the next few years wastage would exceed recruitment.

Annual firing practice was not resumed until 18 December 1950 and then only for 'A' Division which was a special case because of the number of armed points that it covered. The abbreviated pistol course at the City of London Police range in Bishopsgate consisted of eight rounds practice and another eight free position. A total of 191 men participated and although 58 of them managed to score double figures, another fifteen missed the target with all sixteen shots from a distance of twenty yards. However, faulty ammunition may have been responsible for some of the misses. On 21 March 1951 an instruction was sent to all Divisions that 'Examination of certain stocks of ammunition has revealed that a number of rounds have become faulty as the result of age and exposure to the atmosphere, and it has been decided to examine all Divisional stocks centrally.'

Meanwhile the Metropolitan Police had managed to lose another three pistols, or rather they had been lost by other people. On 4 July 1951 Special Branch reported that a pistol check had shown that three of their weapons were missing. One had been lent to Admiral Halsey in 1921, one to Lord Greenwood in 1925 and the third to Sir Samuel Hoare in 1940. Approval had been given by the Commissioner on the last occasion, but there was no record of any covering authority for the first two loans. As Sir Samuel had mislaid his pistol and Halsey and Greenwood were both dead there seemed little chance of recovering the weapons and they were written off.

In a minute to the Receiver, asking for this to be done, one of the Assistant Commissioners wrote, 'I think you will agree that there is no alternative to writing off the three pistols which were undoubtedly handed to persons going abroad on dangerous missions, and were therefore used in the national interest.' Vice-Admiral Halsey had been Comptroller of the Prince of Wales's household from 1920 to 1926, and Lord Greenwood, one time Chief Secretary for Ireland, was the MP for Walthamstow in 1925. Presumably the loan to Sir Samuel Hoare in 1940 coincided with his departure for Madrid to take up his appointment as British Ambassador to Spain. It is difficult to equate these various posts with 'dangerous missions', unless the true facts are hidden in one of the secret files. Strangely enough, none of the senior officers' minutes on the file question the inordinate length of thirty years before the first loss was discovered.

In July 1951, again at Bishopsgate, 114 Special Branch officers attended a short course on the .32 service pistol and this group was followed by another 42 men in November. The weapon, according to a consensus within the Branch, was 'old, clumsy and badly designed'. Special Branch personnel now carried out their own tests, first of all with a .38 Colt, but this was too bulky to be concealed under a jacket. Further trials were then made with a .32 Colt revolver, which was satisfactory but not available in the UK. Robert Churchill, the gunsmith, was consulted, but advised against a revolver and indicated that a self-loading pistol was a better weapon for protection officers. Churchill recommended the .380 Colt pistol, as carried by bodyguards in the USA, which he could supply at £8 each.

This was the start of a lengthy correspondence which began on 8 February 1952 when one of the Assistant Commissioners wrote to the Home Office. In a long letter he explained why the Branch needed another weapon, other than the Webley & Scott .32 pistol, which he stated (wrongly) had been issued in 1910, and asked for authority to buy twenty .380 Colt pistols. The Home Office eventually replied on 6 June, 'We have been in consultation with the War Office about this and feel considerable doubt about the proposal.' The British Army was soon to adopt the 9mm Browning pistol as its handgun '. . . which they regarded as being in every way superior to the Colt, particularly as regards reliability and stopping power'. The letter suggested that it would not be difficult to obtain stocks of this weapon for the police and, in the meantime, all existing .32 police pistols should be examined by the army.

On 3 July the Commissioner wrote personally to the Home Secretary, 'The issue seems to have been confused by a reference to the weapons held in reserve for the use of police generally and it may well be that the new 9 m.m. Browning automatic . . . will be quite suitable for this purpose. But it may or may not be suitable for the Special Branch men who do not want the fact that they are armed to be at all obtrusive . . .' On 7 August the Home Office about-turned and wrote, 'We have been in touch with the War Office who have advised us that the 9 mm Beretta would be a better weapon for the Special Branch,' and gave authority to buy twenty. Branch officers made a last-minute attempt to get the gun they wanted and reported on 3 November that they had borrowed twenty .380 Colt, Model M, pistols from the Director of Armaments at the War Office. A request for supplies of ammunition to carry out trials was apparently granted for the weapons were retained until April 1965.

A telephone call to Croydon Police Station at 9.15 p.m. on Sunday, 2 November 1952, from a man who had seen two men climb a gate into a confectionery warehouse in Tamworth Road, led to the death of yet another policeman. Six local officers responded to the call and one of them, Detective Constable Fairfax, climbed onto the roof and saw two figures behind the head of the lift-shaft. He approached to within six feet of the two intruders, told them that he was a police officer and that they should come out from behind the lift-head. One of the two, Christopher Craig, shouted 'If you want us, – – – – – – – well come and get us.' Fairfax rushed forward and grabbed the second man, Derek Bentley, who shouted 'Let him have it, Chris.' At his trial the defence stated that these words meant that Craig should surrender his gun to police; the prosecution alleged that they were an invitation to shoot. Craig fired and the bullet struck Fairfax a glancing blow in the shoulder and pushed him over. Despite his injury he got up and again seized Bentley, knocked him down and dragged him behind a roof-light. Bentley was searched and a knife and a knuckleduster were found on him, but not a gun.

On the farther side of the warehouse, P.C. Harrison was crawling up the sloping roof when Craig saw him and fired, possibly twice, but missed. Another officer, P.C. Macdonald, had clambered up a drainpipe and as Fairfax helped him over the parapet Macdonald asked him what type of gun was being used. The question was answered by Bentley, 'He's got a 45 Colt and plenty of ammo for it.' In fact, Craig was firing a .455 Colt revolver with a sawn-off barrel and loaded with .44 ammunition. At this point the other officers, led by P.C. Sidney Miles, burst through a door and onto the roof. Craig fired again and Miles dropped dead as a bullet hit him between the eyes and came out the back of his head. Another shot was fired towards the door as Harrison stepped over his dead colleague and threw his truncheon and then a bottle at the killer; both missed. The gunman was shouting, 'I am Craig. You've just given my brother twelve years. Come on you coppers, I'm only sixteen,' and fired two more shots.

Meanwhile the station officer at Croydon had sent over eight ancient .32 Webley & Scott pistols, and Fairfax, who had taken Bentley down to the ground floor, equipped himself with a service pistol. Accompanied by other officers with pistols he returned to the roof and told Craig to drop his gun as the police were now armed. Fairfax apparently fired two shots, which both missed, and in response came four clicks from Craig's gun followed by a shot. Craig then dived off the roof and fell twenty feet. As he lay on the ground with a fractured spine he said, 'I hope I have killed the – – – – lot.'

Next morning's edition of the *Daily Mail* carried a long story on the previous night's incident, which must have astonished the participants. 'CHICAGO GUN BATTLE IN LONDON' read the headline: 'Gangsters with machine-gun on roof-top killed detective, wounded another.' Twenty-four paragraphs informed readers that the London crime wave had reached a new peak as gangsters armed with a Sten gun fired at everything – police, ambulances and fire brigade officers. 'Get them at all costs,' was the order to the 200 police in the battle, 30 of them armed with revolvers. The gunmen fired for nearly an hour and seemed to have an unlimited supply of ammunition as bursts from the Sten gun hit the streets. Finally their ammunition ran out and there was a hand-to-hand battle on the roof before the two men were handcuffed and brought down to street level. When the shooting began, Scotland Yard mobilized all police officers and CID men from Kent and the Metropolitan area. 'Gun flashes from the roof continued even after two of the gunmen had been overpowered. Police believe there may have been four or five gunmen.' It was an impressive exercise in journalistic fiction.

Both Craig and Bentley were found guilty of murder. Craig, a semi-illiterate 16-year-old, was too young to be hanged, as well he knew, and was sentenced to be detained during Her Majesty's pleasure. However, HM's pleasure rarely lasts for ever and Craig was released from prison some years ago and is now living under an assumed name. In the case of Bentley, wholly illiterate and easily led, the jury added a recommendation for mercy, but contrary to the hopes of many he was not reprieved and died on the gallows at the age of nineteen. Although both were legally guilty of murder, Bentley was not carrying a gun and was already in police custody when Miles was killed. Most of the public and many policemen thought it a pity that the law did not allow Craig to hang and Bentley to be imprisoned – instead of the other way about.

Fairfax was awarded the George Cross while Harrison and Macdonald both received the George Medal. P.C. Jaggs, another of the officers on the warehouse roof, received the British Empire Medal. P.C. Miles was given a service funeral and a posthumous King's Police Medal. His widow was given a pension of £2 16s 4d a week.

The case of Bentley has always caused concern and controversy because he was hanged for a murder which he, personally, did not commit. It has provided material for a number of articles and at least one book in which the author seeks to prove that P.C. Miles was killed by a police bullet. Unfortunately for this theory the service pistols arrived after Miles was dead. The latest offering appeared in the *Mail on Sunday* dated 19 May 1985. The article begins, 'Sensational new evidence in a video movie may help to pardon Derek Bentley.' Apparently a film is being made at his own expense by Mr Philip Huxley, a pensioner, who watched the shooting from his bedroom window. A scale model of the warehouse has been built and the film will prove a miscarriage of justice. Mr Huxley did not give evidence at the trial, but has twice urged the authorities to pardon Bentley.' It will be interesting to learn why he has waited 33 years before coming forward with vital information – no doubt all will be revealed in the video.

Following the Home Office correspondence in 1952, the entire stock of .32 pistols held by the Metropolitan Police was checked by examiners of the Inspectorate of Armaments early in 1953. The results were quite alarming. A total of 94 pistols failed to fire because of various defects and 21 would probably have malfunctioned due to short strikers (the firing-pin barely touches the cap in the base of the round, which fails to detonate). Another 54 were unsafe when loaded, even with the safety catch applied. A stoppage invariably occurred after firing the first round in thirty of the weapons, and four were completely unsafe to fire because of bulged or damaged barrels. In three cases the butt housing failed to hold the magazine, which fell out, and two of the pistols were so old that there were no magazines to fit them; hence they could only function as single-shot weapons. In addition, 420 pistols needed minor repairs or some form of servicing. Not surprisingly one of the Assistant Commissioners wrote in a minute on 28 May 1953, 'These reports bring to light fairly clearly the wretched condition of the .32 Webley Scott pistols distributed throughout the Force . . . The obvious initial reaction is to recall at once all unsafe and unserviceable pistols and the unserviceable magazines before anyone attempts to use them . . . When this has been done you might think that the full facts should be put before the Home Office with a view to the replacement of all the .32 Webley Scott pistols with a weapon which is safer and more reliable.'

Sir Harold Scott resigned in August 1953 and was succeeded by his deputy, Sir John Nott-Bower, on the 31st of that month. Scott had inherited some formidable problems at the beginning of his term of office and many of the problems were just as formidable by the time he left.

A decision about Force firearms was made by the Commissioner and on 29 August 1953 the file was minuted as follows:

'1. The main provision of firearms should be revolvers. Apart from the fact that the Webley pistols now held are unserviceable, inaccurate and dangerous, the revolver is the more suitable weapon for use by the semi-skilled and is more reliable.
2. Automatic pistols of a good type are necessary for Special Branch and for officers on special security duties in 'A' Division. Apart from the high cost of such automatic pistols they are only necessary for men on special duty who have to carry them either in concealed slings (shoulder holsters) or in the pocket, generally the latter.
3. A letter to be sent to the Home Office asking authority for 1,200 revolvers for general use in the Force and 50 Colt .38 automatics for Special Branch and 'A' Division security duties.

4. We should also ask Home Office authority for 1,200 webbing belts and holsters. At present pistols drawn from a Station in an emergency have to be carried either in the pocket or in the hand. This is not desirable and at any rate the Smith and Wesson revolvers which can be obtained from War Office are the 6-inch type (barrel) and can only be conveniently carried in a holster on a belt.'

In October the Receiver, quite properly trying to save taxpayers' money, queried whether the Force needed so many weapons and suggested that revolvers could be supplied to Special Branch and 'A' Division instead of pistols. According to his personal experience a revolver could be carried in a shoulder holster with reasonable comfort even when wearing a dinner-jacket, and with no discomfort at all in a lounge suit. As a result, the Commissioner asked one of the Assistant Commissioners for his views and he replied on 17 November, 'I agree with you that the shoulder holster would be no good with a serge (uniform tunic). I cannot agree that a revolver in holster would be comfortable and inconspicuous when carried by a man wearing all forms of mufti. Special Branch, or officers on Royalty protection duty, have to look reasonably well-dressed. In well-fitting evening clothes, it would be impossible to wear a revolver in holster without it showing. In this country we do not like the thought of police being armed and we do not like the public to know they are. Personally, I hate automatic pistols. I have had a good deal of experience with them in the Army and I look upon them as most dangerous, particularly in the hands of semi-trained men. All the same, I can see nothing for it but to have them for Special Branch and Royalty protection officers. I suggest "A" Div. officers on Downing Street, etc. must also carry pistols for the reasons you have stated.' He added that the number of weapons could be reduced by cutting down the total issued to Divisional reserves.

There are one or two interesting points in this minute about the supposed public reaction to police and guns and the writer 'hating' automatic pistols. His attitude seems to confirm that the army had small regard for handguns, especially self-loading pistols, and military personnel were never properly trained in their use. Even today, however, the average police team will usually beat its military counterpart in any handgun shooting competition. Certainly a pistol, or any other weapon, is dangerous in the hands of a semi-trained man, but then so is a wood chisel.

In October 1953 the Branch Boards requested that the provisions for pistol target practice and proficiency tests be extended to apply to all members of the Force, at three-yearly intervals. The Commissioner replied that he was considering an early resumption of annual firing practice, but he was not prepared to increase the number of authorized shots. Possibly because of this reminder, a resumption of annual pistol practice was authorized as from 1 January 1954, to be completed by 30 September.

On 17 November 1953 the Commissioner agreed to supply pistols to Special Branch and 'A' Division officers employed on armed posts or protection, and .38 revolvers for the rest of the Force. By December the choice of weapon was again changed and authority was sought to purchase 750 Smith & Wesson .38 revolvers at £14 15s each and 70 Colt pistols from the War Office to replace the worn-out .32 pistols. The military had a large stockpile of American Lend-Lease weapons, some of which they were prepared to unload onto the Metropolitan Police.

By April 1954 the revolvers were still being sorted and the War Office had only been able to find fifteen Colt pistols. Accordingly the Ministry of Supply was approached and they offered a 1941-pattern Beretta with the butt protrusion removed so that it could be accommodated in a shoulder holster. A sample was tested and approved by Special Branch officers and on 15 June Home Office authority was given to purchase 70 Beretta self-loading pistols at a cost of approximately £550. There was further correspondence, chiefly on the question of a suitable shoulder holster, and it was not until 8 September 1955 that the Beretta pistols and their holsters were available for issue.

A two-page Police Order published on 8 March 1955 gave details of a revised yearly practice and test. The number of rounds for firing practice was increased from sixteen to 24 for revolvers and sixteen to 28 for pistols. However, ammunition used in the proficiency test was reduced from sixteen to twelve in the case of revolvers and sixteen to fourteen for pistols. The revolver practice consisted of six rounds aimed, right-handed, and another six aimed with the left hand, all twelve at a range of fifteen yards. This was followed, at a distance of ten yards, with six rounds fired by sense of direction 'in bursts of two rounds fired in quick succession' right-handed, and another six fired in a similar fashion with the left-hand. The proficiency test now consisted of six aimed shots using either hand at fifteen yards, and another six fired by sense of direction, left- or right-handed, at ten yards. The practice and test for pistol users was similar except that seven rounds were fired instead of six.

An acceptable standard of proficiency is shown as 33 per cent hits for sense of direction and 50 per cent hits for aimed shots; which must have been difficult to score in the case of pistol shots who fired seven rounds. The order is interesting in that, for the first time, policemen were taught to fire paired shots from waist level at close range, without raising the weapon to their eyes and sighting. Unfortunately, the order repeats the sentence which first appeared in 1936 to the effect that it was not absolutely essential to pass the test, as long as the officer clearly proved capable of handling the weapon.

Towards the end of September 1955 the War Office agreed that their .38 Smith & Wesson revolvers were in such a poor state that they could not be brought to a standard acceptable for use. They had considered refunding the purchase price, but were now examining the possibility of offering an equivalent number of surplus .38 Enfield revolvers. In the event they were unable to muster sufficient Enfields and offered instead war-time .38 Webleys. The sample appeared to be satisfactory, but on the advice of the Inspectorate of Armaments at the Ministry of Supply, police insisted that each weapon should be check tested before acceptance. This produced some interesting results. Obviously it would be quite improper to accuse the War Office of attempting to use the Metropolitan Police as a dumping ground for surplus arms in second-rate condition, but the file was minuted on 9 January 1956 as follows: 'The .38 Webley & Scott revolver referred to in the previous minute were, of course, second-hand weapons to be supplied by the War Office. Negotiations with that department have subsequently been broken off, and new weapons with 4″ barrels are being obtained direct from the manufacturers.'

At about this time it came to notice that the blind were leading the sighted; a number of Inspectors who were taking charge of annual firing parties had never been trained themselves. It was therefore arranged, with the co-operation of London District Provost Company, to put one Inspector per Division through a one-day course.

Between January and September 1956, 500 new .38 Webley Mark IV revolvers were issued to Divisions. The second full annual firing practice, since before the war, was held in April 1956. Another decade would pass before police and police firearms became the subject of a professional approach.

13

Chelsea to Epping Forest

Police Orders on 26 July 1957 announced that the pistol booklet had been revised and would now be issued in two parts, (i) for the 9mm Beretta self-loading pistol and (ii) covering the .38in Webley-Scott revolver. Copies of (i) were sent to Special Branch and 'A' Divison and one copy of (ii) to each Divisional office and station – not a generous allocation. The revolver booklet consisted of eleven pages and, for the first time, carried illustrations (with some quite excruciating line-drawings) of the grip, weapon parts and various firing positions. A useful section on common shooting faults was also included. Although both booklets left much to be desired they were still a vast improvement on anything previously issued.

Sir John Nott-Bower resigned on 31 August 1958. His departure was marked in the Metropolitan Police with the same degree of indifference that had greeted his appointment five years earlier. The new incumbent, Sir Joseph Simpson, took office on 1 September 1958. He was the first Commissioner to rise from the ranks and the first professional policeman to hold such a post. Strength of the Force stood at 16,661.

In July 1959 a woman complained to Chelsea police that an unknown man had telephoned on three occasions and was trying to blackmail her over a domestic issue. A 'tap' was installed on the complainant's telephone and on 13 July at 4 p.m. another similar call was made and traced to a public kiosk at South Kensington Underground Station. Detective Sergeants Sandford and Purdy went to the call-box and detained a man for questioning, but as they walked out to the pavement the suspect suddenly took to his heels and bolted. Chased by the two detectives in a commandeered taxi, he ran into the hall of a block of flats in Onslow Square and was caught as he attempted to climb out through a window. Sandford spoke about transport to Purdy, who turned his head to answer his colleague, and the suspect's hand went inside his jacket. Sandford's shouted warning that he might have a gun came too late; the man drew a pistol and shot Raymond Purdy through the heart. As the sergeant fell dying the killer raced out of the building and disappeared from sight.

Apart from his description, which was circulated, there was nothing to identify the murderer. However, when the dead sergeant's personal property was examined, police found a small black notebook which was similar to the one he had taken from the prospective blackmailer in the call-box. Each address and telephone number in the book was checked, and several people, particularly in night-clubs, had recently met a man whom some thought was a Canadian, and others a German, who answered the description of the wanted man. A fingerprint found on the notebook was circulated through Interpol and the Canadian police furnished details and a photograph of Guenther Fritz Podola, aged 30, born in Berlin and a former member of the Hitler Youth. He had landed in Canada as an immigrant from Germany in 1952 and had been deported as an undesirable alien three years later, after serving two years for housebreaking offences.

Police were told that a man similar to Podola, but calling himself Paul Camay from Montreal, had booked a room in a small hotel in Kensington on 15 June. Four days after the murder police surrounded the hotel and a party of seven officers, four of them armed, and accompanied by an Alsatian police dog, quietly went upstairs to Podola's room. There was no response to a shout of 'Police, open the door,' and DS Chambers, weighing 16½ stones, shoulder charged the door. As it burst open it hit Podola in the face (he had been hiding behind the door) causing a cut over his left eye. As he stumbled backwards over a chair Chambers fell full length on top of him and Podola, kicking and struggling, was eventually handcuffed. Police searched the hotel and hidden in the attic they found a 9mm Radom Viz pistol, serial no. D8017, and forty rounds of ammunition. Forensic examination later established that a bullet from this gun had killed DS Purdy. The weapon took its name from Radom Arsenal in Poland where it was originally made for the Polish cavalry. When the Germans over-ran Poland in 1939 they appropriated every Radom pistol they could find and overstamped the frame with a Nazi eagle and swastika.

The doctor who examined the prisoner at Chelsea Police Station found that he was in a state of shock and not fit to be charged. Accordingly he recommended that he be removed to hospital for observation. The headlines in next morning's *Daily Mail* read, 'Armed detectives burst into London hotel, arrest barefoot Fritz in bed' and in capitals, '2 am: PODOLA IN HOSPITAL'.

Podola's black eye and his four days' stay in hospital, which was due to his mental condition and not because of physical injury, produced an extraordinary reaction in the Press and Parliament. Questions to the Home Secretary, and his replies, in the House of Commons filled ten columns in *Hansard* on 20 July. Among the astonishing statements conjured out of thin air by the members was one put by Mr Reginald Paget, a Socialist MP. 'I am not concerned about the charge against Guenther Podola. I am concerned about the people who beat him unconscious. Have charges been preferred against them?' According to the *Daily Mail* on 21 July, 'There was uproar in the House, with some Socialist back-benchers applauding Mr Paget and many Tories shouting disapproval of his remark.' Three days later Lord Stoneham entered the fray in the House of Lords and wanted to know how Podola received his injuries and, referring to his appearance in court on 20 July, why his general condition was such that 'when walking he had to be supported by two officers and dragged his feet slowly'. Someone should have told the noble lord that Podola had been given a lumbar puncture in hospital and hence could only move slowly. Amid the uproar perhaps, hopefully, someone spared a thought for the murdered officer, his widow and three children.

When the trial opened at the Old Bailey on 10 September it was suggested by the defence that the prisoner had lost his memory of all events prior to 17 June, the date he was arrested, and was not fit to plead. This issue, including medical evidence that Podola's bruised eye was consistent with being struck in the face by a door, occupied the court until 22 September. On that day the jury found that Podola was not suffering from a genuine loss of memory. The prisoner was found guilty on the 24th and sentenced to death. Efforts to obtain a reprieve included evidence that Podola had a double, who had committed the murder, or alternatively that Purdy had been killed by another policeman. The first came from one of HM's prisons and the second emanated from a lunatic asylum. Podola was executed at Wandsworth on 5 November 1959.

On 2 June 1959 a letter from the Receiver asked the Inspectorate of Armaments to examine all Force weapons as some of them 'mainly the Berettas, have been found to be defective'. In March 1960 the Inspectorate reported that the condition of the .38 Webley & Scott revolvers was generally good and only eleven out of 750 needed repairs. However, the Berettas were, 'generally in very poor condition' and 15

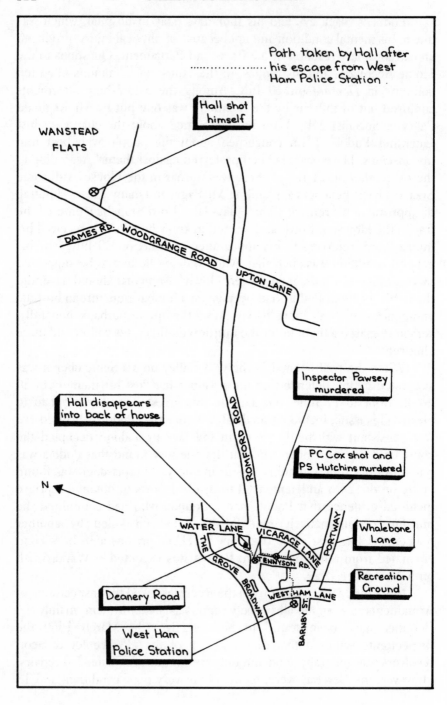

Path taken by Hall after his escape from West Ham Police Station.

Hall shot himself

WANSTEAD FLATS

DAMES RD. WOODGRANGE ROAD

UPTON LANE

Inspector Pawsey murdered

Hall disappears into back of house

PC Cox shot and PS Hutchins murdered

ROMFORD ROAD

N

WATER LANE

VICARAGE LANE

THE GROVE

TENNYSON RD.

PORTWAY

Whalebone Lane

Recreation Ground

Deanery Road

BROADWAY

WEST HAM LANE

BARNBY ST.

West Ham Police Station

per cent of the 68 weapons were unserviceable. The remainder had pitted bores, all were well worn, and their accuracy was suspect.

A minute from the Receiver's office giving the facts to the appropriate Assistant Commissioner mentioned that the Berettas had been purchased second-hand from the Ministry of Supply in 1954 [in fact it was 1955], only because no other suitable weapon was available at the time. 'It is essential that officers engaged on protection duty should have pistols which are both reliable and accurate and for that reason you will probably consider that the time has come when we should seek authority to replace the Berettas with new weapons of a more modern design.' The minute added that the City of London police were using the 9mm Walther for which a price of £15 was quoted last year. On 1 April 1960 agreement was reached that the 9mm Walther should replace the worn-out Berettas, but it was not until July 1961 that the new weapon was taken into use.

Friday night is often lively in the East End of London and Friday 2 June 1961 was no exception. During a domestic row at his mother-in-law's house in Tavistock Road, Stratford, a man lashed out with a chair injuring her, his wife of nine weeks and her younger sister. By the time police arrived the man had decamped, but the complaint was duly recorded at the local police station in West Ham Lane. At 12.45 p.m. the next day, John Hall, alias Helmwigg, telephoned the CID office and asked if he could see the officer dealing with the case whom he understood wished to speak to him about his chair wielding. The Detective Inspector invited Hall to call at the station, which he did. There he was told that he would be charged with causing grievous bodily harm to one of the women, who was quite badly hurt. When the prisoner was asked to empty his pockets he carefully placed on one of the desks six rounds of pistol ammunition and then produced a 9mm Walther pistol from his right-hand trouser pocket. As the D.I. and his sergeant tried to reason with him Hall said, 'You're not keeping me here,' backed through the door and ran down the stairs and out of the station.

Two uniform officers gave chase, one on foot and the other on his light-weight motor cycle, and the suspect was seen to run across the recreation ground and climb a fence into Whalebone Lane. The foot constable, Cox, was now joined by Sergeant Frederick Hutchins, off duty and in plain clothes, and they were told by a small boy that their man had run into Tennyson Road. Both officers caught up with the suspect and the sergeant jumped on the man's back and tried to grab the gun. The powerfully built gunman, over six feet tall, flung him off and as Hutchins tried to tackle him again he was shot in the chest at point-blank range. P.C. Cox unhesitatingly moved forward, but was shot in the stomach. As he fell to the ground Hutchins, staggering under the impact of the bullet, collapsed across his legs.

Meanwhile the escape of an armed man had been passed to all wireless cars by Information Room and this message was undoubtedly heard by Inspector Pawsey driving a duty officer's car fitted with radio. Ironically Pawsey was only covering West Ham Sub-Division for the last two hours of his tour of duty which finished at 2 p.m. – his usual area was Ilford. As the inspector drove into Tennyson Road he saw the suspect, gun in hand, running towards him; the time was 1.40 p.m. As the suspect was passing the car Pawsey opened the door and started to get out. The gunman turned and shot him through the heart from a distance of three feet. For Philip Pawsey, an 8th Army veteran who had survived four years in a German prisoner-of-war camp, luck had finally run out and he fell dying across the seat, reaching for the radio handset.

P.C. England on a light-weight motor cycle, who had been in the chase since Hall fled from the police station, saw the killer run into Deanery Road and thence into the back of a house in Romford Road. At this point faulty information led police to believe that the wanted man had jumped on an east-bound lorry and the trail went cold. Scores of armed police now joined the hunt in the vicinity of Romford Road; his known haunts were under observation and more armed officers scoured nearby Wanstead Flats and kept watch on his parents' house in South Woodford.

Both P.C. Cox and Sergeant Hutchins had been taken to Queen Mary's Hospital, Stratford. Cox was lucky – a bullet was extracted from his stomach and he lived. Hutchins was unlucky – despite cardiac massage, artificial respiration and blood transfusions, he died at 4.30 p.m. He had served 28 years and would have celebrated his 50th birthday with his wife and children in eight days' time.

At 8.30 pm that evening the crime reporter of a Sunday newspaper received a telephone call from a man who said, 'I am the killer. I am the man who killed a policeman.' The journalist kept the man talking and persuaded him to give the telephone number of the kiosk from which he was speaking – Wanstead 4199. A colleague listening on a link telephone passed the information to Scotland Yard and armed police converged on the kiosk at the edge of Wanstead Flats. As they moved in towards Hall, fourteen minutes after he had begun his conversation with the reporter, the murderer shot himself with the same Walther pistol, serial no. 3571, which he had used that afternoon.

On 5 June, the *Daily Mail* under 'Line of Duty' paid tribute to the dead officers and expressed profound sympathy for their dependants. One of the paragraphs read, 'Danger, injury – death. These may come to any policeman on any beat. Here is something to remember now that relations between police and public are said to be bad, and when so much mud is thrown at the force.' The indicator, which had pointed to 'anti-police' for much of the 1950s, was beginning to swing the other way under the impetus of policeman slain on duty. It was a familiar pattern.

Hall was taken to Whipps Cross Hospital where he died the following Saturday. P.C. Charles Cox received the George Medal and P.C. England a British Empire Medal. Inspector Pawsey and Sergeant Hutchins were each awarded a posthumous Queen's Police Medal.

Following the Stratford shootings, the Branch Boards forwarded a resolution that all members of the Force should take a short course in the use of firearms; supplemented by an annual period of firing practice. In addition, special provisions should be made to facilitate this training in respect of all duty officers, i.e., Inspectors. This was discussed by the Commissioner and some of his senior officers, but they decided not to extend the scope of training. However, they did agree that two Inspectors per Division would attend an Army course [this training had been completed by May 1962] and all Inspectors should be trained in the use of firearms.

Returning to the mundane, Police Order dated 29 September 1961 announced that a safety certificate had been issued by the military authorities in respect of a new indoor range at City Road police station. Annual practices which had been held at Bishopsgate would now take place at City Road.

In January 1964, pending the 5-yearly inspection of all Force weapons, a complete check on firearms turned up twenty extra pistols and 80 revolvers. These weapons, from thirteen different manufacturers, had been selected from those surrendered during the last amnesty. They were held together with 2,000 rounds of surrendered ammunition, at Scotland Yard as an operational reserve in case of emergency. The inspection revealed that 25 per cent of the weapons were unserviceable and, in addition, all the ammunition was suspect. The twenty Colt pistols borrowed by the Special Branch also appeared, marked on the return as 'On loan from the War Office'. Fifteen of these pistols were declared unusable and some of the ammunition dated 1951 and 1953 was tarnished by age and had to be replaced.

On Friday, 12 August 1966 the *Daily Mirror*, concerned with the state of crime in the Metropolis, stated 'Four out of every ten cases to go before the jury are ending in acquittal. We can be happy about that only if we are mad enough to believe that in four out of every ten cases, police are nabbing the wrong man.' At 3.15 that afternoon a 'Q' car (unmarked police car with a crew in plain clothes) turned into Braybrook Street, Hammersmith, in the shadow of Wormwood Scrubs Prison. The car, call-sign 'Foxtrot one-one', was driven by P.C. Geoffrey Fox, a father of three and the oldest member of the crew, with sixteen years' service. Detective Sergeant Christopher Head sat beside him in the wireless operator's position and the youngest officer, Temporary Detective Constable David Wombwell, aged 27, father of two young children, occupied the back seat. Many years previously, Wombwell's great-uncle, also a Metropolitan Police constable, had been killed on duty by a criminal – history was about to repeat itself.

The officers saw a blue Vanguard estate car, index number PGT 726, with three male occupants, parked in front of them. Unbeknown to the police, the vehicle also contained three loaded handguns – an Enfield no. 2 Mark I .38 revolver, serial 19210, a Colt .380 pistol, serial no. 17515 and a 1918 9mm Luger pistol, no. 206. Subsequently it was established that the Vanguard's driver was John Witney and the man beside him was Harry Maurice Roberts. John Duddy was in the back and all three men were convicted criminals. D.S. Head and T.D.C. Wombwell approached the car and while Wombwell was speaking to the driver, the sergeant walked towards the back of the vehicle. Roberts produced the Enfield revolver and fired through the driver's open window; the bullet entered Wombwell's left eye and he fell dead. The detective sergeant apparently started to run back towards Foxtrot one-one as Roberts got out of the car and fired at him. The first shot missed, but the second hit him in the back and he fell dying in front of the police car. At that moment Duddy, holding the Colt pistol, left the Vanguard, ran towards the surviving police officer and fired through the rear nearside window at P.C. Fox. He then fired two more shots, probably through the open passenger window of the police car, and one of the bullets passed through Fox's head and killed him. The Q car was a Triumph 2000 automatic and the engine was still running. As Fox slumped in the driving seat his foot depressed the accelerator and the vehicle moved forward, running over the dead body of D.S. Head. Roberts and Duddy ran back to the Vanguard, which was driven away.

John Witney, the Vanguard's owner, was arrested at his home in Fernhead Road, Paddington, at 9 p.m. the same day. According to Witney he had sold the vehicle to a stranger some hours before the killing, but late on Saturday night the car was found in garage no. 103 under a railway arch in Vauxhall. The garage was rented by Witney and the Vanguard contained equipment for crime and three expended cartridge cases.

Saturday morning's *Daily Mirror* carried banner headlines nearly two inches high 'MASSACRED IN THE LINE OF DUTY', above a horrific photograph of Head and Wombwell lying dead in the road. Massacre, meaning indiscriminate slaughter, was the right word. On the same day the *Daily Mail* asked, 'Is it time to give the policeman a gun?' which headed a balanced article on the question of arming the police. The Secretary of the Police Federation was quoted as saying, 'Either make a policeman's murder a hanging offence or give him arms to defend himself. Preferably the former.'

On Monday, 15 August, the *Daily Mail* carried a front page column headed 'ITV SAYS SORRY OVER POLICE PROGRAMME'. Apparently viewers had telephoned to protest that a programme in which criticisms were levelled at police, screened at 6.55 the previous evening, was in bad taste so soon after Braybrook Street. One of the speakers, Mr George Target, had complained that after being issued 'with a uniform and a big hat' police hit people with sticks. The newspaper report added that at home in Hastings on the same night Mr Target, a pacifist, said '. . . I do not condone the murder of the three policemen, but people are being sentimental about it'.

Two days later John Duddy was arrested in Glasgow, but the third member of the trio, Harry Roberts, had dropped out of sight. Despite more than 6,000 alleged sightings in different parts of the country Roberts, a former army marksman who had soldiered in Malaya, could not be found.

Police now received information that on 15 August, three days after the murders, Roberts had bought a sleeping-bag, haversack and tinned food and taken a Green Line bus to the Wake Arms roundabout on

Epping New Road, in the middle of Epping Forest. Scotland Yard issued a photograph of the wanted man and a new description '. . . He may be dressed in a khaki combat jacket, khaki drill trousers, a dark-green shirt, or a multi-coloured brown shirt, and a pair of Spanish boots in green felt . . .' The public were warned not to approach him as he might still be armed.

The Metropolitan Police was about to launch its biggest armed operation since 1911 – but serious flaws were already showing in the system. On the evening of the 17th, after yet another Roberts sighting, two pairs of policemen armed with Webley revolvers were sent to search one of the more secluded parts of Epping Forest. As one of the pairs, an inspector and a constable, alighted at the rendezvous, the P.C. asked the inspector to show him how to load his revolver. Somewhat taken aback his colleague queried whether he was an authorized shot. 'Oh yes,' said the P.C., 'but that was in 'A' Division with a pistol. I've never had one of these things before.' The inspector duly loaded the revolver for him, gave the P.C. a quick lesson on the weapon, and advised him to sit in the car and keep radio watch. However, the constable, stout fellow, refused to allow his inspector to plunge into the undergrowth by himself and insisted on accompanying him. With one eye open for Roberts and the other eye on his partner, who was armed with a loaded 'thing' he had never handled before, the inspector moved into the forest. Fortunately for all concerned Harry Roberts failed to make an appearance.

At dawn on 18 August more than 500 police, including dog-handlers and CID officers, assembled on the outskirts of Epping Forest. Although there was a shortage of revolvers there was an even greater shortage of authorized shots, and a scene at a 'J' Division police station was probably repeated elsewhere. After the men had been briefed there were six revolvers waiting to be issued, but there were only two trained men in the group. The superintendent stared thoughtfully at the remaining four weapons and then asked if anyone had ever handled a revolver in the armed forces. Two right hands slowly rose and two guns were issued. Finally those assembled were asked if anyone would like 'to have a go' and two volunteers, who were certainly unfamiliar with firearms, were each handed a revolver and twelve rounds of ammunition. As one of the waiting officers was heard to remark, 'This is going to be the biggest b – – – – up since the siege of Sidney Street.'

Although there must have been some form of system in the search pattern, which was not apparent to the searchers, it soon broke down

...ove: September 1975,
...ference in the basement of
...aghetti House restaurant.
...ree D.11 officers on the
...t. (Met)
...ght: Interior of the storeroom
...ere the hostages were held.
...et)

Top left: Balcombe Street, 12 December 1975. Mrs Matthews escorted by a hooded gunman. (Met)
Bottom left: Balcombe Street – surrender. The blur to the right in the large window is the masked terrorist leader taking instructions from police by telephone. (Met)
Bottom Right: The Balcombe Street witch, suitably cased. (Met)
Above: Additional ranges at Lippitts Hill training camp were far from rainproof. The cartoon showing an instructor and his student moving forward to check targets appeared on a D.11 noticeboard alongside a note from a senior officer. The latter's memorandum read, 'During the wet season some trouble in the ranges has been experienced'.
Below: Field training with D.11 instructors wearing steel helmets. Casualty being placed on a stretcher mounted behind a mobile armoured shield.

Top left: Libyan People's Bureau, Easter 1984. D.11 personnel discussed various methods of entry should this be necessary. Option 1.

Above: All officers moving through the shielding screen and into the danger area were required to show their warrant cards. D.11's cartoonist allowed his imagination free play.

Top centre: Libyan People's Bureau siege – D.11 marksman on adjoining roof top. (Syndication International)

Top right: D.11 cover the front door of the Libyan embassy, 25 yards away, as a messenger prepares to deliver food.

Right: The long walk, 27 April 1984. Occupants of the Libyan People's Bureau leave the building in spaced groups of six. (Met)

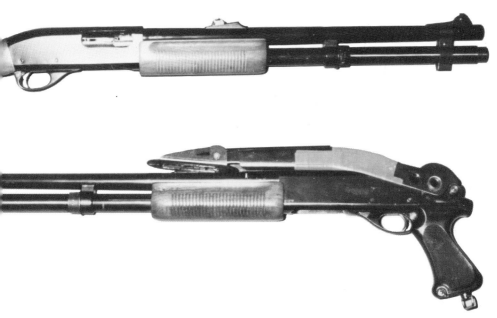

Top left: One of the Metropolitan Police indoor
ranges. Firing from the 25-metre point. (Met)
Bottom left: Shotgun training – D.11 instructors.
Top right: Students' shotgun indoctrination.

Police camera records Press camera. (Met)
Above: Remington 870 12 bore pump-action
shotgun. The same model fitted with a folding
stock. (Met)

Top: Heckler & Koch MP5 A3 9mm
submachine-gun with retracting butt stock. 15- to
30-round magazine. (Met)
Centre: Similar model, but silenced. MP5 SD1.
(Met)

Bottom: Heckler & Koch MP 5K 9mm
submachine-gun for protection officers. Capable
of single shots, 3-round bursts or fully automatic.
(Met)

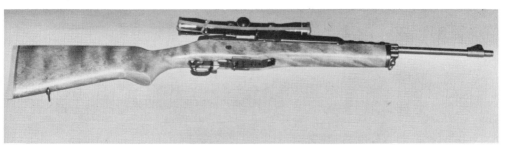

Top: Enfield 'Enforcer' 7.62mm sniper rifle fitted with image intensifier for use at night. (Met)
Centre: Enfield 'Enforcer' with Pecar telescope – daylight usage. (Met)

Heckler & Koch 93 .223 self-loading rifle with a Zeiss telescope. (Met)
Bottom: Ruger mini 14R model. .223 rifle and telescope. (Met)

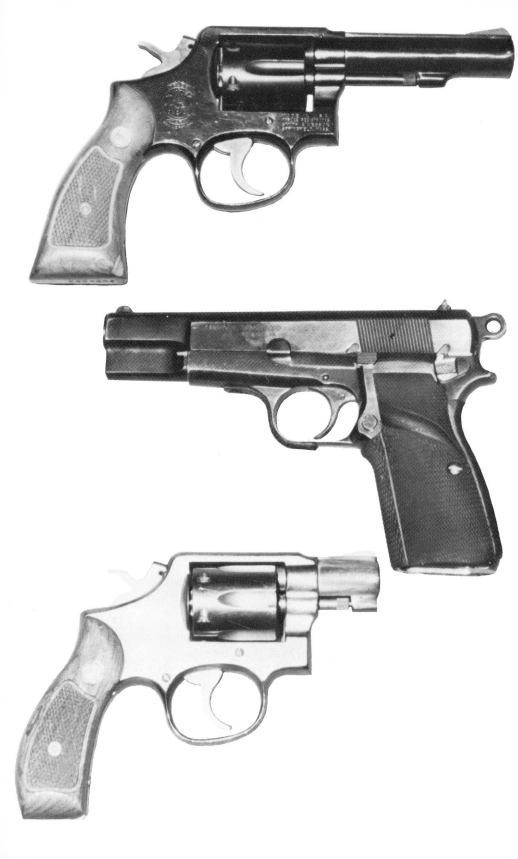

Top left: Smith & Wesson .38 Special revolver, model 10, standard issue. (Met)

Centre left: Browning 9mm pistol. (Met)

Bottom left: Smith & Wesson .38 Special, model 64, carried by plain clothes officers. (Met)

Right: F.B.I. Academy, Virginia, U.S.A. D.11 officer practices his quick-draw routine. Notice the finger outside the trigger guard until the last possible moment.

Below: Two-handed grip, double-action shooting.

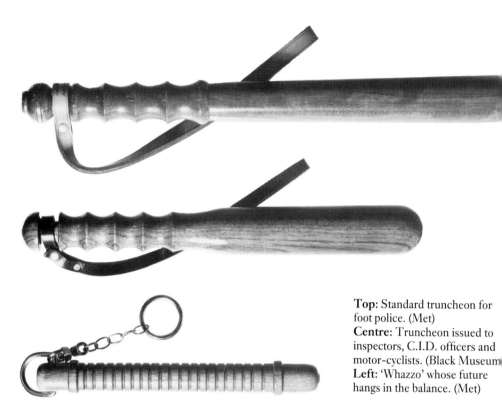

Top: Standard truncheon for foot police. (Met)
Centre: Truncheon issued to inspectors, C.I.D. officers and motor-cyclists. (Black Museum)
Left: 'Whazzo' whose future hangs in the balance. (Met)

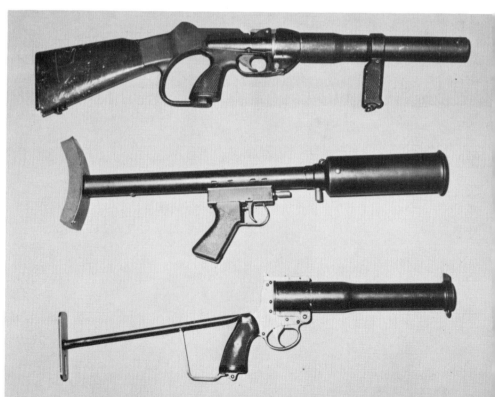

Top left: On the strength of this photograph most Metropolitan Police dog-handlers' were eventually disarmed. (Syndication International)
Left: Distraction devices' used for the first time in London – Boxing Day, 1985. (Met)
Above: Police submachine-gunners at Heathrow Airport, January 1986. (Syndication International)

Fantasy 1886 – Reality 1986.
Above: In 1886 *Punch* portrays a policeman of the future.
Left: P.C.s wearing riot helmets with visors and flame-resistant overalls. The shield lettered POLICE is carried by members of arrest squads and was first used operationally on 28 April 1982 in Notting Hill. The transparent shield on the left was an experimental version. (Met)

through lack of adequate communications. By the end of the first day disconnected lines and groups of men, and women, were beating through the undergrowth and flushing out other police groups. Some of the armed men had holsters, some not, and a number carried unloaded guns and ammunition in separate pockets. In contrast, at least one CID officer carried a loaded and cocked revolver thrust casually into his waistband, until it was pointed out that he stood a good chance of damaging a delicate part of his anatomy! The search continued for two days but Roberts had already moved north through the forest and into Hertfordshire.

The funeral of the murdered policemen was held on 31 August and on the same day Scotland Yard offered a reward of £1,000 for information leading to the arrest of Roberts. Posters carrying this appeal and a photograph of the wanted man were displayed outside police stations throughout the country. These posters were often pinned up alongside reward bills which offered £1,400 for the recovery of stolen jewellery and £1,750 in the case of a furs theft. Property was still worth more than lives. A memorial service for the slain officers was held in Westminster Abbey on 6 September and some of the 1,000-strong crowd outside carried banners calling for the restoration of capital punishment for the murder of police and prison officers.

Roberts was arrested by Hertfordshire officers near his camouflaged hideout in Thorley Wood, outside Bishop's Stortford, on 15 November. 'Please don't shoot,' begged the bold killer, 'You won't get any trouble from me. I've had enough.' A Luger pistol with a fully charged magazine was found in his sleeping-bag and the Colt pistol in his rucksack. The Enfield revolver had been buried by Roberts and Duddy on Hampstead Heath, whence it was disinterred. Forensic tests confirmed that the Enfield and Colt were the two guns used in Braybrook Street.

The trial opened on Tuesday, 6 December and the judge completed his summing-up on the following Monday. It took the jury just thirty minutes to find the three accused men guilty of murdering the three policemen. They were sentenced to life imprisonment and Mr Justice Glyn-Jones added a recommendation that each of them serve a period of thirty years. Four months later a Cypriot, Christos Costas, who had sold the three guns to Roberts, was sentenced to six years imprisonment for firearms offences.

14

A Firearms Wing

Following the searches in Epping Forest it was obvious that fundamental changes were necessary to ensure that only properly authorized men would have access to weapons. The Commissioner therefore decided that all future firearms training would be the province of qualified instructors and, in addition, the number of authorized shots was to be substantially increased. In addition to all Inspectors, it was proposed to train sixty men per Division, plus a number of men from Special Branch, Central Traffic Division, Flying Squad, Special Patrol Group and Headquarters staff. Each man would undergo a four-day basic training course and, thereafter, attend a one-day refresher course every four months.

As training on this scale constituted a continuous process, the task was given to D.6 Branch which dealt with Civil Defence and communications. This was in line with a recommendation by the Police War Duties Committee on the arming of police in time of war which, if implemented, would also be the responsibility of that department. Police Order 20 of 2 December 1966 stated that ten firearms instructors would be attached to D.6 to undertake all firearms training within the Force. Applications were invited from Inspectors, Sergeants and Constables '. . . who volunteer and can be recommended for this important specialist work. Previous experience in the handling and use of firearms, particularly revolvers and automatic pistols, is desirable. Superintendents should include in their recommendations an assessment of each applicant's potential as an instructor, and his power of leadership, bearing in mind the considerable responsibility attached to this duty as regards the safety of personnel under training and the maintenance of a high standard of range discipline.' Successful applicants were to attend a residential course at the Small Arms Wing of the School of Infantry, Hythe, in January 1967. The ghost of Superintendent Wakeford was probably giving an approving nod.

A large number of men volunteered and the ex-service background of the selected ten was supplied by the Royal Marines, Brigade of

Guards, Rifle Brigade, Parachute Regiment, Royal West African Frontier Force and the RAF Regiment. Working dress for the course consisted of a blue boiler suit, gumboots, a webbing belt and holster containing a .38 revolver, and a canvas shoulder holster holding a Walther pistol – all worn at the same time. The citizens of Hythe had seen nothing like it since their town became one of the Cinque Ports. On their return from the course some of the new instructors sat in an annex to Scotland Yard and drafted training programmes, safety rules and a drill book, drawing on the expertise of the Royal Ulster Constabulary, FBI, Shanghai Police and other armed law enforcement agencies. The firearms wing became responsible for all firearms courses within the Metropolitan Police from 1 April 1967, despite a last-ditch stand by Special Branch officers who wished to continue with their own training syllabus.

A basic course lasted four days with two instructors for every ten students, and the primary aim was to teach men to handle a weapon with safety to members of the public, themselves and their colleagues. The first half-day was spent in the classroom where the introduction dealt with the law and armed police, based on the 'defence only' clause first formulated in 1882. Then followed the necessary drill sequences which were practised with dummy rounds and de-activated weapons. Finally, proper emphasis was given to the correct grip, trigger squeeze and sight picture. Students were also required to learn, and continually observe, six standard safety rules. The first of these rules should have been compulsory reading for some of the 14,934 holders of current firearms certificates in the Metropolis – 'ALWAYS prove your weapon is unloaded whenever you pick it up, hand it to, or take it from any person.'

During the course each student fired 108 full-bore rounds, which included a classification test. This consisted of ten rounds fired by sense of direction in paired shots from the 7-yard line in 24 seconds; ten aimed shots from four different positions at 25 yards and ten rounds from the 15-yard firing-point – one shot at each 2-second exposure of a turning target. Simulated brick walls at 15 and 25 yards accustomed the firer to using cover and also provided support when shooting. A two-handed grip was used for all the sequences which were fired double-action, i.e., without cocking the hammer. In sense of direction shooting at close range, dominated by a feeling of urgency and without using the sights, both eyes remained open and the weapon was punched forward like a pointing forefinger.

For the first time the Metropolitan Police also graduated a firer's skill – 28 to 30 hits (maximum) a marksman, 25 to 27 a first-class shot and 18 to 24, second-class. Under eighteen, the student failed, irrespective of his rank or branch. Unlike the Army, FBI and many overseas forces, there were no scoring rings, or kill or wound areas, on the torso-shaped targets which were covered in plain grey paper. A man was never taught to kill, or wound, or aim for a specific mark. Instead, he would always shoot at the largest exposed part of his adversary in order to stop him. The only exceptions to plain grey were the moving targets which represented 'shoot' or 'don't shoot' situations. These appeared in the windows of the facade of a house on one of the small-bore ranges where students spent an afternoon and each fired 60 rounds from a .22 pistol. The situations were quite obvious as all the villains cuddled sawn-off shotguns or bristled with pistols while the innocent bystanders in 'don't shoot' circumstances included a vicar, mother and child, and P.C. Plod.

One day of the course was devoted to fieldcraft at Lippitts Hill training camp. This was fairly elementary, at least to ex-servicemen, and dealt with fire and movement, the use of cover, team work and search situations. There was always keen competition in the class to score off an instructor (physically if possible) and this not only promoted *esprit de corps* among the trainees, but also encouraged nimbleness of mind and body in those who instructed. In addition to the instructors, a small number of men from Divisions were trained in the use of the .303 Lee-Enfield No. 4 rifle. Four stations, each centrally situated in a police district, were each issued with two rifles and the remaining twelve were held in D.6 armoury. The production of a new loose-leaf firearms handbook enabled each successful student to be issued with the relevant section on the weapon for which he was authorized, i.e., revolver, pistol or rifle.

In 1967 the officer in charge of reserve amnesty weapons at Scotland Yard was still trying to regularize his position in case of an emergency. The only instructions he had ever been given were verbal and there was no apparent authority to retain the arms in the first place. The superintendent asked that they be removed, or written instructions be given which clearly defined responsibility for issue. After some lengthy correspondence, 36 of these weapons formed the nucleus of D.6 instructional museum, a number of revolvers were cannibalized as drill weapons, and the remainder were destroyed.

In July one of the Yard's periodical reshuffles turned D.6 into D.11, by which designation it has since been known. Training continued throughout the year despite numerous demonstrations, including the first pro-North Vietnam and anti-USA riot in October. Demonstrators, using park benches as battering rams, metal fencing as pikes and wielding banner poles as quarterstaffs, tried to break into the American Embassy in Grosvenor Square.

By 1968 the protest industry was in full production – Biafra, Vietnam, Rhodesia, anti-apartheid and nuclear disarmament. The second meeting organized by the Vietnam Solidarity Campaign began in Trafalgar Square on Sunday 17 March with an assortment of film stars and routine protesters making routine speeches. Some of the supporters wore white headbands as identification, but the German contingent (who had been trained in the Fatherland and knew a thing or two) were equipped with light-weight crash-helmets. On the outskirts of London police stopped several coach-loads of students *en route* to the Square and removed marbles destined to be thrown under horses' hooves, pepper for throwing in the eyes of policemen, and their horses, and sachets of red paint for simulating wounds inflicted by the brutal constabulary.

The mob made its way to Grosvenor Square where a determined attempt was made to storm the US Embassy. An outer police cordon broke when the helmeted Germans linked arms and charged, but order was eventually restored. Casualty figures were police 117 and demonstrators 45 (excluding red paint and tomato sauce). Most of Monday's newspapers reflected the opinion of the British public at large. The front page of the *Daily Mail* featured demonstrators trying to drag a helmet-less policeman from his horse, above a byline '200 held in clash at US Embassy'. The *Daily Mirror* headlined '80 POLICE INJURED IN "PEACE" RIOT', above a photograph captioned 'A Victim of the Battle' showing an unconscious constable being placed on a stretcher. The entire centre-page spread was devoted to pictures of the fighting and the comment 'This is Lunacy'. The *Daily Mail* returned to the theme the next day with an article 'This POISON spread in the name of peace'. By Tuesday morning thousands of congratulatory letters began to arrive at Scotland Yard from members of the public, all of them horrified by the scenes of orchestrated violence which they had seen on their television screens. The hoodlums responsible for turning Grosvenor Square into a battleground had badly overreached themselves.

Three days after the riots Sir Joseph Simpson died of a heart attack. A dedicated public servant, he was the first Commissioner to die in office since Richard Mayne, a hundred years previously. Sir John Waldron, the Deputy Commissioner, picked up the reins on 21 March 1968. Strength of the Force stood at 20,539.

In July a meeting at the Yard discussed the forthcoming inspection of Force weapons. Manpower reductions prevented the usual practice of the inspectorate staff attending police stations and hence the weapons would have to be sent to Enfield. As it was impracticable to denude Divisions of their revolvers, the Inspectorate of Armaments suggested a loan of 150 Enfield No. 2 revolvers to fill the gap. A D.11 minute dated 29 October points out that the first 50 Enfields had been examined by the D.11 armourer and, '. . . a number were not up to the standard of accuracy required for police purposes'. The inspection was completed by May 1969 and the 150 revolvers returned to Enfield. During this inspection it was found that fourteen of the 9mm Walther pistols (mixed French and German manufacture) used in training had each sustained a body fracture across the forward end of the left slide rib. This fault was potentially dangerous and it was doubtful whether it could be repaired.

During this period D.11 staff also test-fired a variety of the US stockpile revolvers, albeit using British 2Z ammunition, to ascertain whether they were suitable as training weapons. The results were fairly horrifying. In many cases bullets fell short of the target and occasionally barely managed to tumble out of the muzzle. In one or two cases the bullet failed to clear the barrel and had to be reamed out by the armourer. Bulged barrels and pitted bores were not uncommon and one specimen, now in the instructional museum, has been halved to show five bullets, one behind the other, all lodged in the bore. These weapons were promptly dubbed 'suicide specials' and it was felt that the US official who had unloaded this lot onto war-time Britain had done well by the American taxpayers.

Training continued throughout 1967/68 and included, for the first time, exposure to CS capsules at Lippitts Hill camp and gas-gun training at Woolwich Arsenal. The gas was developed in 1928 by two American inventors, Carson and Stoughton, hence CS, and causes copious weeping and some nasal irritation. In a few cases the person affected may vomit, but recovers completely within five to eight minutes.

On instructions from the Home Office, the CS irritant was never to be called gas, but always referred to as tear-smoke. Presumably anyone temporarily incapacitated by smoke would feel much happier than if he had been gassed. In addition, stringent regulations were laid down that it was to be used solely to enable a criminal to be arrested when not to use it would endanger the lives of the criminal, the police or the public. [Policemen felt that this should have been the other way about with the public first and the criminal last]. It was not to be used against persons other than armed besieged criminals or violently insane persons in buildings, except as a means of self-defence in cases of absolute necessity. Under no circumstances would it be used for the control of disturbances. In the Metropolis it could only be used by D.11 instructors. Animal lovers were pleased to learn that CS does not affect horses or dogs.

Not unnaturally articles about CS appeared in newspapers and the matter was raised in Parliament. In July 1968 the Home Secretary, Mr Callaghan, was asked what instructions he had given the Metropolitan Police about the use of CS gas. His answer triggered several other questions including a query as to whether CS might not be lethal in a confined space. He agreed that it was potent, but at the same time was less toxic than other gases, and the number of occasions when it was used were rare. He was then asked, 'If this gas is rarely used, and if there are serious doubts about its effects, why is the Home Secretary authorizing its use at all?' Mr Callaghan replied, 'Because there may be occasions when it would be extremely dangerous for the Police to operate without it.' His answer appears to have quashed a promising issue for debate.

However, despite the concern about CS, this was not the first time that the Metropolitan Police had been given access to gas weapons. Back in 1943, on 12 August, Owen Munro fired at police with a double-barrelled shotgun and then barricaded himself in the attic of a house in Barry Road, East Dulwich. In addition to the shotgun he was also armed with two swords and other weapons. Armed police surrounded the building but repeated calls to surrender were ignored. The man had taken his sister as a hostage, but released her in the early hours of the next morning. When CN tear-gas canisters, obtained from the army, were thrown into the house, Munro donned his civilian issue gas mask and continued to hold police at bay. Finally, fourteen hours after the siege started, he was found dead in the attic with self-inflicted gunshot wounds.

Following this affair the question of gas was considered by the Metropolitan Police, and one of the Assistant Commissioners, Sir John

Nott-Bower, expressed the view that its use would not be in accordance with the traditions of the English police. He added that he had '. . . an instinctive dislike of introducing as a regular feature of police work anything remotely savouring of American gangster films'.

On another occasion a supply of tear-gas was taken to an incident but not used. Following a disturbance during the evening of 12 March 1957, the man involved, Benedict Obinini, locked himself in his room on the third floor of a cheap tenement-house in Shrewsbury Road, Notting Hill. He was armed with two knives and was known to be of unsound mind and extremely violent.

Police were called but could not persuade him to surrender. At 1 a.m. the next morning two dog-handlers and their dogs attempted to enter the room but withdrew after Obinini knifed one of the constables and his dog. Tear-gas grenades had been requested, but there was some delay while the duty officer at the local barracks queried the authority for supplying gas to the civil force. Eventually the canisters arrived but were not used because at 7.15 a.m. Obinini gave up his knives and agreed to accompany police and the Mental Welfare Officer to hospital. However, as they were about to leave the room the man changed his mind and there was a fierce struggle, in which all concerned were injured, before he was overpowered.

Gas was again reviewed by the Metropolitan Police and culminated in an instruction dated 29 September 1958 on the use of gas in the apprehension of violent persons. A stock of tear-gas grenades for police was to be held at Kensington Palace Barracks and a trained NCO would always be on duty. Requests for assistance were only to be made in exceptional circumstances, 'when all other means of overpowering such persons had failed'. A further order on 16 October 1958 emphasized that the responsibility for using gas rested upon police; and the officer in charge at the incident, who must be of not less rank than a super-intendent, would direct army personnel when and where the grenades were to be discharged.

However, in February 1959 the military expressed concern about their position in law. Although willing to supply army grenades for police use, they now insisted that the canisters should be thrown by a police officer and not by a soldier. As a result, all constables employed in Back Hall at New Scotland Yard, plus certain divisional officers on a relieving rota, were instructed in the use of tear-gas grenades by the Royal Military Police. Arrangements were also made for the canisters to be exchanged every three years – the limit of their 'shelf' life.

On 2 April 1962 a demonstration of various types of gas equipment was held at Porton Down and was attended by representatives from the Metropolitan Police. One of the weapons displayed was a Webley & Scott handgun with a 1½-inch bore, of the type commonly called a flare pistol. It fired a millboard cartridge, designated L2A2, containing two ounces of CS smoke, equivalent to half an ounce of CS gas. These pistols and a supply of cartridges were later added to the armoury available for police and held at Kensington Palace Barracks.

By 1965 the search for a more accurate gas discharger had led the research and planning branch to a purpose-designed gun, which fired a variety of projectiles, manufactured in the USA by Federal Laboratories Inc. In December 1966 authority was sought from the Home Office to purchase five of these weapons and a supply of ammunition. Permission was given on 27 April 1967 to buy two, not five, and the two gas guns in their huge carrying cases finally arrived by sea in the UK on 10 July 1967. From this date the Back Hall officers ceased to be responsible for the use of CS in London and the duty passed to D.6, later D.11 Branch.

The newly arrived American gas gun was a 1½-inch self-cocking, breech-loading, smooth-bore weapon which discharged a missile fitted with stabilizing fins which opened in flight. According to certain senior officers this gun was a precise weapon, despite the black powder propellant, capable of placing a shell through a given window pane at 50 yards. Unfortunately this was not the experience of the firers who found that the shell not only often missed the pane but also the window, and sometimes the building. After instructors had set fire to part of the Thames north bank, and on another occasion narrowly missed a tugboat which was minding it's own business, it was obvious that this particular missile had been developed for riot control and not precision work in a built-up area.

The Firearms Act of 1968 came into force on 1 August 1968. A major change of policy was the requirement in Section 2 of the Act that the owner of a shotgun now needed a certificate. However, as criminals have always had access to firearms, without the formality of a certificate, the new provision did little to inhibit the occasions when shotguns were used during the commission of a crime.

By 1969 a number of men from provincial forces had been trained in the use of CS and this two-day course included gas inoculation. The students and staff, all wearing respirators, assembled in a disused warehouse and threw a number of grenades which completely filled the building with CS smoke. Each student then moved towards the door and at a given point removed his gas mask and walked the last 25 yards unprotected. As the weeping figures came out into the fresh air the staff ensured that the same number of bodies that had entered also emerged. Reaction and length of incapacity varied between individuals, but the consensus among those gassed was that CS was less lethal than swallowing diesel and petrol fumes on traffic point-duty.

Also in this year the instructors began moving towards a dual operational/training role. Police Order 28 of 9 May read, 'Occasions may arise when the services of a specially qualified officer is desirable. In such circumstances, the officer in command may ask for the assistance of one or more of the firearm instructors, each of whom is experienced in the use of all types of weapons issued to the Force, i.e., revolvers, rifles and semi-automatic weapons. Requests should be made to D.11 . . . or to Information Room.'

The quality of training improved with the installation of cine equipment, with sound-control mechanism, installed in one of the indoor ranges. Every time a shot was fired at the screen the sound was picked up by a microphone, a heat shutter operated, and the film stopped. Lights behind the screen illuminated the bullet hole and enabled the firer's action and shooting ability to be analysed. Re-starting the film automatically moved the triple-layered screen and covered the last bullet hole. Training films for this cinema, scripted and acted by instructors, were made in Epping Forest and one of the London docks. D.11 was also responsible for writing the script for a film on the use and dangers of CS, which was given a professional commentator.

In 1970, Special Air Service pistol courses were attended by several instructors who thereby increased their skills and awareness of danger. The latter was certainly the case with an ex-Royal Marine in the 'killing room' when a bullet passed through a fold in his shirt. Unfortunately, he was wearing it at the time. Another instructor completed a sniper instructor's course at the Skill-at-Arms Division, School of Infantry, and later attended an instructor's course in firearms and defensive tactics held at the FBI Academy in Virginia. This was the start of a programme which continues to this day, whereby D.11 staff attend outside courses for snipers, bodyguard training and other specialist activities.

Calibre .303 ammunition had not been manufactured since 1956, and the Commissioner, himself a rifleman, was uneasy about the standard of rifle shooting in the Force. Training, which was limited to a one-day practice twice a year, was unlikely to develop marksmen. He was anxious that police riflemen should be of the highest possible standard, a need emphasized by the possibility of planes being hijacked at London Airport. In 1969, the British Airports Authority Constabulary had been refused permission to hold firearms and, as a safeguard, D.11 had provided 24-hour coverage; a duty subsequently taken over by 'T' and 'X' Divisions. A decision was therefore taken to train specialist teams, each man to be equipped with a 7.62mm L42A1 rifle fitted with a no. 32 telescope, initially borrowed from the Ministry of Defence at a hire charge of £310 per annum. Personal binoculars and other equipment were also included, and the riflemen would be trained in a dual sniper/counter-sniper role.

The Force was circulated for volunteers and a staggering 900 applicants came forward. Elimination tests reduced this number to the 30 best shots, which included twelve instructors. Three rifle courses were held in 1971. Each lasted three weeks and took the student in progressive stages from 100 to 800 yards. The classification tests were held at 300 and 600 yards; ten rounds application and ten rounds snap on head and shoulder targets at 300 and torso targets at 600 yards. At each distance the snap target was exposed for three seconds. Every firer was obliged to score a minimum of 46 out of 50 on each practice and at each distance. In addition, he was also required to pass a judging distance test varying from 100 to 600 yards. The pass mark was accuracy on five out of eight within a margin of error of 15 per cent.

Students usually did their homework in the evenings, and some police wives became almost as conversant with such mysteries as the minute of angle elevation table and wind allowance as their husbands. The object of each course was to fret, spelled 'FRHET', a pnuemonic for 'First Round Hit Every Time'. This was essential in view of the major difference between the training for a military sniper and instruction for a police rifleman. In the case of the former, if a bullet passed through his primary target and struck someone else on the same side it was a bonus: for a policeman it would be a disaster. Thus special attention was paid to backdrop and lie of the land. This had a practical application. On an exercise at London Airport it was realized that one of the marshalling positions could only be covered from a particular point.

Any bullet fired from that point, which missed the target, would precisely follow the curvature of the ground and finish in one of the high-octane fuel tanks. There was some hasty revision of lines of fire.

In the early hours of Friday, 30 July 1971, police used CS gas for the first time in London. The previous evening police had answered a 'disturbance' call to a house in Olive Road, Cricklewood. There they found the dead bodies of the occupier, his wife, and son-in-law, a petty officer in the US Navy. They had all been knifed to death. The daughter of the house, aged 19, had also been stabbed but was still alive, although seriously injured. The person responsible, Michael McKenzie, son of the dead couple and brother-in-law of the serviceman, had barricaded himself in a top floor back bedroom. After a four-hour siege two D.11 men climbed into the loft and fired a CS missile into the room through a hole in the ceiling. As CS smoke gushed out, the powerfully built killer tore away furniture piled against the door and burst through the doorway with considerable force. Detective Constable Arnold, weighing 17½ stones, who was immediately outside the door, took the full force of the impact from McKenzie. The impetus carried them both through a group of four officers on the landing and still locked together they fell down the stairs. During the ensuing struggle in the hallway with the murderer, who still had a carving knife in each hand, four of the officers lost their respirators and were affected by tear-smoke. A doctor who entered the house to treat D.C. Arnold for stab wounds and bruises was also affected by CS. The only person who suffered no ill effects was the prisoner.

Press reaction was surprisingly muted. Friday's *Evening News* reported the incident on page 7 under a byline 'CS gas ends siege after triple killing. Fumes Hit Four Policemen'. There was a short factual account of the operation, and photographs, including one of a constable wearing a respirator. On Saturday the *Daily Express* reported the affair under 'Death siege: CS gas not for use in riots' and an assurance that CS would never be used by police for controlling riots.

There was, however, one unusual side-effect to this case. The local authority refused to be responsible for decontaminating the premises and police were therefore left with the task. Hence the D.11 sergeant and constable who had used the gas spent the next two days in the Olive Road house washing carpets and curtains and generally spring-cleaning. Colleagues who inquired whether the two proposed to extend the service into off-duty hours to include baby-sitting and washing-up were given some rather dusty answers.

Sir John Waldron, the 'caretaker' Commissioner, retired on 16 April 1972 and was succeeded by his Deputy, Sir Robert Mark. The citizens of London had just acquired an outstanding chief of police – although a number of corrupt officers may not have agreed. The strength of the Force stood at 22,203.

15
Rifles and Raids

By the beginning of 1972 the Firearms Wing had been beset with teething problems for nearly five years. These included limited training facilities, difficulties with ammunition supplies and an unacceptable rise in the lead level in some instructors' blood. The enclosed indoor ranges, which had been constructed for occasional club shooting, usually small bore, were not designed to cope with the volume of full-bore ammunition which was being fired in training. Thus certain classes were now switched to outdoor service ranges and instructors were suspended from indoor training when their blood/lead levels exceeded 80 micrograms per 100 millilitres of blood (the average town dweller carries about 23 to 30 micrograms).

Even more problems arose over the question of rifles. A working-party on firearms for police use in peacetime, on which the Home Office, Ministry of Defence and various police forces were represented, had been formed in 1970. The committee published an interim report on 20 September 1971 and, as a result, Home Office circular 176/72 dated 29 September 1972 recommended that police be equipped with the L39A1 7.62mm rifle, fitted with a commercial telescope. Model L39 was identical with the L42 apart from minor modifications and an alteration to the trigger mechanism. Both models had been converted from the No. 4 Lee-Enfield, Mk I or II, service rifle, which chambered .303 ammunition, a much less powerful round.

However, the experience of the Metropolitan Police with the L42 indicated that it left much to be desired. Twenty of the first batch hired from the Ministry of Defence were returned, before use, after inspection by the Force armourer. A further five were returned to the Royal Small Arms Factory at Enfield during the following year. On 2 August 1972 an inspecting officer from the Weapons Branch, Technical Group, Woolwich, examined the rifles on loan and certified that 17 out of 30 needed workshop adjustment. Out of that number, nine were unsafe to use even for training purposes. The suspect seventeen weapons were out of commission for six weeks at the REME workshops in Donnington. According to the armourer, pressure generated by the more powerful 7.62mm round in the chamber of a converted .303 rifle caused undue stress on the bolt locking lugs and resistance column. This was borne out in the spring of 1972 at the School of Infantry when bolts fractured on three L42A1 7.62mm conversions as the rifles were fired. The possibility had now to be considered that part of the broken firing bolt might be driven back into the firer's face.

Because of the poor performance of the L42A1, D.11 had considered various commercial rifles, including a Parker-Hale Safari rifle fitted with a heavy barrel and Mauser bolt action. The heavy barrel made for greater accuracy and the Mauser bolt had a triple locking system compared to the double device on the Enfield. A total of 1,200 rounds were fired through the trial weapon in nine days (far in excess of the number of rounds put through an L42 in 18 months) and the Safari was consistently accurate at all ranges up to 600 yards. Equally important, the rifle showed no signs of wear or defects. Bearing in mind the heavy responsibility resting on the shoulders of a police rifleman, the Metropolitan Police were apprehensive that the faults experienced in the L42 would also appear in the L39. Therefore, on 16 November 1972 the Receiver wrote to the Home Office seeking authority to purchase 40 Safari modified rifles at an estimated cost of £3,000.

Following a meeting between interested parties with the RSAF staff, the Assistant Under-Secretary of State at the Home Office wrote direct to the Commissioner early in 1974, asking him to accept delivery of the L39A1 instead of the Safari. He pointed out that the L42 rifles on hire to the Metropolitan Police were among the earliest conversions from .303 to 7.62mm and the weapons themselves were of wartime manufacture, with all that was implied by those words. Furthermore, future L39 rifles for police would be converted only from selected weapons which had been made in peacetime.

As the armed forces had lived off the huge stock of wartime rifles since 1945 it is difficult to visualize where the 'peacetime' weapons and selected components were to be found. It is to be hoped that a very senior civil servant had not been deliberately misinformed on this point. Incidentally the delivery date was worse than for the Safari and the L39s would cost more.

A police rifleman may be asked to undertake a role which might result in the loss of life, possibly also putting his own life at risk, and it was essential (and still is) that he have complete faith in his equipment.

D.11 staff were not convinced that the L39 would be superior to the L42, especially as a provincial force had already experienced difficulties with their 'new' L39s. However, politics took precedence over performance and Metropolitan Police riflemen signed for their Enfield 'Enforcer' rifles (son of the L39, grandson of L42, all with a common ancestor in the .303 Lee-Enfield) on 28 March 1974.

Another recommendation from the working-party concerned handguns. The .38 Webley revolver used by the Metropolitan Police, and other forces, was a rugged and accurate weapon which stood up well to the immense number of training rounds which were poured through the barrel, plus any rough handling to which it was subjected. Unfortunately, it was increasingly difficult to find adequate supplies of .38 standard ammunition which was being supplanted by the .38 special, a more powerful round. The committee agreed that the Smith & Wesson .38 special, Model 10 with a 4-inch barrel, should be adopted for general police use. Continuously armed officers would be equipped with a S & W .38 special, Model 36 with a 2-inch barrel, or the Walther pistol in 7.62mm or 9mm (short) calibre. London police disagreed with the choice of a Walther in view of the hairline cracks which had appeared on frames of some training weapons. The Model 36 was not only easier to teach and use, but also chambered the same calibre round as the Model 10, thus obviating the bugbear of mixed ammunition.

Unfortunately, .38 special bullets were not manufactured in this country and, in order to guarantee supplies of a consistent quality, the Home Office was asked to consult the Ministry of Defence and examine the possibility of one of the Royal Ordnance factories producing this calibre round. The working-party had recommended a bullet that would immediately incapacitate an armed criminal, but without passing through the target and striking a bystander, or ricochetting in the event of a miss. This could only be achieved by a semi-wad cutter hollow-point round (with a cavity in the top of the lead bullet), as opposed to the conventional jacketted type. After it was agreed that Radway Green factory would produce this type of ammunition for British police forces, the emotive words 'dum-dum bullets' began to appear in the Press.

'Bullets penetrate the Law', headed a three-column article in *The Times* dated 22 September 1974. 'Expanding bullets, which have been illegal in wartime since the Hague Convention of 1907, are being considered for use by the British police. A secret Home Office working-party, on "Firearms for Police Use in Peacetime", has come down in favour of them after several types of bullet have been tested . . . The Home Secretary still has to decide whether to accept the working-party's recommendation.' The article went on to explain the difference between jacketted and expanding bullets and quite fairly pointed out that the Hague Convention had never been signed by criminals. It might also have added that the provisions only applied to military forces, and not law enforcement agencies. Although the working-party was never 'secret' in the accepted sense of the word, it would be interesting to know who leaked the information – and why.

In the event the round was never adopted. It was felt that there would be severe criticism of police if they were armed with hollow-point ammunition and the Home Secretary was not prepared to defend its use. Those provincial forces already using this type of bullet presumably fired off their stock in training. The executive at Radway Green also discovered that they were not able to re-tool for manufacturing .38 special, even conventional rounds. This, as it transpired, was a blessing in disguise as the Metropolitan Police and many other forces were eventually obliged to make their own ammunition and save the rate-payers a good deal of money over the years.

One of the other important issues arising from the working-party's recommendations concerned the supply of Smith & Wesson .38 special revolvers. In 1973 Webley & Scott wrote to the Commissioner asking if the force proposed to re-equip with American weapons instead of their firm's product. They were informed that the decision had been made at national level in order to standardize police arms. The firm had already been approached and asked if they were prepared to produce a .38 special handgun, to police requirements, but at the time they were unable to give such an undertaking. It was a great pity that British police could not carry British guns which, among other things, would have saved heavy dollar purchases in the USA.

A consultative panel of firearms instructors had been formed on 15 June 1971 and they produced an interim report in September 1972 and a second report two years later. Needless to say there was a fair measure of disagreement between members of this panel and their bosses who sat on the working-party. Much of the difference of opinion centred on the length of time needed to train a safe and competent shot and the amount of practice necessary for him to retain those skills. There were very wide variations between forces, both in the proportion of men trained and in the standard and frequency of re-training. One Chief Constable, for example, said that a police rifleman could be trained in two days and practice thereafter once a year. The instructors thought it could not be done in under three weeks, with further regular training every month.

The other matter which caused alarm and despondency was the question, raised by the panel, of senior officers attending seminars on the tactical deployment of armed police. A number of police chiefs were convinced that their senior men could not be spared for this purpose, even for a day. Thus in many forces there was now a danger that the tail would wag the dog and those who were led were far better trained than those who led, and made command decisions. The lessons of Sidney Street had long since been forgotten. Fortunately the light has now dawned in many places, including the Metropolitan Police area.

While committee members digested coffee and excellent biscuits in the hallowed halls of the Home Office, ordinary policemen were still up at the sharp end – out on the streets. Two days after Christmas 1972, P.C. 531B Slimon, in uniform, was returning to his armed protection post at Palace Green, Kensington, which housed a number of foreign embassies. The officer was carrying a loaded .38 Webley revolver in the right-hand pocket of his overcoat. At about 11.30 a.m., as he approached the National Westminster bank on the corner of Kensington High Street and Campden Hill Road, he heard an alarm claxon blaring and was told that the bank was being raided by armed robbers. The season of good will to all men had ended earlier than usual.

Slimon drew his revolver and ran to the bank entrance shouting to the bandits that he was armed. One of the raiders, later identified as Robert Hart, pointed a sawn-off shotgun at the officer and both men appeared to have fired simultaneously. The P.C. hit his opponent, but at the same instant was himself wounded in both arms and thrown back out of the doorway by the impact. As he picked himself up and turned towards the entrance a number of bandits emerged, one with a pistol trained on him. Slimon, who was losing blood and the strength from his right hand, was only able to fire one shot, which hit another gunman.

The gang boarded a Bedford van which was driven away north along Campden Hill Road. It stopped in Pitt Street, a short distance from the bank, and the occupants began to transfer themselves and their loot into two waiting vehicles. As they were helping the last of the wounded men into one of the cars a police dog patrol van drove into the street. The raiders dumped their wounded gang member in the road and made off. Two hours later the dead body of Robert Hart, aged 33, the first bandit to be shot, was found on the fifth floor of a multi-storey car-park in Young Street, where he had been abandoned by his companions. When the body was searched, police found a loaded Luger pistol with the safety catch off and a cartridge in the breech.

Obviously the gun battle featured on the front pages of most of the daily papers on the 29th. 'Wounded Pc Kills Bank Raider. Gun battle as gang snatches £25,000,' announced the *Daily Telegraph*. 'P.C. kills gunman. Wounded – then he shoots it out,' stated the *Daily Express*. The *Daily Mirror* devoted the whole of page 11 to the affair and revealed that the dead man had nine previous convictions and was believed to have taken part in at least four other armed robberies. He was described as 'a highly dangerous criminal who shoots first'. Headed 'The Police and their Guns', the main article on the page stated, 'A new controversy over the arming of Britain's policemen flared yesterday following the cop-and-robber gun battle at a London bank on Wednesday . . . Labour's spokesman on home affairs, Mr John Fraser, said: "I think we need to know how many police are now carrying firearms. We want to know how many police guarding embassies carry guns and what is the justification for it." 'The Labour MP for Hackney Central warned of the possibility of Britain's police becoming armed, 'Through a process of stealth'.

Some of the more fatuous remarks made in Parliament and elsewhere caused the *Daily Telegraph* to comment (referring to the constable), 'The suggestion that he should have hurried to his post, leaving the staff and customers of the National Westminster bank to their fate, or, alternatively, that he should have gone to the nearest telephone kiosk to get the approval of his superiors for intervention in the raid, is clearly absurd. It belongs to the realm of liberal fantasy.'

An inquest on the dead man was held on 19 January and an unfortunate Yugoslav tourist, who had been shot by one of the raiders, told the court that at the time he thought it was a carnival because all the men wore masks. The jury returned a verdict of Justifiable Homicide on Hart, and P.C. Slimon was later awarded a well-earned George Medal.

In the following month another shooting incident added fresh fuel to the armed police controversy. On 20 February 1973 at about 9.30 a.m., three Pakistanis, Basharat Hussain and Mohammed Hanif Hussain both aged 19 years, who were not related despite the same surname, and a 15-year-old schoolboy, Dalamar Khan, forced their way into India House, Aldwych, the offices of the Indian High Commission. The three intruders were all wearing stocking masks and had armed themselves with two revolvers, three knives, a sword and a spray containing concentrated nitric acid. They seized nine hostages, including a woman, some of whom were bound and the others assaulted. The most seriously injured victim received two sword wounds, one of which fractured his skull. Surgeons subsequently removed a sliver of bone from the fracture. The assailants then smashed a window to display the hostages whom they threatened to kill.

The first policemen on the scene, armed with truncheons, arrived at 9.37 a.m., but retreated under threat from the two handguns. However, during the confusion one of the hostages escaped by hurling himself bodily through a plate-glass window and a second hostage followed him through the broken glass. Special Patrol Group officers with revolvers, who had received information that armed masked men were holding prisoners in the building, entered the reception hall at 9.42 a.m. and heard the terrified hostages screaming for help. A masked man pointed a handgun at the officers shouting, 'I'll kill the lot of you.' He was told that police were armed and he was to drop his revolver and surrender. A second masked man, holding a gun and a knife, ran towards the cowering hostages shouting, 'I will kill them, I will kill the bastards.' This second man was shot and killed by a constable. At this point the first masked man took cover behind a pillar, pointing his revolver at police. Unarmed police officers who had entered the building from another direction called on him to surrender but he yelled back, 'Don't come in or you will all be killed. You will all be shot.' Another armed officer, edging round towards the pillar, shot and hit the first masked man when he was apparently about to fire at him. The masked schoolboy who was struggling with two of the office staff dropped his sword and was arrested by other officers. It was then discovered that the raiders' handguns, which appeared to be Smith & Wesson short-barrelled revolvers, were imitations. Cavities in the revolving cylinders held plastic caps containing a small charge which simulated a gun shot when the trigger was squeezed.

London's newspapers generally presented a balanced account of the incident and many journalists drew attention to the numerous replica firearms that were readily available. Headlines obviously differed and ranged from a sober 'Armed Police Kill Raiders' in the *Daily Telegraph* to 'The Toy Gun Terrorist' on the front page of the *Daily Mirror*. The latter also explained to its readers that, '. . . the men of the Special Patrol Group are known as the Blue Cobras – because they can strike fast'. This undoubtedly surprised members of the group who had never heard of the blue cobras. Neither had anyone else.

On 22 February the *Daily Telegraph* reported, 'The Metropolitan Police should be armed with guns which fire rubber bullets, and not lethal weapons, Mrs Shirley Williams, Shadow Home Secretary, said yesterday . . . Organized crime and terrorism imported from abroad were eroding the "gentleman's agreement" between English petty criminals and the police not to carry firearms . . . Referring to Tuesday's killings at India House . . . she asked if it might not have been possible to shoot at the intruders to wound rather than kill'. The long line of policemen slain on duty had obviously not been parties to the 'gentleman's agreement'.

Five years later another armchair expert entered the lists in the weekly journal of the Law Society, *Guardian Gazette*, dated 20 December 1978. In the course of an article headed 'A Call to Arms?', the writer commented on the events at India House in the following terms: 'It was a matter of surprise to some that when armed police were called into a disturbance by students at the Indian High Commission in recent years, an officer shot dead a student who was found to be in possession of a toy gun. It was clearly not necessary in those circumstances for the officer to use a firearm and although he could not have known that the young man was not armed, he would have known that no shots had been fired and that it would be possible in such circumstances to obtain a surrender by tactics of patience.' No doubt the writer, Timothy Lawrence, would have felt differently had he been one of the terrified hostages.

This article triggered a reaction in the *Daily Mirror* which leapt into the fray on 3 January 1979 and stated: '. . . the Law Society warned in its official newspaper of the dangers of allowing police too wide a use of firearms. The warning is coupled with a demand that Parliament should probe the whole problem of police and guns. The Law Society is right. The more our police carry guns the more the criminals are likely to respond with bullets. And with firearms disturbingly easy to obtain the threat is very real.'

A policy of appeasement, which the paper appears to advocate, had as much chance of success with an armed criminal as it did with Adolf Hitler. The *Daily Mirror* might have performed a service for its readers by pressing for the judiciary to hand out some realistic sentences to those found guilty of crimes of violence against the community.

16

Bodyguards and Bombs

Although over the years there have been many attempts to assassinate members of the British Royal Family (Queen Victoria appears to have survived at least five such attacks), the kidnapping of 'Royals' has not been practised for some centuries. This happy state of affairs was interrupted on Wednesday, 20 March 1974.

At 7.55 p.m. a Rolls-Royce chauffeured by Alexander Callender was travelling along the Mall towards Buckingham Palace. The passengers were HRH Princess Anne, sitting in the back, with her husband, Captain Mark Phillips on her left. Miss Brassey, the Lady-in-Waiting, sat facing Captain Phillips. Inspector Beaton, the Princess's personal protection officer, occupied the front nearside seat next to the driver. As the vehicle approached the junction with Marlborough Road it was overtaken by a white Ford Escort motor car, driven by Ian Ball, unemployed and of no fixed abode, who swerved sharply in front of the Rolls and forced it to stop. Ball left the Ford and ran back towards the royal car.

The occupants of the Rolls assumed that Ball was an irate driver who was about to remonstrate with their chauffeur and Inspector Beaton alighted in order to intervene. However, the rear of the Ford was so close to the Rolls that Beaton was obliged to walk round the back of the royal car. As he reached the rear offside he saw for the first time that instead of confronting a disgruntled driver he was facing a man holding a .38 revolver. As the officer approached, the gunman fired three shots, one of which hit the bodyguard in his right shoulder. Beaton drew his Walther pistol, which chambered 9mm short ammunition, and fired at Ball, but missed. He attempted to fire a second shot, but the gun malfunctioned and Beaton went to the nearside of the Rolls and attempted to clear the jam. Meanwhile Ball, still holding a revolver, was trying to open the rear offside door of the royal car with his free hand and demanding that the Princess leave the Rolls and go with him. As Princess Anne and her husband struggled to keep the door closed Miss Brassey was able to leave the vehicle by the rear nearside door. At this point the gunman told Beaton to drop his pistol or he would shoot the Princess. As the officer had not been able to remedy the stoppage he dropped the gun and then entered the car to try and interpose himself between his principal and Ball.

John McConnell, a freelance journalist, was a passenger in a taxi being driven westwards along the Mall when he heard the three shots. He told the driver to stop and returned on foot to the two stationary cars. Ball was in the roadway talking to someone inside the Rolls as McConnell appeared and asked him for his gun. By this time the gunman had produced another revolver, a .22 Astra, with which he shot the journalist in the chest at a range of about twelve feet. The wounded man reeled across the pavement and collapsed. During this episode the occupants of the royal car had managed to close the rear offside door. The gunman now raised his revolver and threatened to shoot unless the door was opened. Inspector Beaton thrust his right arm in front of the Princess to protect her as Ball fired through the window, breaking the glass, and hitting the officer's right hand.

P.C. 736A Hills, who was on duty at St. James's Palace, hurried to the scene of the shooting, using his personal radio to raise the alarm at Cannon Row Police Station. He approached Ball with the intention of disarming him, but the gunman took careful aim and shot him in the stomach from close range. Hills managed to stagger to the rear of the Rolls and call on his radio for urgent assistance. He saw Beaton's discarded pistol lying on the ground and picked it up intending to shoot the would-be kidnapper. However, because of his injury he was unable to focus on his target and he collapsed against the nearside of the car. Having disposed of him, Ball opened the rear offside door of the Rolls and deliberately shot Inspector Beaton in the stomach. Beaton had now been wounded three times, the last being the most serious, and he was bleeding quite badly both from his hand and shoulder and also internally. He fell out of the offside door onto the road. At some point during the action round the car the chauffeur had been shot in the chest and he too was out of the fight.

Another chauffeur, Glenmore Martin, now drove a Jaguar car in front of the Ford to prevent Ball from escaping. Martin alighted and went to the royal car, but instead of shooting him on sight Ball merely stuck a gun muzzle into his ribs and told him to clear off. Although Martin wisely retreated under threat he remained at the scene and assisted the wounded constable. Yet another taxi passenger, Ronald

Russell, arrived and punched Ball as he was trying to drag Princess Anne from her car. The gunman fired at him, but the bullet missed and shatered a window in Russell's taxi. Russell then ran to the rear of the car thinking to arm himself with P.C. Hill's truncheon. He was unsuccessful in this attempt so he returned to the royal car where Ball was still trying to drag the Princess out of the rear offside door. He again punched the gunman in the head and, as both men stumbled, a number of police cars arrived.

Ball ran away, still carrying a revolver, but was brought down in a rugby tackle by temporary Detective Constable Edmonds, attached to 'A' Division Crime Squad. When the gunman was searched police found a ransom note for three million pounds and a free pardon exonerating him from any crimes which he would commit in connection with kidnapping the Princess. He was also in possession of four pairs of handcuffs, to restrain his victim, plus nineteen .38 and thirty-nine .22 rounds of ammunition. The serial numbers had been filed off both revolvers, but inquiries revealed that the Astra, serial 140930, had been purchased in Madrid, and he also held a Spanish police permit for a .38 revolver, no. 142893. Under a false name he had rented a house in Fleet in Hampshire which was stocked with bedding, food and drink ready for occupation by his intended prisoner.

On 22 May 1974 Ball pleaded guilty at the Central Criminal Court to two counts of attempted murder, two counts of wounding with intent and one of attempted kidnapping. He was ordered to be detained under Section 60 of the Mental Health Act 1959. Inspector Beaton was awarded the George Cross, Russell and Hills each received a George Medal and the Queen's Gallantry Medal went to McConnell and Callender.

Beaton's jammed Walther caused an immediate reaction at Scotland Yard. Within days D.11 staff had been ordered to implement a crash training programme to instruct protection officers on the Smith & Wesson .38 Special, Model 36 – a short-barrelled revolver. One of the problems associated with a self-loading pistol had always been the time required to clear a stoppage and fire another shot. If a round failed to fire in a revolver the firer merely squeezed the trigger again, which caused the cylinder to revolve and brought another round in line with the firing-pin. By contrast, when a pistol malfunctioned it was necessary to pull back the slide to its fullest extent, which ejected the unfired round, and then release the slide. As the slide moved forward under spring pressure it picked up another cartridge from the magazine and fed it into the breech, when the firer again operated the trigger. Failure to pull the slide fully back against the stop, either through stress, injury or maladroitness, resulted in the dud round's failing to be thrown clear through the ejection port. Thus, the slide moved forward carrying a fresh round which jammed against the unfired cartridge. After they had taken .38 Specials into service the royalty protection officers began to attend properly constituted bodyguard courses.

In the meantime violence was still loose on the streets of London, especially in Red Lion Square, W.C.1 on 15 June 1974. A meeting of the extreme right-wing organization, National Front, clashed with a counter-demonstration by a number of organizations calling themselves 'Liberation'. Police, playing in their usual position as piggy in the middle, were violently attacked by the International Marxist Group allegedly as the result of a prearranged signal to the mob. In the ensuing battle an unfortunate student fell among the crowd and, although dragged clear by some policemen, later died of his injuries.

Left-wing spokesmen claimed that in effect the young man had been murdered by police brutality. Mr Bidwell, Labour MP for Southall, said that mounted police attacked the crowd and that he would be writing to the Home Secretary. He also alleged that police attacked a small body of demonstrators 'with great ferocity' as they tried to break the police cordon. All quite predictable. The ratio of casualties was equally predictable – 46 police officers as against twelve demonstrators. On 17 June, under a by-line 'Student Hitlers', the *Daily Telegraph* reported, '. . . the result was a fierce street battle in which police casualties greatly outnumbered those suffered by the demonstrators, with the inevitable consequence that police are accused of brutality. Everything suggests that this was a calculated attack on public order . . .' On the same day the *Daily Mirror* stated, '. . . The right to demonstrate is an important part of freedom. Saturday's provocative affair was the kind of demonstration which could undermine that freedom . . .'

Instead of waiting for the usual orchestrated campaign against police, the Commissioner asked for an inquiry into the conduct of his men and the death of the young student. Lord Justice Scarman presided over the inquiry which lasted 27 days and cost the ratepayers a great deal of money. The legal bill alone for the attendance of lawyers totalled £33,642. Sir Robert Mark has noted that one quarter of this amount would, in his opinion, have been gross overpayment. An account of the published result appeared on page 11 of the *Daily Mail* on 28 February 1975 under the heading, 'Police cleared over student who died in Red Lion Square. Marxists blamed for fatal riot.' The report stated that the disorders started with an 'unexpected, unprovoked and viciously violent' attack on police cordoning off the square to prevent rival factions clashing. On the same page reference was made to a guide which had been sent to the presidents of 700 student unions by the left wing-controlled National Union of Students. The byline read, 'Students told how to stage a demo.'

However, violence on the streets of London was not confined to crime and demonstrations. By 1974 the capital city had been subjected to continuing terrorist outrages which had started in August 1967 with a hit-and-run machine-gun attack on the American Embassy in Grosvenor Square. On 3 March 1968 bombs exploded outside the Spanish Embassy and the American Officers' Club in Lancaster Gate. Between then and August 1970 there were six further bomb attacks in London, all but one directed against Spanish targets, including an aircraft at Heathrow. On 30 August a bomb exploded outside the Commissioner's house in Putney, followed nine days later by another explosion at the flat of the Attorney-General.

Bomb attacks continued throughout 1971 and on 1 July led to the formation of the Bomb Squad, later to be renamed the Anti-Terrorist Branch. The 'First of May Group', dedicated to the cause of Spanish and Italian revolutionaries, became the 'Angry Brigade'. In 1972 eight members of the brigade stood trial charged with conspiracy to cause explosions – but as one threat was removed another took its place. On 18 September the 'Black September' movement, an Arab terrorist group, moved into the space vacated by the Angry Brigade. In the four months to 25 January 1973 forty-three letter-bombs were posted to Jewish individuals or organizations. Most of these bombs were intercepted or defuzed on receipt, apart from the first missive which killed an official at the Israeli Embassy.

On 8 March 1973 the IRA returned to the mainland. Four massive car bombs, each vehicle packed with 150 pounds of explosives connected by an electrical circuit to an alarm clock, were shipped across from Dublin to London. Ten members of the Provisional IRA accompanied the murder weapons. The first was left by the post office opposite New Scotland Yard, the second outside the Old Bailey, a third near the Army Recruiting Office in Great Scotland Yard and the fourth at the British Forces Broadcasting offices in Dean Stanley Street, Westminster. All the timing devices had been set for 3 p.m.

At about 8.30 a.m., two sharp-eyed S.P.G. constables on duty outside New Scotland Yard noticed a Ford Corsair without a tax disc and bearing registration plates which did not tally with the year of manufacture. Explosives officers were called from across the road and found the rear compartment packed with home-made explosives and sticks of gelignite. Within half an hour the lethal load had been defuzed and the first of the car bombs rendered harmless.

All ports and air terminals in England were sealed off and eight of the ten Irish bombers were arrested at Heathrow airport as they enjoyed a hearty breakfast. A team of that size suggested that there were other car bombs in the Metropolis. If this were the case it was probable that all the timing devices, in common with the Scotland Yard bomb, were set for 3 p.m. that day.

Shortly before 2 p.m. *The Times'* news desk received garbled details about the four bombs. The caller, who was probably telephoning from Eire, was obviously not aware that the first car had been discovered. By 2.30 p.m. the remaining vehicles had been located and a Vauxhall Viva in Dean Stanley Street was defuzed and made safe. At 2.44 p.m., while explosives officers were making preliminary tests on a Hillman Hunter in Great Scotland Yard, the vehicle exploded. There were 61 casualties, fortunately most of them were slight. Seven minutes later the fourth bomb, packed in a Ford Cortina outside the Old Bailey, detonated. It caused 162 casualties, many of them serious.

A new wave of attacks started on 8 August 1973 with a number of incendiary devices left at Harrods and other large department stores, principally in Oxford Street. When these failed to have the desired effect on public morale the IRA reverted to bombs and in the summer of 1974 their targets included the Tower of London and the Houses of Parliament. The explosion at the Tower caused one fatality and injured 37, some of them seriously and including children. Happily the incident at Westminster Hall resulted in only a few minor injuries, although the building was badly damaged.

Photographs, all of them reminiscent of the 'Blitz', showing flames and clouds of black smoke billowing around Big Ben appeared in the Press on 18 June. However, the Mother of Parliaments, which had survived Zeppelins in the First World War and the *Luftwaffe* in the Second, still stood. Throughout this period, Bomb Squad officers, and others, were habitually armed.

17
Sieges and Outrages

In 1975, the name of Stephen Andrew Tibble, married for two years and a policeman for six months, was added to the Roll of Honour in New Scotland Yard. On Wednesday afternoon, 26 February, he was off duty and riding his 175cc motor-cycle in Charleville Road, Hammersmith, when he saw three of his colleagues from Fulham police station chasing a man wearing a brown jacket and trousers. Tibble overtook the suspect and then jumped off his machine at the junction with Gledstanes Road. As the young officer moved in the man shot him twice in the chest at point-blank range. A third bullet missed and buried itself in a nearby doorway; the killer made off into Baron's Court underground station. Despite intense activity by armed police who sealed off all the tube stations in the area and boarded trains, manned road-blocks and searched lodging-houses, the man in brown escaped. P.C. Tibble died in Charing Cross Hospital, Fulham, at 4.40 p.m. the same day.

The murder made the front page of every newspaper the next morning. A typical presentation was given by the *Daily Mail* with inch-high headlines, 'THE KILLING OF PC 178'. On 28 February the headline in the same paper read, 'KILLER'S TATTOO OF HATE', and the report stated that the man who had killed Tibble was a scarred IRA bomber with 'Hate' tattooed on one of his hands. 'He ran a bomb factory in a sleazy basement bed-sitter only 300 yards from where the policeman was murdered.' Months later the gun which had been used in the killing was found, following another incident which featured prominently in the national Press.

By June 1975 top-level discussions were being held on the question of dealing with cases of serious armed crime or terrorist attacks. In the latter instance a military presence would always respond, but there was bound to be a time-lag before a Special Air Service group could arrive and be briefed. Hence the danger, during this hiatus, of hostages being systematically murdered because terrorist demands were not being met. If this occurred it was essential that police be in a position to take positive action. Therefore, although the police task would normally be restricted to containment, it might suddenly be switched to an offensive role in order to remove the risk to hostages as soon as possible. Such police teams would require above-average marksmanship, weaponry and training; the obvious choice was the D.11 instructors – all of whom volunteered.

Furthermore, in order that the selected teams be able to meet terrorist firepower on equal terms they would need automatic and silenced submachine-guns, plus regular training in close-quarter combat. In addition they required more shotguns – ideal close-support weapons. The first two pump-action shotguns had been purchased in November 1972 for the purpose of firing CS cartridges, known as 'Ferrets'. Although these missiles contained less CS than the conventional 1½-inch shells they were extremely accurate and had sufficient power to penetrate a wooden door. Another advantage was the fact that they could not be picked up by the recipient and thrown back.

In August a proposal was made to the Home Office that four such D.11 teams could be made available. Team members should also have body armour, and other special clothing, and the use of an armoured vehicle. While the Home Office considered these suggestions, a bungled robbery gave the future teams a 'dry run' rehearsal.

During the early hours of Sunday, 28 September nine staff members from various restaurants had gathered at the Spaghetti House Restaurant, the main office of the company in Knightsbridge, to check and pay into a local bank the takings for the previous two nights. This amounted to about £13,000 and after the money had been counted it was packed into two briefcases. By 1.40 a.m. only the security lights were on and the nine men prepared to leave; the general manager and a company director each carrying one of the brief-cases. As they reached the main door three coloured men entered from the street and demanded the takings at gunpoint. One was armed with a double-barrelled sawn-off shotgun and the other two with handguns. Taking advantage of the dim light the two men with brief-cases slid them under some tables where they remained unnoticed by the gunmen.

The nine men, all Italians, were then taken down a short flight of stairs in the basement. Here the general manager escaped unseen in the darkness and gained a rear staircase. He reached the ground floor and ran to a nearby hotel where he raised the alarm. The call was received in Information Room at 1.46 a.m. and a message was passed to the local police station at Gerald Road and the area wireless car that an armed robbery was in progress. Meanwhile the remaining eight Italians were made to empty their pockets and remove their coats, at gunpoint, obviously in an effort to find the money intended for the bank. During this search police were heard to arrive on the ground floor and the gunmen herded their eight hostages into a basement storeroom, shouting to the police to keep away or they would fire. The storeroom was immediately located and the intended robbery had become a siege.

Conversation with the occupants of the store revealed the names of the hostages and the identity of the gunmen's leader. He claimed to be Franklin Peter Davis, a Nigerian and a 'captain' (self-promoted to 'major' two day later) in the 'Black Liberation Front'. He boasted that he had been released from prison in April after serving a term for armed robbery. An invitation to surrender was declined, rather rudely.

Police build-up continued throughout the night and by 7 a.m. all support services, including a mobile canteen, were in position. Vehicular and pedestrian traffic was excluded from Knightsbridge, between Wilton Place and William Street, by barriers manned by foot police, and an ambulance and fire brigade units were standing by. A police control van was removed after a control post had been established and equipped with radio, lighting and telephones in empty first-floor premises opposite the restaurant. Armed police sealed the front and back of the siege building and the basement was cleared of obstruction and occupied by D.11 officers and dog-handlers.

During the course of negotiations the gunmen made several demands which included the release of black defendants in current criminal proceedings, the presence of the Home Secretary, an aircraft to be placed at their disposal and a radio in the storeroom. They were successful only with the last request. It was made clear to them that their demands were not negotiable and that they would leave the restaurant only as prisoners.

Obviously the affair provided a feast for the Press and on 30 September the front page of the *Daily Express* carried headlines, 'Ordeal inside the hell-hole. SIEGE GUN MAN NAMED'. Alongside was a sketch reconstruction of the Spaghetti House basement showing the positions of the principal players. Four armed policemen were all depicted standing with handguns pointing down at their own feet – a stance which in reality would have earned them a fair-sized rocket. In fact, the number of armed officers in the room varied from time to time and occasionally there was only one. The day shift worked two hours on and two hours off from 8 a.m. to midnight and at meal times the team had their food in the next room. Only the team leader stayed on watch, eating his meal at the raised cash desk dais which dominated the basement and the black door of the storeroom. Various devices had been installed which required the leader to wear headphones in order to hear and relay conversation from inside the storeroom, and a visual probe gave him a live picture on a television screen. It was all quite civilized apart from the gun on his hip and a loaded pump-action shotgun lying beside the wine glass (which held tonic water). The visual monitor proved invaluable at 9.2 p.m. on 30 September when a shot was fired inside the storeroom, but was seen to be accidental. If police had not been able to establish this fact they might well have taken offensive action in the belief that a hostage had been harmed.

As the siege dragged on, police enlisted the help of the Italian Ambassador and his Consul-General; the acting High Commissioner for Jamaica; a representative from the Nigerian High Commission; and a consultant psychiatrist, all of whom attended the scene and gave invaluable help. By the evening of Monday the 29th two hostages had been released and police had considered the available options in case they were forced to assault the storeroom. The room in question measured 13½ by 15 feet and was stoutly constructed of bricks and breeze-blocks. Unfortunately, the only means of entry, or exit, was through a strong wooden door, 6½ by 2½ feet, which was locked and barred on the inside. Use of CS had already been discounted, chiefly because of possible risk to the hostages trapped in a confined space with three irritable gunmen. Similarly, it was not feasible to use a controlled explosion to blow the facing wall because of almost certain injury to the Italians' ear-drums. The object, as the Commissioner told the basement group, was to arrest the gunmen without incurring casualties among the hostages or police; a remark which certainly endeared him to the D.11 men. It would probably have endeared him even more to the hostages had they been able to hear the conversation.

Supplies of coffee, water and cigarettes were regularly sent in to the besieged, all of which the Italians were forced to taste or smoke first, in case they were drugged. By Thursday, 2 October the three gunmen were suffering bouts of bad temper and their dialogue with the police, always insulting, was becoming irrational. Assistance in reassuring the hostages was again provided by Dr Manca, the Italian Consul-General. Excellent CID work led to the arrests of both the organizer of the attempted robbery and the Sicilian who had provided the inside information about the takings. Naturally these two arrests were made known to the gunmen.

At 2.55 a.m. on Friday the 3rd, the light inside the storeroom was switched off for the first time during the siege and this was followed by a long discussion and argument between the bandits. At 3.45 a.m. one of them announced that the hostages would be released and the six Italians, unharmed, emerged from the storeroom at 3.56 a.m. Two of the robbers then indicated that they wished to surrender, but before they could do so a muffled gun-shot was heard from inside the storeroom. An old sawn-off, double-barrelled, 16 bore shotgun and an Austrian 9mm Steyr pistol loaded with five vintage rounds (dating from the first World War; a collector's item) were pushed out of the doorway and into the basement. Two of the gunmen were then talked out, one at a time with their hands up, and were arrested and searched. Police entered the storeroom and found Davis lying on the floor suffering with a self-inflicted gun-shot wound in the abdomen. He had shot himself with an ancient .22 rim-fire revolver of the type with a folding trigger. The organizer had obviously not bothered with modern arms and ammunition for his bandit crew. All the criminals concerned, including the driver of the get-away car, were subsequently tried and convicted.

For once there were no dissenters, when the news broke in Saturday's newspapers, that the Metropolitan Police had correctly handled a potentially dangerous situation. However, the normally factual *Daily Telegraph* did find space for a byline on page 3, 'Rebuke for Pc who stormed siege room'. According to the report a uniformed officer who leapt inside the storeroom after hearing the shot was later reprimanded – "gently" – because he had gone in despite orders that nobody was to enter the room before all the gunmen had come out. A pleasant little story with the human touch – a pity it wasn't true!

Meanwhile the IRA continued to murder the innocent and the useful members of society. Victims included Gordon Hamilton, a distinguished cancer specialist and Captain Roger Goad, BEM, one of the Yard's explosives officers. Captain Goad was blown to pieces while attempting to defuze a bomb left in a Kensington doorway. He was awarded a posthumous George Cross. On the day of his funeral a bomb exploded in the foyer of the Hilton Hotel in Park Lane, killing two people and injuring many more. In November a bomb was thrown into a crowded restaurant in Walton Street, Chelsea, causing more deaths and injuries. Later that month Ross McWhirter, a fearless journalist, was shot and killed in front of his wife on his own doorstep.

During an evening in early December a trap, which involved the deployment of 700 police, was set for the IRA terrorists. The operation was to have been mounted two weeks earlier, but after the initial briefing at Scotland Yard an informant blew the story, undoubtedly for money, to the *Evening News*. The newspaper promptly splashed its 'scoop' across the front page. The bombers were thus forewarned and a very costly plan to protect London's citizens, which would have saved at least one life, was temporarily shelved. Unfortunately, the Yard's Judas was never traced and the name of the editorial staff member who authorized publication was not revealed.

On Saturday, 6 December at about 8 p.m., four men in a stolen car drove slowly past the front of Scotts Restaurant in Mount Street, Mayfair – the scene of a bombing three weeks earlier – and opened fire on the premises with automatic weapons. Particulars of the suspect vehicle were given on personal radio networks and the car was sighted in Portman Square by two officers on foot. They gave chase in a taxi along Gloucester Place, Park Road and Alpha Close. The stolen car was then abandoned by the four men who ran along Rossmore Road firing handguns at the two policemen, who had left the cab and continued the chase on foot. One of the suspects dropped a bag which was found to contain a dismantled Sten gun.

Two Special Patrol Group carriers arrived at the scene; the first vehicle pulled in front of the running men and the second carrier drew level with them. As officers from this carrier left the vehicle they were shot at by the suspects, fortunately without effect. Two members of the crew who were armed returned fire, but missed. The four men now turned tail and ran back towards their original pursuers, an inspector and a sergeant who, being unarmed, took cover in a doorway. As the suspects approached, still shooting, an unmarked car containing Flying Squad officers turned the corner and forced the hunted men to scatter. The four gunmen, still being chased by police, ran along Taunton Street, down the steps into Boston Place and thence into Balcombe Street where they were lost to view.

When police arrived outside the council flats in Balcombe Street they were told that four men had just run into the basement below the flats. By 9.25 p.m. the area had been cordoned off and armed police and dog-handlers were posted at the front and back of the building. Police

Plan of siege positions at 22ᴮ Balcombe Street.

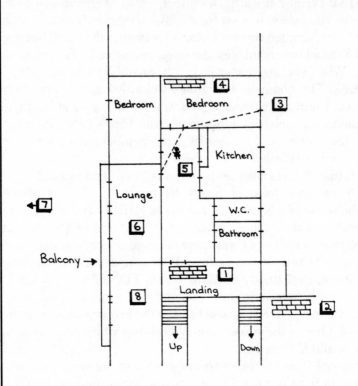

[1]   'Fort Sharpend'. Sandbagged position outside front door manned by two D11 shotgunners.

[2]   Sandbagged rifle position overlooking rear.

[3]   Window used by D11 as an entry point.

[4]   Sandbagged position used as retreat point.

[5]   Witchy Poo doll hanging on a cord attached to door handle.

[6]   Terrorists held their two hostages here.

[7]   Negotiators, rifle position and video cameras across the street.

[8]   Flat used by D11 to receive prisoners.

then began a systematic search of the basement area and flats and finally identified 22B, a first-floor flat, as the place where the gunmen had taken refuge. They had forced their way into the flat and were holding the occupants, Mr and Mrs Matthews, in the lounge as hostages. Well-oiled siege machinery was immediately set in motion.

The first D.11 team was in position that same evening and the build-up of resources, including the deployment of divisional riflemen, continued throughout the night. By the next day a telephone had been lowered into the flat, followed by drinking-water and a portable lavatory. All D.11 personnel had examined the layout of identical flats above and below the siege flat, and photographs of the hostages had been distributed. In the early hours of Monday morning Special Air Service troops, accompanied by D.11 men, reconnoitred the area while one of the Yard's less well-known branches installed certain devices. At 9 a.m. police began sandbagging the rear sniper positions under the super-vision of a D.11 instructor, formerly an assault pioneer platoon sergeant-major. A smaller sandbagged emplacement was erected on the front landing facing the front door of 22B, an open space devoid of cover, which was christened 'Fort Sharpend'.

Page 2 of the *Daily Mail* on Tuesday 9 December, carried an excellent photograph of the first of the rear sandbagged positions being built. Much of page 4 in the same issue was devoted to an article headed 'The Blue Berets' which informed the readership that they were the men in dark-blue battle-smocks and berets at the siege of Balcombe Street who had been noticed for the first time in action. 'The fact that the siege has made the public realize London has this élite force of professional marksmen ready to kill or maim if necessary is bound to raise the question: "Are we moving too quickly towards other countries which have permanent para-military police units?" Strength could be added to that argument because the marksmen, known as the D.11 group, were themselves allowed to choose their own para-military uniform, suggest and get the guns they want, and are completely in control of training methods.' An artist's illustration showed a D.11 man carrying a standard British Army 7.62mm 20-shot rifle. All this must have surprised the general public – but not half so much as it surprised the D.11 teams. Presumably these details had been garnered from the *Daily Mail*'s pet policeman. Whatever the size of his tax-free handout, the newspaper was entitled to an 80 per cent refund for the false information he supplied.

An interesting side-effect of this article was the number of dog-handlers who began to sport similar headgear to D.11 officers, presumably attracted by the spurious glamour of the blue beret tag. D.11 personnel approved of all these extra berets; working on the principle that a live man in specialist uniform is even better than a cardboard cut-out for diluting the opposition's firepower. However, it was soon noticed by the brass, and the canine blue berets were returned to their hatstands.

Throughout the siege various D.11 officers and other men had, on occasions, entered the flat and on one of these nocturnal excursions a cord was tied to the lounge door handle and secured across the passage. A small doll in the form of a witch, one of the ornaments in the hall, was fixed to the cord. Thus, any attempt to turn the door handle from the inside caused the witch to move and alert the garrison of 'Fort Sharpend'. The witch was later cased, given a suitable inscription, and presented to D.11 by Mr and Mrs Matthews.

At 2.12 p.m. on Friday 12 December, by arrangement with the gunmen, Mrs Matthews came out onto the balcony and was helped into Flat 28 next door and thence to hospital. She and her husband had borne their captivity with fortitude. Two hours later the first terrorist surrendered and was led away. The next person to emerge, on police instructions, was Mr Matthews. The remaining hooded bombers came out, one at a time with their hands in the air, and were searched and handcuffed.

Next morning's newspapers gave front page prominence to photographs of the gunmen surrendering, covered by the guns of D.11 sergeants on the balcony. The *Daily Telegraph* correctly described how the gunmen, '. . . defiance ground to despair, came cringing from the tiny, stinking room that had been their prison without dignity and without drama'. Page 2 in the same edition carried a thoughtful article headed 'Gun law arrives in Britain, says MP'. According to Mr Eldon Griffiths, Conservative MP and consultant to the Police Federation, 'Balcombe Street revealed the extent to which our once unarmed police are now armed. But what the public as a whole has not appreciated is the sheer number and the growing normality of guns . . . The number of guns now being carried and used by professional criminals and terrorists on the one hand and policemen on the other is quite likely 100 times greater today than it was when we abolished the death penalty . . .'

Weapons recovered from the Balcombe Street flat, and elsewhere, included a Sten gun, an Armalite rifle, two .30 carbines, three .357

Magnum revolvers, two .38 Colt revolvers and two pistols. Test-fired bullets from the Sten gun tied the weapon to four previous shooting incidents in London from 11 December 1974 to 19 January 1975. Ballistic results from the other guns showed that they had been used in a number of murders, including that of Ross McWhirter on 27 November 1975.

The four bombers, all members of the Provisional IRA, later stood trial at the Central Criminal Court charged on an indictment containing 25 counts consisting of murder, causing explosions with intent to endanger life, possessing firearms with intent to endanger life, assault, unlawfully detaining persons, and conspiracy to cause explosions in the United Kingdom. The trial lasted two weeks and all four were convicted and each sentenced to life imprisonment with a recommendation that they serve not less than 30 years. It was a small, a very small, price to pay for the misery and suffering caused in more than 50 separate incidents of bombing, assassination, shooting and kidnapping for which these four men were responsible.

18

Shotguns and Pike Drill

By the beginning of 1976 the Home Office had agreed in principle to the dual instructional/operations role of D.11. On 28 May a four-page police order was devoted to firearms and began with a paragraph in capital letters which warned that a police officer could only use a firearm as a means of defence for himself or others. The order generally consolidated previous instructions dealing with the issue, use and return of firearms, and repeated the six standard safety rules. For the first time the destruction of dangerous animals was mentioned and the fact that shotguns were available for use by D.11 personnel.

The latter was no doubt prompted by two separate incidents towards the end of the previous year involving escaped bullocks. The first animal had been quietly disposed of at the side of a reservoir, but the second escapee caused a fair amount of consternation. The headline in the *Waltham Telegraph* dated 14 November 1975 read, 'Terror Hunt as Slaughterhouse Bullock runs amok near Town'. This particular Hereford bullock had an exceptionally thick skull and was only stunned, and not killed, by the humane killer in the abattoir. Instead of dropping dead the beast, justifiably annoyed at the attempt to drive an iron bolt into his head, flattened two large iron gates and stampeded onto the public road.

During the escape bid he managed to unseat a motor-cyclist, charge four horses, causing one to throw its rider, and finally scatter some players on West Essex golf-course before disappearing into Epping Forest. Half a ton of beef on the hoof looks quite impressive, especially when viewed frontally, and it was some time before the animal was cornered in a garden on the edge of the forest. After a deaf gardener working next door, who was in the line of fire, had been convinced that he would be safer elsewhere, the bold bullock was killed with a rifled slug (a solid lead projectile weighing nearly one ounce) from a shotgun. A few months later, three bullocks escaped together and moved briskly in line abreast along the road – which did not leave much room for anything else. Their demise on a nearby roundabout ended an operation which resembled a cross between an amateur rodeo and a Keystone Cops film.

Another item in the same police order announced that copies of a new Firearms Training Manual were in the course of distribution to Divisions and Branches. The manual was in eleven parts: safety rules and precautions; investigation of firearms accidents; revolvers, self-loading pistols; the firing of handguns; rifles; gas guns; shotguns; firearms training courses; ammunition; and operational deployment of armed police. It was a giant step forward when compared with anything else that had been seen in police circles.

Back on the streets in Notting Hill, during the Bank Holiday weekend of 29–30 August 1976, a festival which began as a carnival ended in a riot. Four hundred policemen and more than 200 members of the public were injured, shops were looted and many vehicles, both police and private, were set on fire or destroyed. Total damage was estimated at a quarter of a million pounds. The mob attacked with an assortment of weapons ranging from coping-stones to ammonia sprays, and the dustbin lids and milk crates with which policemen guarded themselves heralded the dawn of riot shields on the streets of London. There were more than 200 reported cases of robbery, assault and theft, mostly committed by young blacks against respectable people of their own colour – two-thirds of the victims were women and girls. 'Rampage at the Carnival' and 'Carnival of Fury' were two of the headlines in the national Press on the 31st.

Predictably, it was all the fault of the Metropolitan Police for having too many officers on duty at the carnival (in fact, there were fewer than the total that policed an average Wembley Cup Final). On 31 August the *Daily Mirror* reported a statement from community worker Cecil Gutzmore: '. . . With such heavy policing there was sure to be provocation. And the coloured people who went to enjoy themselves had the normal human response to provocation . . . and defended their rights.' Presumably the rights included picking pockets and stabbing those victims who protested.

In the following year Sir Robert Mark retired on 12 March. He had been a memorable and articulate Commissioner who would be remembered with respect and affection by his men. It was a hard act to follow. His successor was Sir David McNee, former Chief Constable of Strathclyde, who had been a detective chief inspector in Glasgow only seven years previously. His promotion record was probably the equivalent of a major making the long leap to field marshal in a similarly short period. There is a story, possibly apocryphal, that the new Commissioner asked to see copies of all police messages transmitted within his Force area during the previous 24 hours – a practice he had followed in Strathclyde. The next morning he struggled to reach his desk through piles of forms (there is a great deal of paper as well as action in the Metropolitan Police) and the idea was abandoned. Paper apart, he still had the dual advantage of being both a hard-headed Scot and a professional policeman. He was to need both qualities in the years ahead. Strength of the Force stood at 22,430.

A small industrial dispute which started at Grunwick Processing Laboratories, Willesden, in August 1976 had escalated to massive proportions, amid a blaze of publicity, by the summer and autumn of 1977. Shirley Williams and Denis Howell, both Government Ministers, and Arthur Scargill, President of the National Union of Mineworkers, were among the well-known personalities who joined the picket line at one time or another. On 11 July the number of demonstrators was estimated at 20,000 and as many as 4,500 police, or more than 20 per cent of London's total uniformed force, were needed to contain the violence. By the end of the year more than 300 officers had been injured and it was realized that the traditional helmet offered little protection against a thrown brick. Shortly afterwards a new type of semi-crash helmet was taken into experimental use.

Public order, or rather disorder, continued to absorb police manpower. During a National Front march at Lewisham in August 1977, left-wing militants made concerted attacks on police as they struggled to keep the rival factions apart. A total of 270 police officers were injured, despite the use of protective shields. On 15 August the *Daily Express* carried the headline, 'Thug Law' alongside a photograph showing some of the weapons used in the Battle of Lewisham. These included a stave studded with nails, a machete and a plastic container which held ammonia instead of washing-up liquid. The centre-page opinion column stated, 'A section of the extreme Left are out to discredit and demoralize the police force. Not everyone who travelled to South London was there to swell a peaceful counter-demonstration to the National Front march. As the pictures we publish show, many of them came armed with weapons designed to cause serious injury. The targets and the victims were the police . . .' Nothing had changed since the Battle of Coldbath Fields in 1833.

On Monday 24 October, police accompanied bailiffs to a council flat in Worthington House, Myddleton Passage, Islington, near Sadler's Wells theatre. The occupant, Stuart Brickell, aged 43 and a keep-fit enthusiast, objected to being moved and indicated his displeasure by arming himself with a machete, a dagger, a knife and a cut-throat razor. One officer suffered a fractured skull from the machete and a sergeant was slashed about the head and stabbed in the stomach. When a constable tried to protect his injured colleagues by using a protective shield and his truncheon, he was attacked with such force that his truncheon was chopped in half by the machete and the force of the impact sprained his wrist. Police machinery was set in motion and a D.11 team arrived but was not allowed to use CS, the obvious solution. The machete man took refuge in a small bedroom and threatened anyone who approached. Police barricaded the doorway with a makeshift wood and barbed wire frame, and a mini-siege was in progress.

Police were now faced with a problem. Although there was enough fire-power to engage an infantry section, obviously it could not be used in these circumstances even to incapacitate Brickell. Nor, following the doctrine of minimal force, could the man be rushed with the assistance of 'hard' dogs. According to a report in the *Daily Telegraph* on Wednesday 26 October, the besieged was described by his neighbours as 'gentle and refined'. No doubt the bailiffs' escorts, who were still in hospital, disagreed. Mattresses were placed on the grass beneath the bedroom window in case Brickell jumped, but after he had leaned out of the window shouting and brandishing his machete there were fears that he might reach the ground and run amok. The window was therefore boarded over by police working from the roof.

As the affair continued the prisoner refused to eat and accepted very little water. His adoptive father, friends and a doctor spoke to him from the other side of the barricade but there was no positive response. Police considered the use of a tranquillizing dart, but in the absence of certain vital information which Brickell refused to supply (body weight, last intake of food and so forth) there was a danger that the subject would receive an overdose and might die. In the meantime one of the D.11 sergeants suggested using a heavy wire mesh folding cage which could be extended into the room, a section at a time. Other officers with long poles inserted through the mesh would keep the prisoner, and the machete tied to his wrist, away from the men manhandling the cage.

The sergeant's brainchild originated from his previous experience on a Scottish farm, where Highland cattle had sometimes to be contained. The first prototype was not satisfactory and was returned to the workshops for the handles to be re-positioned.

By Monday the 31st, the prisoner was obviously tiring, partly because of the police efforts to keep him awake and partly due to the energy he had dissipated in trying to chop away the barricade. On that day he finally consented to provide a urine sample which was taken away for analysis. He also agreed to surrender but afterwards changed his mind. When the result of the test was made known the next day it indicated traces of albumen in the urine, indicative of kidney trouble. Brickell was told that he was risking his life, but he still refused to accept water or medical treatment. The point had now been reached where the man was liable to die while technically in police custody.

On Wednesday 2 November, five local officers (one for each arm and leg and another for the throat) were briefed and drilled by the D.11 sergeant in the use of their pikes. These were 9-feet long, made of tubular steel, and fitted at the ends with rubber-covered semi-circular arcs of steel, large enough to pinion an arm or leg. The apparatus was assembled, poles positioned, and the cage operators with their supporting pikemen advanced into the room. After the first few showers of sparks, caused by the prisoner's machete as he tried to reach the cage manipulators, the pikemen became quite adept at manoeuvring their cumbersome poles. Just before noon Brickell was trapped in a corner of the room, enveloped in the folding cage and pinned to the wall by his wrists and ankles. The inventor slid behind the cage, removed the machete man's weapons and handcuffed him. Another siege was over and a folding wire cage and some pikes had been added to the Metropolitan Police armoury. Brickell was later tried at the Old Bailey and sentenced to five years' imprisonment.

Returning to terrorism, an interesting article appeared in the *Radio Times* on 11 February 1978. Headed, 'The hidden dissuaders' the first paragraph read, 'Top security advisers now believed it is only a question of time before international terrorists, other than the IRA, mount an operation in Britain. The attack could come from Japanese Red Army, Baader-Meinhof, Black September or any one of the extremist groups now active round the world.' The writer continued, 'When the hit comes, the men in the front line will be the police', and went on to enumerate the various units available in the Metropolis. These included the Anti-Terrorist Squad, the Special Patrol Group and the Diplomatic Protection Group, the latter with a responsibility for guarding foreign embassies and missions. Following a list of available weaponry (three out of the six were wrong), mention was made of D.11, '. . . who made their first unforgettable public appearance at the Balcombe Street siege, training guns . . . on the windows where the four IRA terrorists held their hostages'. In fact the 'gun trainers' were Special Patrol Group men, D.11 officers were already inside the building, but no matter. 'They (D.11) are linked by radio earpieces to a firemaster whose order is the only one they are allowed to obey.'

The last sentence was incorrect, for obvious reasons. However, it was certainly true that D.11 and the divisional riflemen had experimented with a fire controller for situations where it is vital that all terrorists in a group be incapacitated at the same instant. The type of incidents in mind were the hostage/terrorist situations which had occurred on the Continent. But this was not to be the solution. It presupposed that the riflemen not only had a clear view of their targets, but that the hostages and their captors could be identified, one from another. If, for example, they are all hooded and intermingled, with guns and grenades kept out of sight, then which was which? Furthermore, did 'Z', the extreme left-hand sniper engage terrorist no. 1 who was on the extreme right of his group, and so on along the line. If this were the case, and no. 1 changed his position, did 'Z' track him through his telescope or did he shift target and re-align on the next right-hand gunman. These, and other problems, caused the idea to be abandoned and other methods adopted.

In addition, the article stated, 'At the Home Office a senior official said there was no question of forming paramilitary police units to meet the terrorist threat. We totally reject the idea of a third force and are completely confident in the ability of the police to handle terrorists. The lines of demarcation between police and army are quite clear – if terrorists start throwing grenades or using missiles, it is clearly a job for the army.'

If this was correctly reported, the senior official appears to have overlooked the D.11 teams authorized three years previously. History provides many instances where a relieving force, through no fault of the unit concerned, has failed to reach the besieged in time to save them. In a military context this means to save them from becoming prisoners of war – in the case of hostages the failure may mean death. Transport and weather problems aside, there is the growing fear that the special army teams might be too few in number to cope with a multiplicity of terrorist incidents orchestrated to start at the same time. Demarcation lines between the army and police are always clear – on paper. Possibly the lines would blur if all the hostages were senior civil servants from the Home Office.

The year 1978 also saw different Arab groups at war in London. Two employees of the Syrian Embassy were killed when a bomb exploded in their car, and the P.L.O. representative was murdered as he sat in his central London office. The former Prime Minster of Iraq was shot dead outside a London hotel in July, and later that month a bomb was thrown at the Iraqi Ambassador's car. In August an El Al coach was attacked with machine-gun fire and hand-grenades ouside a Mayfair hotel; one of the terrorists was killed and a second arrested. In December, IRA activity resumed and two car bombs exploded and a third was successfully defuzed. Thankfully there were no serious casualties.

Unfortunately, London had more than enough local armed crime without the addition of foreign imports. On Saturday 9 December 1978 in Eltham, as the result of 22 armed robberies in the area during the past eleven months, three detectives were in an unmarked car on robbery patrol. The team leader, a detective sergeant, was armed with a .38 service revolver. Just before 5.30 p.m. the police car was parked in Passey Place while the officers kept casual observation on a Securicor vehicle standing outside the front entrance of a supermarket. The three-man crew were collecting cash-bags from the premises.

At this point a stolen Rover motor car was driven alongside the Securicor van and two men wearing long white coats and carrying sawn-off shotguns jumped out of the Rover and attacked one of the guards who was carrying a canvas money-sack. The detective sergeant and one of his men got out of their car and ran towards the scene, the sergeant shouting that he was an armed police officer and that the bandits were to drop their guns. As the two officers drew level with the Rover the front nearside passenger pointed a sawn-off shotgun at them. The sergeant fired two shots by sense of direction, which apparently missed the gunman but hit the car. He again shouted a warning that he was armed and the car began to move. One of the attackers, later identified as Michael Frank Calvey, who was trying to board the get-away car, suddenly pivoted and aimed his shotgun towards the two detectives and a security guard. The D.S. instinctively fired two shots, one of which hit Calvey. His mates drove away at high speed leaving him lying in the middle of the road. During the gunfight, the second member of the gang had made off on foot, dumping his white coat, balaclava helmet and shotgun as he ran. Calvey was found to be wearing a wig, false moustache and surgical gloves. A shotgun lying by his side was loaded in both barrels and one of the hammers was cocked. The bandit was taken to Brook General Hospital where he died from a gunshot wound in the abdomen at 6.15 p.m.

At the coroner's inquest on 15 February 1979, Calvey, aged 37, was stated to have a number of previous convictions as an adult, including two for armed robbery. The jury returned a verdict of justifiable homicide.

Towards the end of 1978, two Glasgow-bred criminals, Gary Miller and Robert Morris, both aged 18 years, moved to London and found an ideal 'squat' in a disused fire station in Blackstock Road, Highbury. As they liked girls and glue sniffing they found it difficult to manage on Social Security handouts and supplemented their income by armed robberies in the Holloway/Islington/Kings Cross triangle. The method they adopted was simple, effective and potentially fatal. They entered a shop together and while one threatened the staff with a sawn-off double-barrelled shotgun, produced from a carrier-bag or from under his coat, the other took cash from the till.

On 10 December 1978, they decided to work nearer home, and at about 8.30 p.m. visited an off-licence in Mountgrove Road, Highbury. Using their well-tried technique, the gun was produced in order to frighten the manager, which it did because it was fired at a member of his staff when she threatened to call police. Happily the spread of shot missed her. One of the bandits grabbed about £100, despite a spirited attempt by the lady assistant to slam his fingers in the till, and both men ran. However, the shot had been heard and they were challenged by a patrolling police sergeant. The officer dived out of the line of fire when Miller pointed the shotgun at him and apparently pulled the trigger. Fortunately, he fingered the trigger of the barrel which he had already fired. The two gunmen ran back to their 'squat' where police reinforcements were called, backed by a D.11 team, and the area was sealed off.

By next morning there was still no response to loudhailer calls inviting surrender, and the police had to make sure that the quarry were still in residence. After visiting a nearby shop, a policeman fired marbles from a catapult (shades of Sidney Street) at three of the windows on the fugitives' floor. This failed to draw any movement and a police dog was then sent into the building. After a suitable interval, which failed to produce barking or other signs of contact, such as fearful cries, the dog was withdrawn. There was now an uneasy feeling that the two gunmen might have escaped during the night, and senior police officers retired to the local police station to consider the next move. While the conference was in progress a piece of white towelling was waved on the end of a stick through one of the broken windows. The only officers in a position to see what was happening were a D.11 sergeant and a constable on the opposite balcony who passed on the information by radio and then talked the two men out into the street to be searched.

Both youths admitted to six armed robberies between 14 November and 10 December 1978. They were later sentenced to seven years' imprisonment, concurrent on each count. Naturally the surrender featured in the national Press and there were numerous photographs of the bandits with their hands in the air or lying in the roadway and being handcuffed. One of these photographs was to cause problems within the Force.

The front page of the *Daily Mirror* on 12 December carried a picture of a dog-handler holding a revolver, albeit with his finger outside the trigger guard, and his dog. Camera angle falsely showed the gun muzzle to be pointed at the animal. It was captioned, 'Armed to the teeth: One man, his gun and his dog at the North London siege', and the headline read, 'Portrait of a British Policeman Today'. On the strength of this photograph all Metropolitan Police dog-handlers, other than members of London Airport dog section, were eventually disarmed. The argument ran that a man cannot handle a dog and a gun at the same time. Hence district dog-handlers, although still trained by D.11 in room search techniques and the like, are unarmed when they accompany armed officers in high-risk situations. Not unnaturally, the handlers are not too happy with this state of affairs and have advanced some sound reasons why their guns should be returned. Basically, of course, a dog, in common with a gun, is only as good as its handler and there will always be a variation in both skills. The debate continues.

Gunfire at Eltham and the Highbury incident, following on each others heels, led to the usual questions in Parliament and the usual articles in the Press. Many of these deplored the ease with which shotguns could be purchased and others voiced disquiet at the possibility of members of the public caught in a cross-fire between police and villains. However, one newspaper stated quite fairly, 'When an armed policeman is faced with an armed criminal he would be a courageous fool not to shoot first.' It omitted to mention that the criminal was first invariably warned and given the opportunity to drop his gun. Hence, in those circumstances a police officer who failed to fire would not only be courageous, and a fool, but dead into the bargain.

19

Into the Eighties

In January 1979 the Provisional IRA detonated a bomb at Greenwich gas works. Thankfully there was no loss of life, but worse was to come. On 30 March, as Mr Airey Neave, MP drove his Vauxhall car up the ramp from the House of Commons underground car-park, a bomb, clamped underneath the vehicle, exploded. The victim, a much decorated war hero, was trapped in the wreckage for half an hour before being released and taken to Westminster Hospital. He died eight minutes after admission. Next morning the *Daily Telegraph* clearly spelled out the issues involved: '. . . it must be recognized that the only effective deterrence against terrorist murder is capital punishment. No prison sentence, however long, can deter a man who believes that some future political settlement will include his own amnesty. Thirdly, it is likely that this crime was committed by men who would once have been interned. Is not internment a much lesser evil than continued terrorism? . . .'

The following month there was another death, but this time as the result of mob violence. On Monday 23 April, the National Front was to hold a parliamentary election meeting in the town hall at Southall, the centre of London's largest Asian community. The opposition was determined that it would not take place. One socialist journal stated, 'We will not be intimidated by police. We will use any means necessary to stop the meeting.' Nearly 3,000 police were on duty to keep the peace, and from 6 p.m. onwards concerted and vicious attacks were made on the police ranks. Everything, from lumps of concrete and smoke-bombs to folding chairs, were thrown in an attempt to break the police lines and one officer was stabbed.

At about 7 p.m., a group of young Asians had started throwing missiles at a police cordon across the Broadway; one constable was hit in the face by a brick and his jaw was broken in three places. A Special Patrol Group unit responded to the call for assistance and chased the attackers down a side-street. It was then that Blair Peach, a New Zealand schoolteacher and left-wing militant, was found injured. He was taken to Ealing Hospital where he died as the result of a fractured skull. Inevitably members of the Special Patrol Group concerned were very properly rigorously interrogated, but under circumstances that would have led to another general strike had they been trade unionists. Apart from the unfortunate New Zealander, the day's casualty roll showed the usual ratio in the hospital treatment for injuries – 25 demonstrators against 97 police officers. A top-level inquiry failed to establish who, or for that matter what, had struck the fatal blow on the dead man's abnormally thin skull.

Back at Lippitts Hill, a series of four-day courses in vehicular convoy protection were held at the training camp during early summer. Students were drawn from the Special Escort Group (responsible for the protection of high risk convoys), Special Branch, Diplomatic Protection Group (charged with the protection of embassies and consulates), Royalty officers and certain specialized units. Among the guest speakers was an explosives officer whose slides and material usually frightened his audience (especially after the live booby-trap demonstration), a senior Special Branch man who spoke on assassination and a SEG inspector who dealt with convoy control. D.11's contribution, apart from running the courses, included a horrifying session on the vulnerability of motor vehicles and their occupants to the firepower of various weapons. Fortunately, a breaker's yard and a low-loader were available as the cars under attack never lasted longer than one lesson.

These courses had originated in a series of one-day exercises held in a disused military installation more than two years previously. Doubts expressed by various branches had led to full-blooded ambushes where the victims 'died' in a welter of red-and-white smoke and some very loud bangs. It became painfully obvious to all concerned that assassination in a non-totalitarian society could be very simple.

Police Order 16 of 10 August 1979 dealt with the classification of authorized shots. From September, all shots were obliged to classify on each occasion they attended for training, i.e., every four months, and not once annually as had been the practice in the past. At the same time the category of Class II shot was abolished and only two ratings remained – marksman and standard. Scores of 90 and 70 per cent respectively were needed to classify in these grades and, more importantly, the percentage would be calculated on a full day's shooting. This was a big step towards the goal of a comparatively small number of, but more expert, gun-handlers.

By the end of the year a further police order directed that firearms would only be issued under the direct and personal supervision of an inspector, or higher rank, and in each case the chief superintendent in charge of the Division was to be informed as soon as possible. Another order announced the issue of authorization cards which indicated the type of weapon the card holder was authorized to use. It was the first time a police order had correctly referred to a self-loading pistol instead of an automatic or semi-automatic.

In 1979 the Metropolitan Police celebrated its 150th anniversary with a professionally produced Tattoo in Wembley arena from 12 to 17 October. There were some outstanding displays by various branches and the last item was entitled 'All in a day's work'. This began with a solitary policeman on his beat and ended with his being involved in a bank raid. The villains, and the officer who negotiated their surrender through a loudhailer, were all D.11 staff and this episode was part of the Tattoo later shown on television. A few weeks later, at first light in an East End street, a D.11 team were conducting a similar 'talk out' but this time for real. In the midst of the operation an Indian gentleman, obviously a television enthusiast who had seen the programme, popped out of a nearby house and inquired if this was the second part, and where were the cameras and when would it be on television. He was quite upset when he was hustled back indoors and told that this particular episode was not being filmed!

The New Year was barely under way when at 1.15 a.m. on 7 January 1980 local police were called to a disturbance in Greenfield Road, South Tottenham. While police were talking to the occupier, a man inside the house smashed a window in the front bedroom and fired six shots from a revolver – all of which missed. A cordon was thrown round the house, and police, including a D.11 team, settled down for yet another siege. At 3.30 a.m. a boy appeared at a back bedroom window and a police inspector rescued him, with the aid of a borrowed ladder. The affair ended without bloodshed at about 10.20 a.m. after D.11 men entered the house by a side window while the gunman, a 35-year-old Sicilian, was kept in conversation at the front by a negotiator.

This incident may have been partly responsible for a series of questions about police and firearms which were asked in the House of Commons during January and February. The Home Secretary gave a full written answer to every query other than one about protection officers, which he ducked. According to *Hansard* on 5 February, the

Secretary of State for the Home Department was asked, 'If he will list the number of occasions guns were issued to police for protection duties for every year since 1970.' Mr Whitelaw replied, 'It would not be in the interests of security to publish such figures.'

More urgent matters were soon to engage the attention of MPs. At about 11.25 a.m. on Wednesday 30 April, six Arabs armed with submachine-guns, pistols and hand-grenades, forced their way into the Iranian Embassy in Prince's Gate, Kensington. The armed DPG officer on duty, P.C. Lock, had no time to draw his revolver as he struggled with the first intruder. Bursts of gunfire shattered windows, sending glass into his eyes, and he was pushed inside the entrance hall. The alarm connecting the Embassy to New Scotland Yard was sounded and within minutes armed police had surrounded the building and cordoned off the area. Inside the Embassy, terrorists now held 26 hostages; eighteen Iranians of whom five were female, five British, an Indian, a Pakistani and a Syrian. Contact was made with the gunmen who were dedicated to obtaining independence for Khuzestan, a province in southwest Iran. They demanded the release of 91 prisoners in Iran within 24 hours; an end to the daily mass exterminations in their country and the provision of an aircraft to transport them and their hostages from England. Any police action would endanger their captives, and the building, which would be blown up.

In the massive operation that followed, forward and base controls were established and the entire area was sealed by an outer cordon. An inner ring was manned by D.11 personnel with automatic weapons, accompanied by armed dog-handlers, and divisional riflemen moved into position to cover the front and back of the building. Flats and offices within potential arcs of fire, or liable to blast damage if the terrorists carried out their threat to blow up the Embassy, were evacuated. Communications were installed, including a 'hot line' to the Cabinet Office briefing-room. Skilled negotiators, a consultant psychiatrist, and interpreters in Farsi and Arabic were all available. The usual back-up services of the Metropolitan Police arrived at the scene and last, but certainly not least, a Special Air Service group was placed on immediate standby.

A separate police command post was made responsible for the large number of chanting Iranian demonstrators who congregated by the outer cordon. These supporters were allowed to leave the immediate area, but not to return, a decision which led to protests from their fellow countrymen throughout the world. The violence which erupted from time to time led to several arrests and one constable had his leg broken.

In the next few days protracted negotiations led to the release of five of the hostages, one on the first day, one on the second, two (including a pregnant woman) on the fourth day and one on the fifth. P.C. Trevor Lock, who had managed to retain his revolver unbeknown to his captors, was pressed into service as an intermediary between them and the outside world. One of the released hostages passed a message from Lock to the effect that if the situation deteriorated and shooting began inside the Embassy, he (Lock) would attempt to shoot the first terrorist armed with a machine-gun and he and the other captives would barricade themselves in one of the rooms until released.

By Monday 5 May various deadlines set by the gunmen had come and gone and they had been told that none of the Ambassadors for whom they had asked would attend or assist. Furthermore, there was no aircraft to fly them out of the UK and no other country would give them asylum. They were again urged to release their hostages and surrender themselves to a fair trial under British law. At 1.15 p.m. three shots were heard from inside the Embassy and at 6.42 p.m. another three shots. Three minutes later the dead body of a hostage was pushed out of the front door of the Embassy. At the same time the terrorist leader told police over the telephone that another hostage would shortly be killed. Medical examination of the body indicated that death had occurred some hours previously and there was thus a possibility that the later shots had killed another of the captives.

The Home Secretary authorized the military to be committed and at 7.7 p.m. the Deputy Assistant Commissioner in charge handed formal control of the incident, in writing, to the senior army officer. All units maintained radio silence from 7.14 p.m., and D.11 men moved into close-support positions on the porch, rear patio and first-floor balconies at the front and back of the Embassy. At 7.24 p.m., after detonating a controlled explosion at the front of the building Special Air Service troops launched their assault.

P.C. Lock was found struggling with the terrorist leader, who was killed, as were another four of his band. The sixth gunman was discovered hiding among the women hostages, and taken prisoner. One captive was killed and another wounded by the terrorists; the remaining hostages were rescued unharmed and there were only minor casualties among the SAS. At 7.50 p.m. the military commander returned control to the police and the operation was over. Presumably the letter which came into police hands at the moment troops stormed the building was delivered later to the Embassy staff. This was addressed to the Iranian Embassy from the Foreign and Commonwealth Office and asked that the Embassy flag be half-masted because of the death of President Tito of Yugoslavia.

Congratulations echoed around the world and in Tehran English tourists had their hands kissed by grateful Iranians. In the House of Commons, which was addressed by the Home Secretary on the successful conclusion of the siege, Mr Eldon Griffiths, MP made the point, 'Has not this event – like many others – underlined that the first social service that any Government owes to its people is the maintenance of the Queen's peace? Will my right honourable friend therefore dismiss all those calls that have been heard recently in this House for the abolition of the Special Patrol Group, for the standing down of the Special Air Service, for the reduction of powers under the Prevention of Terrorism Act, for the reduction of MI5 and the security services, and for the control by the borough of Lewisham of the operations of the Metropolitan Police?'

The surviving terrorist was later sentenced to thirty years' imprisonment and Trevor Lock was awarded a George Medal and honoured with the Freedom of the City of London.

A 7-page police order on 29 July 1980 condensed the instructions on Force firearms which had appeared in various orders since 1976. Once again the first paragraph was in capital letters and warned that every police officer to whom a firearm is issued was to be strictly cautioned that it is only to be used in cases of absolute necessity to defend his own life or that of the person he is protecting. Under a side heading, 'Specialized Weapons and Equipment', the order mentioned body armour and the fact that D.11 provides operational five-man teams to advise and assist at serious armed crime or terrorist incidents. The officers are equipped with specialized weapons and equipment and they will be clearly identifiable as police officers at all stages of the incident and cannot be deployed without the authority of the Deputy Assistant Commissioner (Operations). In addition, D.11 also have available anti-sniper armour capable of defeating 7.62mm ball ammunition and a 'Weldmesh' wire screen (shades of the machete man) for use against persons armed with weapons other than firearms or noxious fluids.

The year 1980 ended as it began – with violence. During December, bombs exploded in Hammersmith, including one at the

Territorial Army Centre; bombs planted in Piccadilly at the offices of the French Tourist Board and French Railways were defuzed. An incendiary device was detonated at the Libyan Airlines Office and an unsuccessful attempt was made to destroy a Thames Gas Board installation at Bromley-by-Bow.

On 13 April 1981 the front page of the *Daily Express* carried 1½-inch headlines, 'More Riots Hit Brixton'. Six inside pages supplied further coverage with photographs of vehicles, property and police-held riot shields blazing as the result of petrol bombs thrown by rioters. Fire-appliances and their crews who were trying to douse the flames were attacked and stoned by senseless mobs bent on destruction. Between 6 p.m. on Friday and 11.30 p.m. on Monday the 13th, in quite a small area of Brixton, 415 police officers and 172 members of the public were injured. 122 police vehicles and 91 private vehicles were destroyed or damaged; 28 premises gutted by fire and another 158 were attacked or looted. A total of 779 crimes were reported and 285 people were arrested.

The financial penalties incurred by the rest of London's population were threefold: 1. They paid out millions of pounds in riot damages; 2. They funded an expensive inquiry chaired by Lord Scarman whose terms of reference from the Home Office restricted him to policing methods, without identifying the underlying social and political problems in the district. Hence the inquiry revealed nothing that was not already known. 3. They paid for, and presumably will continue to pay for, fireproofed clothing, riot helmets, fire-resistant shields and other equipment which is now necessary to protect the forces of law and order.

One of the happier events of the year was the Royal Wedding on 29 July. Unfortunately even this occasion for public goodwill and rejoicing carried security undertones. Some time before the event, two D.11 officers walked the procession route from Buckingham Palace to the City boundary by the Royal Courts of Justice in the Strand, back and forth several times. The honeymoon route from the Palace to Waterloo railway station was also examined in detail. Both men were selecting suitable rifle positions from which to protect the Royal couple.

On the big day eighteen counter-sniper teams moved into position, backed by six SPG mobile response teams, and fortified by their 6 a.m. operational breakfast of greasy baked beans and even greasier bacon. Rumours that certain police canteens had been nobbled by the opposition were not substantiated. The route was divided in two and each half was the responsibility of a rifle control point, one of which was on top of Admiralty Arch. This was also one of the camera stations manned by a BBC crew who were in a position to monitor some interesting conversations between sniper control and the riflemen. Actually they behaved like perfect gentlemen, even to the extent of sharing their smoked salmon sandwiches! In order to cover the honeymoon route police riflemen and their spotters re-mustered on fifteen counter-sniper positions and the second control point moved to the top of a building on the south side of Westminster Bridge.

Fearful, as ever, that a photograph might appear in the national Press showing a police rifleman, complete with his rifle, orders were given that the counter-snipers were not to remove weapons from the carrying cases until the procession approached their particular arc of fire. It is certain that if the general public had seen such a photograph in their newspapers they would probably have been pleased, rather than horrified, that the Metropolitan Police took proper precautions to guard the Royal couple, but, as every rifleman knows, it takes time to wind into a support sling, settle in a comfortable firing position and check the telescope. Many of the snipers felt that politics had taken precedence over protection, leaving the latter diminished by some degree.

Firearms featured in three police orders in 1981. From 1 June each authorization card was to be date-stamped to show the expiry date of the holder's authority to be issued with a firearm. Another order in October instructed that a holstered handgun must be carried out of sight. Police Order 14 of 24 November stated that if any authorized shot was concerned in disciplinary proceedings in which a police firearm was in any way involved, his authorization would be immediately suspended pending the outcome of the inquiry.

In the aftermath of Brixton the Metropolitan Police began to consider more effective forms of riot control, including the use of baton rounds (plastic missiles designed for crowd control) or CS tear-smoke. Inevitably questions were asked in Parliament and on 19 October a written reply from Mr Whitelaw, the Home Secretary, stated:

'CS or baton rounds are to be used only with the express authority of the chief officer of police (or, in his absence, his deputy), under the direction and control of a senior officer whom he has designated as officer in charge, and by police officers who have been trained in the use of the equipment and know its characteristics. CS or baton rounds are to be used only as a last resort where conventional methods of policing have been tried and failed, or must from the nature of the circumstances obtaining be unlikely to succeed if tried, and where the chief officer judges such action to be necessary because of the risk of loss of life or serious injury or widespread destruction of property. Wherever practicable, a public warning of their use is to be given. Only CS equipment and baton rounds and riot guns of a type authorized by the Home Office may be used for these purposes. Nothing in the guidelines will affect the principle, to which section 3 of the Criminal Law Act 1967 gives effect, that only the minimum force necessary in the circumstances must be used. The degree of force justified will vary according to the circumstances of each case.'

On 22 October there were a number of questions from MPs in the House of Commons about Metropolitan Police equipment, community relations and policing methods. The shortest reply to any of these queries was given by the Home Secretary in answer to a question from Mr Dubs, Labour MP for Battersea South, who asked, 'Are CS gas, plastic bullets and water-cannon available for use by the Metropolitan Police?'; Mr Whitelaw, 'Yes, Sir'.

Out on the streets London was still a terrorist target and during the afternoon of 26 October police received information that bombs had been planted in three premises in the West End. One of the devices was found by a police officer searching a basement lavatory in the Wimpy Bar in Oxford Street. More than 100 people quickly left the building and the call was answered by Mr Kenneth Howorth, one of the Yard's explosives officers, who was given a description of the package. He entered the basement and the bomb exploded, killing him instantly.

Minutes later another explosives officer, Mr Peter Gurney, knowing full well that his colleague had just been killed, entered Debenhams in Oxford Street to deal with a similar device. The third reported bomb did not exist and appears to have been a false alarm intended to create more confusion.

Mr Howorth was awarded a posthumous George Medal. Mr Gurney, a former Warrant Officer Class I, had already earned a George Medal for bomb disposal in Northern Ireland. In 1973 he was made an MBE for his work as a civilian explosives officer in the Metropolitan Police, and in 1983 he received a bar to his George Medal. Journalists who constantly misuse the word 'hero' in connection with some highly paid footballer or pop star should write about an explosives officer going quietly to work. They will then be able to use 'hero' in the correct context.

Efforts to combat international terrorism resulted in a pilot three-week bodyguard course attended by sixteen students at the end of the year. Basic skills for the course were drawn from the expertise of D.11, Special Branch and other specialists. In addition to varying shooting techniques, the syllabus also covered commercial and home-made explosives, security of vehicles and buildings, personal protection, vehicle escort and anti-ambush drills and practical first aid. Unarmed combat and physical training occupied the last session of each day. These courses are now a standard feature in the Firearms Wing curriculum and have drawn students from as far afield as Gibraltar, Sri Lanka and Australia.

In August 1979, after the murder of Lord Mountbatten, the Commissioner appointed a working-party to examine the protection provided for the Royal Family and their residences, and to recommend improvements. This report was submitted in September 1979 and included a number of recommendations which were put to the Palace and the Home Office. Nearly three years later, despite efforts by Scotland Yard, officials of the Royal Household, the Home Office and the Department of the Environment were still juggling with the hot potato. None of the suggested security measures had been implemented by 6.40 a.m. on Friday 9 July 1982 when Michael Fagan walked into the Queen's bedroom. Fagan was no stranger to Buckingham Palace which he had entered a month previously. On that occasion the court found him not guilty of the offence with which he was charged, but guilty of another matter unconnected with the palace. He was committed to a mental hospital; it had obviously been a short stay.

Just before the lions bounded into the political arena the other Christians hastily quit, leaving the Commissioner in the centre of the sand. Also present was the Home Secretary, unwilling to throw in his lot with the lions but unable to join the Christians. As the storm subsided it became obvious that the whole sorry affair was a series of ifs. If the first alarm beam had not been so easy to evade; if the second had worked; if the third had not been recorded as a false alarm; if the day constable in the apartments had not been replaced, at the wishes of the Royal Household, by a footman; if the said footman had not been walking the dogs; if the duty sergeant had been faster in his response; if, if, if. Above all, if the original recommendations had been accepted Fagan would not have been able to enter the building in the first place. Finally, common sense brought the affair into perspective and it was accepted that grave faults in the security system, which were still to be remedied, had been compounded by human error.

On the morning of 20 July 1982 an improvised car bomb in South Carriage Road, Hyde Park, was detonated by remote control, a device only previously used in Northern Ireland. The switch was thrown as a mounted troop of The Life Guards was passing the vehicle. Four cavalrymen were killed and thirty-one people were injured, including tourists, disabled children and old-age pensioners. Some of the horrific wounds were caused by 4in and 6in nails, 30 pounds of which in weight had been packed in the device. Two hours later another improvised bomb exploded beneath the grandstand in Regent's Park while the stand was occupied by the regimental band of the Royal Green Jackets. Seven bandsmen were killed and another 28 persons injured.

Sir David McNee, who had held his post for longer than the normal five years, retired on 1 October 1982. He had survived the initial shock of the cold and muddy waters of the Metropolis and had done his best for the community he served and the men he led. No man could ask for more. His successor was Sir Kenneth Newman, a former member of the Palestine Police and Chief Constable of the Royal Ulster Constabulary. In common with his immediate four predecessors he was a professional policeman. Strength of the Force stood at 23,886.

20

Submachine-guns and Gas

There was a disastrous start to 1983 when detectives fired at an innocent man and nearly killed him. The man they sought, David Martin aged 35 years, was a cunning and dangerous criminal with a bizarre personality. On 5 August 1982 he was caught late at night after breaking into a West End office. He escaped by shooting his way out, in the course of which a police constable was hit in the groin and severely wounded. A month later, on 15 September, he was arrested while dressed as a woman (one of his favourite ploys) outside a London flat. In the course of a violent struggle Martin drew two loaded handguns which undoubtedly he would have used, had he not been shot in the neck by an armed detective. He recovered in hospital and was later charged with attempted murder of the constable, armed robbery (in which a security guard was shot) and various burglaries and firearms offences.

In one of the burglaries 24 revolvers and pistols, together with a large quantity of ammunition, had been stolen from the premises of a firearms dealer in Covent Garden. Although most of these guns were recovered after his arrest a few were never found and would obviously be available to Martin if he were ever at liberty. On Christmas Eve 1982 he escaped from a cell at Marlborough Street Magistrates Court where he was appearing on remand.

As a result of this escape a special team was formed of local detectives, backed by officers from Criminal Intelligence Branch, for the sole purpose of catching Martin. There were a certain number of leads, one of which was his association with Miss Susan Stephens with whom he had been friendly before his arrest. She had visited him in Brixton Prison while he was on remand and police believed that she had continued to see him after his escape. For that reason she was followed, and her flat in Hampstead was under surveillance, in the hope that she would eventually lead them to the wanted man. Police suspicions were well founded. It later transpired that he had telephoned her several times, they had been to a cinema and, a week or so later, taken a meal together in Hampstead. Needless to say Miss Stephens had not told police about the calls or the meetings.

Just after 6 p.m. on Friday 14 January 1983, team members using various unmarked police vehicles were following a hired Mini car in West London. Miss Stephens was in the back seat, occasionally looking out of the rear window, and the car was being driven by Lester Purdy. The man in the front nearside seat was Steven Waldorf, a freelance film director, who had the misfortune to resemble David Martin. There was, of course, no suggestion that Miss Stephens used him as a decoy to draw the observation team away from Martin. By this time some of the officers were becoming increasingly confident that the passenger was the fugitive gunman and comments were passed about his distinctive nose (a feature shared by both Waldorf and Martin).

In Pembroke Road, near Earls Court, the Mini, travelling in the nearside lane, was practically forced to stop because of heavy traffic congestion. It was dark and the street lighting was reasonable but not particularly good. At this point one of the detectives was sent forward on foot along the pavement to attempt a positive identification. Unfortunately the detective in question was the only officer present who knew Martin. Moreover he had been one of the arresting officers back in September and knew what to expect if the suspect were indeed the gunman. In the event he mistook the passenger for the wanted man and also misread his intention when he reached back into a bag on the rear seat. The detective's revolver was already drawn and he first fired at the nearside rear wheel, and then at the man he believed to be Martin. A second officer left his vehicle to help, and a third D.C., hearing the shots, thought that his colleagues were being attacked and opened fire. Fourteen shots were fired before it was realized that the first officer had made a terrible blunder.

Waldorf's life was saved in St. Stephen's Hospital and he was later awarded substantial damages. The first and third detective constables stood trial for attempted murder and other offences, but the judge upheld a defence submission on behalf of one of the defendants that there was insufficient evidence to proceed with the charge of attempted murder. The jury later found both officers not guilty of all the counts on the indictment. Neither of the officers concerned will ever again carry a service firearm and the echo of those fourteen shots will continue to reverberate for many years.

A shot fired by police received Press coverage on 28 February 1983, but from a different viewpoint. On 3 June 1982, outside the Dorchester Hotel in Park Lane, the Israeli Ambassador to London was shot in the head by a Jordanian, Hussein Said. He was chased by the Ambassador's Special Branch protection officer who eventually fired at Said, and hit him in the neck, after the would-be assassin had turned to shoot at him. The gunman was using a Polish wz63 machine-pistol, capable of automatic fire and loaded with 9mm Makarov semi-armour piercing ammunition. It appears that the weapon jammed after the shot fired at the Ambassador – which undoubtedly saved his life and that of his bodyguard. As far as the unfortunate victim was concerned this was a doubtful blessing since he suffered irreversible brain damage. The terrorist recovered and stood trial, with two companions, for attempted murder.

Mr Justice Mars-Jones, summing up at the Old Bailey, said it had been suggested by Counsel for the defendant that the officer had done something unlawful and improper. 'It would be unlawful for a police officer to shoot a suspect to prevent him from escaping,' said the Judge, 'but in this case there is no doubt that Detective Constable Simpson saw his charge being shot in the head at close range. When the Ambassador fell he chased the gunman up Park Lane while he was still carrying a gun. Then in South Street he called on the person he believed to be the gunman to stop – and he failed to do so. The law is not so stupid as to forbid a police officer in such circumstances to resort to the ultimate remedy of shooting a gunman, and whose failure to do so would allow an armed man who had demonstrated he had a killer instinct to escape with a machine-pistol and to allow the same man to do the same thing again.'

At their trial, the three accused, later identified as members of 'Abu Nidhal', an extremist Palestinian organization, were alleged to have drawn up a 'hit list' of Jewish targets which included Lord Marks of Marks and Spencer fame.

In March 1983 the Home Office issued ten guidelines for police on the issue and use of firearms. Most of the advice was already incorporated in Metropolitan Police orders – with one important exception. Future authority to issue guns should be given by an Assistant Chief Police Officer, equal to the rank of Commander in London. In urgent cases this permission could be given by a Superintendent, which was still a far cry from Inspector rank which had previously authorized issue of firearms. Unfortunately, these guidelines were sent direct to the assistant chief officers who, in the metropolis, now had two conflicting orders. One from their police authority (the Home Office) and another (enforced by the discipline code) from their own Force. The unprecedented speed with which the Home Office had issued this instruction caused a few problems and numerous telephone calls until the matter was resolved by an amended police order.

Also in March 1983 the Association of Chief Police Officers had been responsible for the publication of a new manual of guidance on police use of firearms. More than 150 pages contained in twelve chapters and eleven appendices covered every aspect of police firearms training and operations, and ranged from the law on the subject to cross-force convoys. Even more important was the statement that an authorized shot must satisfy his instructors and supervisors of a stable and mature attitude with firearms under stress; an excellent point, of paramount importance, which would depend chiefly on the man's character and the quality of his training. In an attempt to acclimatize men to this stress factor, battle induction schools during the Second World War used live ammunition and explosives and were permitted a percentage of casualties during training. However, policemen in the eighties are rather scarcer than infantrymen in the forties and, in any case, the reason for the end-product is quite different.

Although certain tests can furnish an estimate, nothing can gauge with certainty a policeman's reaction to the prospect of injury; whether that injury be a punch on the nose or a bullet in the head. Stability is affected by many seemingly insignificant factors – the common cold, a bad night's sleep, domestic worries and so on *ad infinitum*. As a general rule these unbalancing factors can only be offset by longer and more intensive periods of training.

This point was readily taken by a working-party which was convened to examine the issues raised by the Waldorf shooting. Their recommendations included a ten-day basic firearms course (the original four days had been extended to five in June 1980) and more emphasis on tactical training. Another part of the report dealt with the appointment of a clinical psychologist or the introduction of written tests to assess the authorized shot's reaction to stress. Most of the findings of this working-party, plus the Home Office guidelines, and all previous orders dealing with Force firearms were incorporated into an eight-page police order published on 2 August 1983.

From this time the term 'authorized firearms officer' was substituted for 'authorized shot'. In addition, the canine blue berets were taken off the hatstands and they are now official issue to all force riflemen and dog-handlers, in addition to D.11 personnel. The ACPO sub-committee also recommended that this form of headwear be issued to all authorized firearms officers in England and Wales as a means of identifying armed police. If implemented, this would transform public ceremonials such as Trooping the Colour, with every tenth policeman wearing a blue beret and facing inwards towards the crowd. It would also let the opposition know who to shoot first.

Stemming from the working-party's report on psychological guidance, and starting in October 1984, a series of test papers were completed by all students on the first day of their basic firearms course. These trials were an attempt to find a suitable personality profile test paper, or papers, from among those used for military and commercial purposes. Unfortunately, none of the tests proved to be scientifically valid and it was accepted that an experienced instructor's appraisal of his student was a more reliable guide than any written question paper. After eleven months the trials were abandoned.

For many people, as 1983 drew to a close, Christmas would not be a time of rejoicing. On Saturday, 17 December at 12.40 p.m., the London Samaritans' central office received a telephone call from a man with an Irish accent. The caller identified himself with a code word known only to police and the IRA and stated that car bombs were outside Harrods, other bombs were inside the store, and another had been planted at Littlewoods in Oxford Street. The Samaritans' 999 call was received at the Yard at 12.44 p.m. and police began to search both department stores and the surrounding streets. Harrods' management was warned of the alert and made preparations to clear shoppers from the premises. At 1.20 p.m. as police went to investigate an Austin car, KFP 252K, parked in Hans Crescent outside Harrods, the vehicle exploded.

Police Sergeant Noel Lane and W.P.C. Jane Arbuthnott were killed outright, together with a journalist and two women, one of whom was an American. Inspector Stephen Dodd died from his injuries in hospital. P.C. Gordon, a dog-handler, and his dog (which had to be destroyed) both suffered terrible injuries. Gordon lost a leg, in addition to being badly burned by the explosion, and was prematurely declared dead at the scene. During his stay in hospital he lost part of one hand and then his other leg. A year later, thanks to the medical profession and his own guts, he walked unaided. Fourteen other police officers and 85 members of the public were injured by the blast, many seriously.

It was later reported from Dublin that the IRA's so-called army council had not authorized the attack and regretted the civilian casualties. The crocodile tears were probably caused by intense public anger, both at the outrage and the maliciously misleading warning which had preceded the explosion. There were no other devices, other than in the murder car outside Harrods.

Early in 1984 the news that certain Special Branch protection officers were to be trained in the use of submachine-guns, ready for the London economic summit in June, caused a certain amount of uproar both in Parliament and the Press. The weapon in question was the 9mm Heckler & Koch MP5(K), capable of firing single shots, a burst of three rounds, or fully automatic fire, depending on the selector lever position. Ammunition capacity was fifteen or thirty rounds according to the magazine size. 'SAS guns for police,' announced the *Daily Mail* on 2 April, and 'Machine-gun police alarm Kinnock' in the *Daily Telegraph* on the 4th were typical bylines. However, the *Sun* on 3 April stated, 'The decision to allow some police to carry submachine-guns is sad but necessary. The weapons will be issued to specially trained protection squads only after the most stringent safeguards. It's true we have come a long way since the days when bobbies were never armed at all. So, alas, have the criminals and the terrorists.' It was fair comment.

A lively debate among MPs started on 3 April and continued over two days after Mr Kinnock, the Leader of the Opposition, had asked the Prime Minister to withdraw her permission for the proposed automatic weapons. In replying Mrs Thatcher assured the House of Commons that, 'The officers to whom these weapons will be issued will be trained to high standards by the Metropolitan Police Force arms training specialists in techniques appropriate to the role of the police. They will not be trained by military personnel.'

On 5 April, according to *Hansard*, Mr James Callaghan asked, 'In giving permission to the Metropolitan police to acquire submachine-guns, have the Government considered the impact of this serious further step in arming the police on the relationship between the police and the public, and on the very nature of the police service? I recognize the Government's dilemma in protecting foreign Heads of Government, but would not it be preferable in those circumstances to give that responsibility to the regular armed services when the Government are faced with short-term need? If the Metropolitan police are armed with submachine-guns that could change the character of the force and sacrifice a long-term beneficial system of policing to a short-term need.' The Prime Minster replied: '. . . The right honourable Gentleman may recollect, as it is within public knowledge, that as long ago as 1976 the Labour Administration approved the acquisition by the Metropolitan police of a small number of conventional submachine-guns – [Honourable Members: "Ah"] – for possible use in a terrorist emergency – a cause which I feel sure the right honourable Gentleman and the then Home Secretary had very much in mind when they approved that purchase.'

During the brisk verbal duelling which followed the delivery of the Prime Minister's body-blow, Mr Eldon Griffiths stated, '. . . that when the Leader of the Opposition seeks to make mischief and to attack the British police for doing what the Labour Government authorized them to do, he is stabbing in the back the best police service in the world.' Mr Kinnock (when he was eventually able to make himself heard) denied that he had made such an attack on the police, for whom he had every respect. After numerous interruptions the Speaker finally ruled that he did not think the matter should be taken further.

More submachine-gun news came on 8 April from the *Mail on Sunday* which informed its readers, 'Scotland Yard's secret armoury of automatic weapons, includes models from behind the Iron Curtain, it was revealed last night. According to police sources the Czech M61 Skorpion submachine-gun has been available for police use since 1980 . . . D.11's "Blue Beret" marksmen are trained in the use of the Skorpion . . .' This was news indeed to Scotland Yard and D.11 – who had never even seen a Skorpion – let alone trained with it. Presumably the *Mail*'s police informant was still obtaining money by false pretences.

Concern about policemen and automatic weapons was soon to be overtaken by graver matters. On Tuesday 17 April 1984, a number of demonstrators opposed to the Gadaffi régime gathered in St. James's Square, Westminster, outside the Libyan People's Bureau. They were separated by pedestrian barriers from two small groups of pro-Gadaffi supporters standing outside the building. At 10.10 a.m. a five-second burst of automatic fire from one of the first-floor windows of the Bureau struck down W.P.C. Fletcher and ten of the demonstrators. After a moment of stunned horror policemen rushed to help the injured and escort the remaining demonstrators out of the square. As the wounded were removed, armed police moved in to block exits from the Bureau although there was a delay of about ten minutes before the rear of the building was covered. During that time it is possible that two, possibly three, Libyans left the Bureau through an unguarded back entrance.

All the victims were taken to Westminster Hospital where Yvonne Fletcher died on the operating-table at midday. A team of surgeons had struggled for nearly an hour to save her life, but the bullet wound in her abdomen proved fatal.

The Bureau and its 30 occupants, protected by diplomatic immunity, was sealed off by the Diplomatic Protection Group. Personnel from this group, who had been responsible for the initial containment, were deployed around the building and the immediate area throughout the siege. D.11 teams and divisional snipers provided armed heavy support. In Libya three Britons were detained and armed troops surrounded the British Embassy in Tripoli. During the diplomatic deadlock, the declaration of people's power in Libya was marked by five bombs planted in London. Four of these were defuzed by explosives officers, but the fifth detonated at Heathrow airport at 7.55 p.m. on Friday 20 April and injured 25 people.

As the containment continued it was painfully obvious that the killer, or killers, hiding behind the sacred cow of diplomatic immunity, would not be brought to justice. It was equally obvious that the participants in St. James's Square were merely puppets – the real negotiators sat in Whitehall and Tripoli. Above all, there were no captives in the Bureau to be rescued. The hostages were nearly 2,000 miles away in Libya; well out of reach of the Metropolitan Police and too many in number to be helped by the SAS.

Finally, on Friday 27 April, the occupants of the Bureau left the building in groups of five, their progress monitored by watchful, hidden eyes. Each batch was escorted by Muftah Fitouri who had acted as a messenger throughout the affair. The Libyans were taken to Sunningdale for questioning and customs formalities before flying home from Heathrow. Their diplomatic baggage, unsearched, went with them.

The next morning explosives officers searched the vacated building. There were no booby-traps, but every window had been fitted with a padlocked, heavy steel grille. Television scanners covered all the outside approaches, including the roof, and the foyer was protected with armour plate and blast-resistant glass. The Libyan People's HQ in London was a fortress rather than a bureau.

On 28 April the mood of both public and police was expressed by the headline in the *Daily Mirror* which appeared under photographs of the thirty men, 'Who got away with MURDER?' On the same day the *Daily Express*, referring to the Government's attitude to diplomatic immunity, stated, '. . . It must drop the dangerous nonsense – evident in the Home Secretary's statement in the Commons on Wednesday – that the Vienna Convention is Holy Writ . . . That Convention was for civilized countries with civilized diplomats performing civilized duties. The explosion onto the world stage of barbarous régimes like those of Libya and Iran has made it obsolete. It is sheer suicidal madness to let these barbarians use civilized rules to further their uncivilized activities . . .' The byline at the top of the column accurately gauged the reaction of the man in the street, 'Humiliation for Britain'.

On 3 July 1984 the Greater London Council received a recommendation from its police committee seeking approval to commission an inquiry into the issue and use of firearms by police in London. It was suggested that the inquiry should be led by a Queen's Counsel, and fortunately one was available who hoped he could undertake the task during the courts' vacation period. He would be assisted by a junior from his chambers. The committee also envisaged that an appropriate academic person concerned with civil liberty issues should join the inquiry team. A much reduced fee of £5,000 would be paid to the QC, £2,500 to his junior and £3,500 to the academic member. These fees would be supplemented by £2,500 to meet out-of-pocket expenses (travel, secretarial, miscellaneous, overheads). Total cost to London's ratepayers – £13,500.

The rest of 1984 passed quietly enough apart from armed robberies, shootings and bomb incidents in which members of the public, explosives officers and police, both armed and unarmed, had their lives placed at risk.

At 7 a.m. on Thursday 24 January 1985, the occupants of a three-storey house in Gleneldon Road, Streatham, were quietly evacuated from the building by armed detectives. The only resident not approached by police was Toni Baldessare, aged 45, who occupied the attic flat. Baldessare moved to a new address every few months and was described as an armed professional criminal with a long record of violence and crime. He was wanted for questioning about a number of armed robberies, including a bank raid at Petts Wood in the previous August. In this incident a dog-handler had inadvertently appeared on the scene as the robbery was in progress and released his police dog 'Yerba' to tackle the raiders. Baldessare took deliberate aim with a .38 Special revolver and shot the dog twice in the head. As the wounded animal lay dying in the road, the gunman put another aimed bullet into Yerba's back.

Residents were evacuated from surrounding houses and at 8 a.m. the wanted man was woken by a telephone call from a detective inspector who told him that the house was surrounded and urged him to surrender. Baldessare refused, despite pleas from his estranged wife and a solicitor. From remarks he made to the negotiator it appears that he wanted to be remembered as the man who died in a shoot-out with police. Unfortunately no one was prepared to oblige him for the sake of criminal folklore. A D.11 team and a handful of Robbery Squad officers were already in position (rather fewer in number than the 100 armed marksmen mentioned in the Press the next morning) and a siege was in progress.

On Friday smoke was seen pouring from a fanlight in the attic roof and the gunman told the negotiator that he was 'destroying the evidence'. At the time it was thought that this was a trick to lure police into rushing the house, because shortly afterwards the smoke died away. However, it subsequently transpired that the fugitive had actually burned thousands of pounds in banknotes in the kitchen sink. At 11 p.m. that night a solitary shot was heard from the direction of the attic. Two hours later D.11 officers entered the house by smashing their way through the party-wall from next door. They were accompanied by an explosives officer as there were fears that the flat had been booby-trapped. Baldessare had shot himself in the heart with a Colt .38 Special revolver, loaded with lead roundnose bullets, and was lying dead in the living-room.

Three barricades, built from furniture and kitchen equipment, had been positioned in various places, ready for the grand shoot-out that did not materialize. A home-made 12 bore pistol loaded with a no. 6 shot cartridge was resting on a telephone table at the top of the stairs by the first barricade. Near the living-room door lay a 12 bore pump-action sawn-off shotgun with the safety catch off. It was loaded with three cartridges; a rifled slug, a no. 9 and a no. 6 shot. (No. 9 contained a load of 500–600 lead pellets; no. 6, 200–250 pellets.) The suicide weapon was near the body, surrounded by 41 rounds of assorted revolver and shotgun ammunition. Baldessare's epitaph appeared in the *Sunday Mirror* on 27 January under a photograph of his coffin being carried from the house – 'DEATH OF A VILLAIN'.

Two months later there was to be another 'grandstand' suicide. In October 1983, a 34-year-old keep-fit fanatic, James Baigrie, escaped from Saughton Prison in Edinburgh where he was serving a life sentence for murder. Baigrie had killed a barman, by blasting him in the back with a sawn-off shotgun, during a bungled robbery in the same city. At 6 a.m. on 20 March 1985, armed detectives raided a flat in Philbeach Gardens, Earls Court, where the wanted man was believed to be living. However, the killer was not to be quietly captured in bed for he had already dressed and left the premises. A white Transit van, which Baigrie drove for a construction company, was parked outside in the street and when a detective opened the back door of the vehicle he was confronted by the fugitive with a sawn-off shotgun. The officer dived for cover as the gunman threatened to shoot.

The area was sealed off and residents were warned not to look out of their windows. Where necessary they were given armed escorts to and from their homes. D.11 personnel, backed by local divisional armed officers, moved into position and another siege was in being. Despite appeals to surrender there was no response from the gunman until 3.5 p.m. when he shouted, 'All you want to do is send me back to prison' (quite true), but he did agree to accept a telephone link. Next morning the *Daily Express* featured a photograph of a D.11 sergeant placing a portable telephone in a plastic bucket, which Baigrie had pushed out of the back door on the end of a broomstick.

Late in the evening of Thursday 21 March Baigrie, who had refused to speak to police for some hours and was believed to be under the influence of drugs, broke through the partition which separated the body of the van from the driving compartment. The killer now had the opportunity to drive away in the vehicle – a danger to anyone who crossed his path. At 1.40 a.m., two CS ferrets were fired from a shot-gun into the van and he was given another opportunity to surrender – relayed through a loudhailer as he would not answer the telephone. There was no response to the call, but a few seconds later a shot was heard from inside the vehicle. After a pause, during which further calls were made, two D.11 men wearing respirators approached the Transit. Grappling-hooks (borrowed from Thames Division) were used to rip open the back doors of the van, and the murderer was found to have shot himself in the head.

Later that day, according to the *Daily Express*, in the House of Commons, Clive Soley, MP and Opposition spokesman on policing, 'lashed out at the police claiming that the siege seemed to have been handled differently from normal practice. "I would have expected the police to have waited much longer before going in," he said.' The headline in the *Standard* that evening read, 'Why Did Siege End In Death?', and according to the newspaper some of the residents in Philbeach Gardens said that police should have waited. The fact that gas had been used for the third time in London seems almost to have escaped comment from the Press and public.

Fortunately there was also some common sense available. The *Daily Express* on 23 March under a byline, 'Why so puzzled?' stated, 'James Baigrie's self-destruction was regrettable. As was his escape, 16 months ago, from the prison where he was serving a life sentence for a vicious murder with a sawn-off shotgun. However, instant and ill-informed criticism of the way police handled the operation is deplorable . . . What on earth makes the armchair tacticians think they are better judges of a dangerous situation than the men on the spot? There is something rather sinister about the persistent and relentless denigration and villification of the police by people who should know better . . .' On the same date the *Daily Mail* took a similar line. 'As soon as the barest facts were known about the end of the siege of the London gunman the Left were instantly ready to denounce. The report that CS gas had been fired into the gunman's van before he shot himself led them to conclude that the police had acted too soon. Labour MPs rushed to demand an immediate statement from the Home Secretary. Yet in what other country than Britain would the police have waited so patiently or so long? . . .'

Another balanced viewpoint under 'Killers and sense' appeared in the *Sunday Telegraph* on 24 March. 'Many people must have felt that the convicted killer James Baigrie did society a service by killing himself last week, thereby saving us all from having to pay for his incarceration for the rest of his life. Yet Her Majesty's Opposition, in the form of its spokesman on law and order, seems to believe that the police should have done more to prevent this armed and dangerous escaped prisoner from dying by his own hand, presumably by waiting even longer – they had already waited two days – before moving in to recapture him. Nor is Mr Clive Soley alone in his eagerness to question the police handling of this incident. Many other so-called keepers of the national conscience have also expressed equally critical sentiments . . .'

No doubt by now the man in charge of the operation had realized (although he probably already knew) that whatever action is taken by a police officer someone will say it was wrong. If, of course, it was wrong, everyone will say so. In fact, from the moment Baigrie smashed the partition and was able to move the vehicle the number of options open to police were reduced to one. To allow an armed killer to drive away would have been madness and had to be prevented. Shooting out the tyres works well on television, but a vehicle can travel on the rims for some distance. Firing a rifled slug into the engine block was yet another possibility. In either case, if as a result the van crashed and killed the driver, or worse still someone else, what then? Obviously, 'Why didn't the police do something else?' Attaching steel cables to both axles (at great risk) would have held the van, but would not have stopped Baigrie leaving his refuge and shooting as he came. The answer lay in immobilizing the man and not the vehicle and this could only be done with CS.

Why did the siege end in death asked the *Standard*. It ended in death because the killer chose to blow his brains over the wheel arch rather than surrender and stay alive – a choice denied to his victim.

21
A New Era

Back at Lippitts Hill training camp the basic defensive weapons course had been extended from five to ten days, with major changes in the curriculum, as a result of the 1983 recommendations. This was coupled with a rigorous selection procedure for students who were also tested for a reasonable standard of physical fitness. Much of the extra time was allotted to police tactics in armed situations and based on the ACPO manual of guidance. A revised set of instructors' notes was introduced and, significantly, 110 of the 167 pages were devoted to tactical training and exercises. Despite the fact that all the participants carried firearms, these schemes were generally designed to bring an armed incident to a successful conclusion without shots being fired. Finally much greater emphasis was placed on the assessment of students under stress, albeit if only artificially induced.

During the course each student fired 440 full bore rounds which included a 50-rounds classification shoot. The lowest pass mark for a standard shot stayed at 70 per cent with an overall 90 per cent in order to qualify as a marksman. However, this criterion was allied to the introduction of a new target on which a small central area scored 2 for every hit; anywhere else on the target only scored 1. Thus it was possible for a man to hit the target with every one of his 50 shots and still fail to pass, if the central area had not been struck at least twenty times.

The classification now consisted of five practices; the first three starting from the drawn weapon position. (1) ten rounds fired by sense of direction in paired shots from the 7-metre line in 25 seconds at a static target; (2) a similar practice but a pair of shots on each 2-second exposure of a turning target; (3) ten aimed shots, double-action, from the 15-metre line, one shot on each 3-second exposure of a turning target; (4) ten aimed shots, also double-action, from the 25-metre line in 1½ minutes at a static target – two standing fired from the strong hand, two standing using the weak hand, and back to the strong hand for two kneeling, two sitting and two prone. (5) ten aimed shots, single action, again from the 25-metre line – one shot on each 3-second exposure of a turning target – five prone and five standing, kneeling or sitting (firer's choice), changing position halfway through the practice.

These new training techniques produced a surprising number of marksmen even from among those who fired a Smith & Wesson Model 64 revolver with a sight radius of only 3½ inches (i.e., the distance between the backsight and foresight). An error of ¹⁄₁₆in at the muzzle of this weapon multiplies to sixteen inches at the target 25 metres away. A muzzle error of a quarter of an inch at the same range results in a fall of shot more than five feet away from the point of aim. Another by-product of the 1983 working-party was a two-day senior officers' tactics course for all ranks from inspector upwards. These courses had been started at Lippitts Hill late in 1983, and opened with a demonstration of various weapons and their firepower. This was followed by exercises and discussions, often based on actual incidents, which explored the control and command of different types of armed operations.

In July 1985 a number of national newspapers mentioned that the Metropolitan Police was experimenting with a lightweight truncheon, but were wrong in their assumptions that it would be suspended from an officer's belt or that it had been developed for use in public disorder situations. The 'Defender' baton, brainchild of Brigadier Harvey, self-defence adviser to the Force, was originally designed for women police and a three-, four- or five-link chain replaced the leather strap fitted to a conventional truncheon. Weighing 4½ ounces and nicknamed 'Whazzo', the new baton met considerable sales resistance from certain women officers and, at the time of going to print, the fate of 'Whazzo' is still in the balance.

On 14 September, under a byline 'Scotland Yard issued with flat-nosed bullets', the *Daily Telegraph* reported, 'Scotland Yard officers are being issued with a new type of bullet for their guns, designed to expand on impact to stop a gunman in his tracks . . . The new .38 bullets for their Smith and Wesson model ten revolvers are softer and flat nosed so as to spread on impact. The recent change in ammunition, on the recommendation of Home Office researchers, is partly the result of a building society hold-up in London last year, one of the 1,838 occasions when weapons were issued to police. In this case a police bullet went straight through its target, leaving the gunman still on his feet and armed, and posing a continued threat both to the police and to members of the public . . .' The round in question, a 125 grain semi-jacketed semi-wadcutter, had been in use for the past four months and was similar to the type of bullet which had been refused to the Metropolitan Police some twelve years earlier.

However, despite improved weaponry and further training for authorized firearms officers the possibility of human error still remained. Dire consequences followed such an error on the morning of Saturday 28 September 1985 when armed police entered a house in Normandy Road, Brixton. They were searching for a 19-year-old youth who was wanted for questioning about an incident at Kennington two days earlier when a shotgun had been fired. During the initial stage of the search the occupier, Mrs Cherry Groce, was accidently shot and seriously injured by a policeman.

That evening, allegedly as a result of the shooting, parts of Brixton were again burned and looted by the mob. 'Brixton's Revenge' and 'Brixton Ablaze' were two of the typical headlines in the Sunday Press which reported that mobs of black teenagers, some of them hooded, had besieged Brixton police station, built and ignited barricades of over-turned cars, thrown petrol bombs and indiscriminately attacked whites. Despite 149 arrests there were doubts that police strength had been sufficient and Monday's *Daily Express* byline on page 2 read, 'Looting gangs left to go on rampage'.

Unfortunately, events at Brixton were to be overshadowed during the following month by what amounted to urban guerrilla warfare. On Saturday 5 October 1985, a West Indian mother, Mrs Jarrett, collapsed during a police search of her house in Tottenham and was certified dead on arrival at hospital. It was disclosed at the subsequent inquest that she suffered from a serious heart condition and was liable to die at any time. However, the death of the unfortunate Mrs Jarrett was to be made the excuse for mass violence and murder.

On Sunday the 6th, orchestrated street warfare started at 3.15 p.m. and, after a break of some two hours, continued until the evening. During this period the outnumbered police suffered heavy casualties from petrol bombs, paving-stones, shotgun pellets and at least two policemen were shot – one in the stomach by a revolver bullet. By about 10 p.m. the main body of rioters had withdrawn to the Broadwater Farm Estate, a complex of high-rise council flats with raised walkways. The centrepiece of the estate, Tangmere House, built in the form of a flattened pyramid, featured a shopping area in which Asian-owned shops had been looted and fired. At this time the three approach roads to the estate had been sealed off by the mob with burning barricades;

police with riot shields were restricted to a defensive, holding operation. Previous police attempts to gain ground had been repulsed with petrol bombs and missiles from the balconies of the flats, causing more police casualties.

Just before 10 p.m. a small group of policemen, in the charge of a sergeant, was sent into Tangmere House to protect a squad of firemen who were to tackle the fires in the shopping precinct. There were fears that the flames would spread to occupied flats above the shops. However, it appears that the police and firemen were forced to retire when they were attacked by a mob. At the same time another group of rioters surged along the passages behind them and almost cut off their line of retreat. During this precipitate withdrawal one of the officers, P.C. Keith Blakelock, aged 40 and the father of three children, stumbled and was separated from his colleagues. He was then knifed and hacked to death by some of the mob. The injured man was taken to hospital on a fire-engine, as no ambulances were available, but died fifteen minutes later.

Later that evening D.11 units and divisional riflemen equipped with baton guns were deployed in the area, but not used. The final tally of casualties to the police and public totalled 255 against seven and four of the latter were reporters or cameramen. Injuries sustained by policemen included burns, gunshot and stab wounds.

This display of unprecedented savagery on the streets of London inevitably dominated the front pages of the national newspapers on Monday 7 October. At a press conference on the same day the Commissioner issued a statement which included the words [referring to the possible use of plastic bullets], '. . . I wish to put all people of London on notice that I will not shrink from such a decision should I believe it a practical option for restoring peace and preventing crime and injury'.

The feelings of most of London's populace were put into three words, 'Enough is Enough', which headed the *Daily Express* opinion column on 8 October. In this article the writer castigated certain politicians and civil leaders who claimed extenuating circumstances for the orgy of violence and terror. He identified the real cause in the following words: 'This was criminal violence for which there can be no excuse, no sociological explanations, no twentieth-century heart-bleeding clichés. It was urban warfare . . . in London N.15.'

As the echoes of the second Tottenham outrage died away amid calls for more police and better riot equipment, 1985 ended, as it had begun, with bloodshed. At about 11 a.m. on Christmas Day, Errol Walker aged 29, entered a third-floor flat at 62 Poynter Court, Gallery Gardens, Northolt. His estranged wife, Marlene, had already left the premises but her step-sister, Jackie Charles aged 22, her daughter, Carlene, and Walker's own daughter, both aged 4, were still there. Fifteen minutes later Jackie Charles was thrown out onto the balcony and died of stab wounds on her way to hospital. Armed D.11 officers moved into position and after a period of negotiation Patricia Walker was released unharmed.

During the containment which followed, lasting for 29 hours, the *Sun* newspaper reported that Walker had appeared on the balcony several times clutching Carlene, brandishing a carving-knife, and warning police to keep their distance. The end of the siege came at 3.48 p.m. on Boxing Day and was witnessed by television viewers who saw Walker run crouching along the balcony and pick up an abandoned police riot shield. Three D.11 officers appeared from an adjoining flat to his left and attempted to rush him, but Walker managed to block the front door with the shield and regain the flat. A few seconds later two distraction devices were thrown into the flat and the team members forced their way in through the barricaded bathroom and kitchen windows. As a result of what they saw, and heard,Walker was shot in the shoulder and head and the little girl was snatched from his arms. She was taken out of the flat unconscious and suffering from knife wounds to her throat and arm.

The delay of twelve seconds before the police entry provided a field-day for the armchair tacticians who appeared in force and pontificated without knowing the true facts. Unfortunately, the affair is still *sub judice* and it will be some months before what actually happened (as opposed to what apparently happened) can be revealed. According to the *Daily Express* of 27 December, there was 'Uproar over bungled raid' despite the fact that the little hostage had been rescued and a man arrested without harm to police or members of the public. The twin firsts – the first time anyone had been shot by a D.11 marksman (and very good shooting in the circumstances) and the first time distraction devices had been used in London – appear to have passed unnoticed.

However, not everyone was as critical as some politicians or the various self-appointed experts. The day after the siege ended, the D.11 team involved sent Carlene a giant teddy bear with a 'Get well soon' message. A few days later her grandparents replied with a simple card which read, 'Thank you for giving us back Carlene.'

A new era began on 10 January 1986 when pictures appeared in the Press showing D.11 men openly carrying submachine-guns at Heathrow Airport. What the photographs could not show was the fact that the guns would only be used to fire single shots. In any case, the deployment of D.11 personnel was only an interim measure until local officers could be trained in the use of a 9mm carbine.

The presence of these weapons was the result of top discussions on the best way to deter, or counter, the type of terrorist attacks on airports which had been experienced at Vienna and Rome in the previous months. A number of policemen at Heathrow already carried revolvers or pistols, but these were hardly a match for grenades and automatic assault rifles. In addition, any terrorist onset in a crowded area, such as a passenger lounge, would have to be stopped immediately with accurate counter-fire. This might well take place at longer ranges than are usual for handguns.

Rifles were considered, but rejected because the penetrating power of a high-velocity bullet is such that it could pass through the primary target and hit one of the people it was supposed to protect. Shotguns were ruled out for a similar reason; the spread of shot beyond a certain distance increases the chance of hitting a bystander. The solution lay in a single-shot carbine, but with the magazine capacity of a submachine-gun, capable of firing a pistol round with extreme accuracy at medium ranges. This role was filled by the Heckler & Koch MP5, modified so that it could not be used for fully automatic fire.

Predictable dissatisfaction from outside the Force included comments that Scotland Yard had chosen the wrong weapon/unsuitable ammunition/police were inexperienced in the handling of a carbine/it was wrong to carry it openly – and Labour's Home Affairs spokesman called for a public inquiry. Another complaint centred on the fact that the carrying of such a weapon damaged the police image. Presumably the image took precedence over a police potential to safeguard the travelling public.

Meanwhile important changes both in training and operations were in hand. An additional one-day refresher had been introduced for authorized firearms officers in September 1985, thus increasing the number of training days each year from three to four. It seems to have escaped notice that this was in line with a recommendation made over half a century earlier, but it was still short of the eight days proposed after the 1983 enquiry. Furthermore, the cost of eight separate training days per annum for more than 4,000 men would be prohibitive, especially during a period of restricted police expenditure. Therefore, in April 1986, it was announced that the total of AFOs would be reduced to just under 3,000; roughly 10 per cent of the Force.

Coupled with this reduction came the introduction of a three-tier level of armed police response which would vary according to the anticipated degree of expertise required. As in the past, a firearms incident involving one or two men (level 3) would continue to be handled by local armed officers, while at the top of the scale, (level 1), D.11 teams would still be used for terrorism and hostage situations. Police planners now prepared for events at an intermediate level, (2), which would need men with extra skills, beyond those taught to divisional officers, but less than the standards and training demanded of D.11 personnel. To meet this requirement, extra men (who would not necessarily become instructors) were to be recruited into D.11. They, and their similarly trained counterparts in other specialist departments, would deal with all future level 2 operations.

It is anticipated that the response level will be determined by a senior D.11 instructor, or a D.11 trained firearms tactical adviser, who will assist the police officer in charge at the incident. However, there are only limited resources and numbers of men available for the new system. If all the D.11 and level 2 teams are committed to various operations at the same time – not an unremote possibility – who will fill the breach?

There was yet another important development still to come. After the Brixton and Tottenham riots, in which a press photographer and P.C. Blakelock lost their lives and 348 policeman were injured, police were criticized in some quarters for the manner in which the disturbances had been handled. Some of the harshest critics of police tactics, however, were the men at the sharp end who had not been allowed to take positive action. As a result, they had been forced to shelter behind riot shields while the petrol bombers used them as passive and static targets.

In consequence, the Metropolitan Police conducted a searching review into the subject of policing serious public disorder. The findings of this inquiry were published on 30 June 1986 in a Special Police Order, which listed 71 recommendations (distilled from 546). These covered most of the alphabet from armoured vehicles to water cannon and urged that the use of firearms during severe rioting should be examined, together with the weaponry, equipment and training available to police. Among other points, the report also called for improved public order training for senior officers and radical alterations in command and communications channels during riots.

News of the impending changes broke in the Press on 3 July, and several newspapers reported that the Home Secretary, in a written reply to the House of Commons, had stated that he authorized the purchase of 24 bullet-proof vehicles, 80 protected personnel carriers, another 700 radios and 1,500 long truncheons, each measuring 28 inches. In fact the Home Secretary had referred to ballistically protected vehicles, i.e., armoured Land Rovers, generally capable of withstanding fired missiles up to a certain calibre. Unfortunately, no vehicle – be it tracked or wheeled – is wholly proof against bullets and, in particular, the repeated impact of bullets hitting the same spot on various vulnerable parts.

Regrettably, there are no easy options (other than in a totalitarian State) for any police force trying to quell rioting, for riot control has never been an exact science. This is especially true if the rioters have been infiltrated by groups prepared to use firearms to further their own ends. In any case, every riot contains a strong criminal element, which in itself poses a danger to the community. Thus, in the aftermath of the last Brixton riot, more than 900 crimes were reported and 219 people were charged with offences including murder, rape, arson, robbery and grievous bodily harm.

In the final analysis, police counter-measures to restore law and order must always be governed by the degree of violence exercised by the mob. Other countries have long since found the need for specially trained and equipped riot squads – which would be unthinkable in London. However, only a few years ago, London policemen with sub-machine guns, or wearing flame-resistant overalls and carrying riot shields would have been equally unthinkable.

The new era bids to be turbulent.

Postscript

In 1829 a police force was that abomination feared by the populace and denounced by politicians – a Standing Army – the permanent weapon for enforcing the will of government and fatal to the liberty of the subject. The Metropolitan Police, conceived of necessity and reared among the community with whom it worked, generally proved otherwise.

By 1985 the term 'para-military force', when applied to specialist armed police units, carries the same sinister implications as the word 'police' in the early 19th century, although the Metropolitan Police has always firmly rejected the suggestion that D.11 teams are para-military. However, irrespective of nomenclature, there is still a belief in some quarters that such groups should be abolished, leaving only the 'traditional' British Bobby; traditional in this case meaning unarmed.

Unfortunately, if these specialist units were to be disbanded, and the conditions still existed which led to their formation, then the gap would be filled – not by an unarmed civilian force, but by a wholly military presence. Such a vacuum was created in Northern Ireland when the Royal Ulster Constabulary was disarmed. The breach had to be manned by armed British soldiers who, since that time, have patrolled the streets of British cities to give the citizens some semblance of law and order.

'The only liberty I mean is a liberty connected with order; that not only exists along with order and virtue, but which cannot exist at all without them'.
(Edmund Burke, October 1774).

Select Bibliography

Although this is only a short list there are, of course, many other books dealing with various aspects of the Metropolitan Police. Some of these are excellent and others, unless treated as works of fiction, are useless. One author in particular, dealing with the Tottenham Outrage, has managed to transform the continuing police pursuit of Lepidus into a widespread hunt by Special Branch. This culminates in the fugitive's being traced and called upon to surrender by a Branch sergeant. There are a number of similar examples in other books where the alleged facts bear little resemblence to the truth.

Ascoli, David. *The Queen's Peace.* Hamilton, 1979
Bell, Walter G. *London Rediscoveries.* Lane, 1929
Browne, Douglas G. *The Rise of Scotland Yard.* Harrap, 1956
Bushell, Peter. *London's Secret History.* Constable, 1983
Colquhoun, Patrick. *A Treatise on Police of the Metropolis.* London, 7th edn, 1806
Critchley, T. A. *A History of Police in England and Wales.* Constable, new edn, 1978
Fairfax, N. W. H. and Wilkinson, V. L. H. 'History of Metropolitan Police Uniforms and Equipment'. Unpublished MS, 1974
Howgrave-Graham, H. M. *The Metropolitan Police at War.* HMSO, 1947
Mark, Sir Robert. *In the Office of Constable.* Collins, 1978
McNee, Sir David. *McNee's Law.* Collins, 1983
Lee, Captain W. L. Melville. *A History of Police in England.* Methuen, 1901
Reynolds, Gerald W. and Judge, Anthony. *The Night the Police went on Strike.* Weidenfeld & Nicolson, 1968
Rogers, Colin. *The Battle of Stepney.* Hale, 1981
Rumbelow, Donald. *The Houndsditch Murders.* St Martin's Press, 1973
(Rogers and Rumbelow, the latter a City of London Police officer, draw different conclusions about certain aspects of the murders which led to the siege of Sidney Street. Both books make interesting reading).

SOURCE MATERIAL
National newspaper files
New Scotland Yard: Commissioners' annual reports; police orders
Parliamentary debates
Police Review
Public Record Office: MEPO and HO papers.

Appendix I
Arms and Accoutrements

Date	Item	Remarks
1829	Truncheons	18½ inches long and made from West Indian lancewood or male bamboo.
1829	Cutlasses	Steel bladed, brass grips. Carried on the Commissioners's authority for certain duties.
21 December 1829	Flintlock pocket pistols	Order for 50 pairs placed with Parkers of Holborn.
13 August 1836	Flintlock cavalry pistols, truncheons and sabres	Weapons held by Bow Street Horse Patrol and brought into the Metropolitan Police when the Patrol was incorporated as the Mounted Police.
1839	Assorted cutlasses, blunderbusses and flintlock boat pistols	Marine Police weapons taken over by the Metropolitan Police when the river police organization was absorbed and became the Thames Division.
1844	Percussion pistols	No. 22 bore. As sea service model of 1842, but without belt hook. Number unknown.
1852	Ammunition pouches	Fitted to the truncheon-holder on Mounted Police saddles.
1856	Truncheons	17 inches long, turned from lignum vitae, an American evergreen. Replaced the 18½-inch truncheon.
19 August 1856	Percussion pistols and cutlasses	Contract placed with Parker, Field & Company. Some of the pistols may have been double-barrelled.
1864	Truncheon cases	New infantry-style uniform issued. Truncheon carried in a spring-loaded scabbard suspended from the belt.
4 January 1866	Revolvers	Unknown number borrowed as a temporary measure. Probably Adams .450 percussion from the military, but may have included Tranter .44 rimfire revolvers from elsewhere.
29 January 1866	Pistols	All percussion and flintlock pistols, bullet moulds and powder flasks withdrawn.

Date	Item	Remarks
1868	*Sabres*	*Withdrawn from Mounted Police.*
28 August 1868	Revolvers	200 Adams .450 breech-loading revolvers issued from the Tower of London. Weapons borrowed on 4 January 1866 returned.
19 November 1868	Revolvers	Another 200 Adams, as above, also collected from the Tower.
29 January 1869	Revolvers	Last consignment of 222 Adams issued from the Tower of London.
1 December 1882	Revolvers	Twelve Webley .455 'Bulldog' revolvers purchased from P. Webley & Son for protection duties.
January–July 1884	Revolvers	931 Webley .45 gateload revolvers bought from P. Webley & Son for use on outer divisions. Adams revolvers returned to store.
26 June 1884	Rattles	Withdrawn from men in suburban areas and replaced by whistles.
Early 1885	Rattles	Withdrawn from remaining divisions and replaced by whistles.
January 1885	Truncheons	Length reduced to 15½ inches and another size, 12½ inches long, introduced for detective officers. Both models were turned from lancewood which was cheaper than lignum vitae.
March–September 1885	Cutlasses	4,713 cutlasses scrapped; 728 left on divisions.
October 1886	Truncheon-cases	Abolished. Truncheons henceforward carried by foot police in special pocket sewn into the uniform trousers.
October 1886	Truncheons	Trials conducted with Australian cocus and tuart wood. West Indian partridge wood (hard red wood with darker parallel stripes) eventually adopted.
1903	Revolvers	Webley Mark IV revolvers supplied by Naval Ordnance Department for police on duty in dockyards.
1905	Revolvers	Rebounding hammer fitted to 370 Webley gateload revolvers in interests of safety. Remaining gateload weapons withdrawn to store.
February 1909	Pistols	Two Colt 'automatics' purchased from Churchill of Agar Street for protection duties.

Date	Item	Remarks
November/ December 1911	Pistols	920 Webley & Scott .32 self-loading issued to divisions. All .45 gateload and .455 'Bulldog' revolvers withdrawn to store.
1912	Truncheons	New pattern, 21-inch long, baton for mounted officers.
March 1912	Pistols	100 Webley & Scott .22 single-shot pistols purchased for practice purposes.
1913	Pistols	Webley .455 self-loading pistols supplied by Admiralty for police on duty in dockyards.
7 August 1914	Revolvers	281 old Webley .45 gateload revolvers re-issued from store.
29 January 1919	Swords	Withdrawn from inspectors and above, although they were returned to superintendents on 20 December 1920 for use on ceremonial occasions.
1920	Truncheons	36-inch long baton replaced the 21-inch model for mounted police.
1 December 1920	Pistols	300 additional Webley & Scott .32 self-loading pistols purchased.
May 1921	Pistols	Another 300 pistols purchased, as above.
July 1921	Pistols	500 additional weapons purchased as above.
1 December 1926	Revolvers and pistols	All Webley .45 gateload revolvers and some .32 pistols returned to store.
13 April 1934	Pistols	.22 Webley & Scott pistols taken out of service and given to M.P. shooting sections.
28 May 1940	Pistols	.22 Webley & Scott pistols reclaimed from sectons and issued to Divisions.
1 June 1940	Rifles	3,500 Canadian Ross .303 rifles issued to stations. A number were carried on patrol in police vehicles.
22 January 1941	Revolvers	21,000 American-manufactured .32 revolvers issued to stations.
March 1942	Revolvers	124 .45 revolvers, mainly Webley & Scott but some Colt and Smith & Wesson, issued to inspectors and above. Part of the stock of 301 weapons seized from London gun dealers and held by police.
31 July 1945	Firearms	.45 and American .32 revolvers, plus all rifles, withdrawn.

Date	Item	Remarks
3 November 1952	Pistols	Twenty Colt .380, model 'M', self loading pistols lent by War Department to Special Branch. Returned 23 April 1965.
8 September 1955	Pistols	70 second-hand Beretta .32 self-loading pistols purchased for protection posts and duties.
January–September 1956	Revolvers	500 Webley & Scott .380 Mark IV revolvers issued to Divisions.
30 April 1957	Pistols	All Webley & Scott .32 pistols withdrawn to store by this date.
September 1958	CS gas	Grenades available for police and held at Kensington Palace Barracks.
April–December 1960	Pistols	Walther 9mm, model PP, self-loading pistols replaced Beretta pistols for armed posts and protection duties.
April 1962	Pistols	Webley & Scott 1½-inch gas dischargers stored at Kensington Palace Barracks.
1967	Pistols	Browning .22 'Hi-Standard' self-loading pistols used on basic firearms courses. Actual purchase date not known.
24 May 1967	Revolvers	222 Colt .38 'Police Positive' revolvers (war surplus) for issue two per station for C.I.D. Weapons unserviceable.
10 July 1967	Gas guns	Two Federal CP 1½ inch bore gas guns purchased to replace Webley & Scott gas dischargers.
October 1967	Rifles	Twenty Lee-Enfield No. 4 rifles hired for use on divisions.
December 1968	Revolvers	150 Enfield .38 No. 2 revolvers on loan to cover period of routine weapon inspection of Force arms.
September 1969	Gas guns	Two Webley 37mm gas guns purchased as replacements for Federal gas guns.
5 October 1970	Revolvers	Webley & Scott .22 revolvers replace Browning .22 pistols on basic firearms courses.
2 July 1971	Pistols	Browning 9mm self-loading pistols taken into use by certain high risk convoy escorts.
8 March 1972	Shotguns	Two Savage, Model 69, pump-action shotguns purchased for CS gas delivery by D.11.

Date	Item	Remarks
23 March 1972	Shotgun	One Viking double-barrelled shotgun purchased for evaluation – CS delivery by D.11.
13 October 1972	Rifles	Enfield L42A1 7.62mm rifles with telescopic sights replace .303 Lee-Enfields.
30 April 1973	Carbine	One Sterling Mark L34 A1 9mm single-shot carbine purchased for evaluation. Saw some operational service.
1973	Rifles	Ten Enfield Envoy 7.62mm target rifles purchased for training.
20 December 1973	Rifles	Enfield Enforcer 7.62mm sniper rifles collected from Enfield and taken into use on 28 March 1974. Replaced all other rifles on divisions.
October 1974	Revolvers	Smith & Wesson .38 Special revolvers, Models 10 and 36 (six and five chambers respectively) replace all other handguns in Metropolitan Police.
5 July 1976	Pistols	Browning 9mm self-loading pistols for use by D.11 team members.
24 January 1977	Shotguns	Remington Model 870 12 bore pump-action shotguns replace Savage and Viking models.
April 1977	Revolvers	Smith & Wesson .38 Special revolvers, Model 28, for D.11 team use.
1977	Submachine-guns	Heckler & Koch MP5 and MP5 (SD) for D.11 team use.
20 April 1977	Rifles	Twelve Heckler & Koch .223 (HK 93) rifles for divisional and D.11 team use.
3 May 1978	Revolvers	Smith & Wesson .22 revolvers replace Webley & Scott models on basic firearms courses.
8 July 1981	Gas guns	Webley/Schermuly 1½-inch gas gun replaces earlier model.
3 August 1981	Grenade-launchers	L1A1 66mm CS launcher firing L11A1 CS grenade. Only for use in serious public disorder.
12 August 1981	Baton round dischargers	Type L67 discharger. Fires type L5A4 plastic round. Usage as above.
June 1983	Rifles	Ruger .223 Mini 14R Ranch rifles replace the Enfield 7.62mm and Heckler & Koch .223 throughout Metropolitan Police area.

Date	Item	Remarks
October 1983–February 1984	Revolvers	Smith & Wesson .38 Special revolvers, Model 64, replace all S&W Model 36 revolvers in M.P.D.
19 March 1984	Submachine-guns	Twelve Heckler & Koch 9mm MP5 (K) submachine-guns for VIP protection purposes.
February 1986	Carbines	Heckler & Koch 9mm MP5 carbines for airport protection.
1986	Truncheons	Modified, shorter issue for women police.
1986/7?	Truncheons	'Defender' baton (wood and metal links) for issue to women police in the first instance and then to male officers. May eventually replace wooden truncheon for normal duty – not in public disorder situations.

Appendix II
Robberies, 1860–1985

Figures for reported robberies committed in the Metropolis have been taken from the Commissioner's Annual Reports.

			Yearly average
During the 84 years from	1860 to 1944	7,581	90
– and every decade	1945 to 1954	2,973	297
thereafter.	1955 to 1964	5,060	506
	1965 to 1974	23,859	2,385
	1975 to 1984	82,103	8,210
	1985	—	15,184

Annual totals for reported *armed* robberies were first separately shown in 1947, but were not recorded for the years 1964 to 1966.
Therefore, only the figures for the first, and last, fifteen-year periods have been extracted.

1947 to 1961	386	25
1970 to 1984	12,439	829
1985	—	1,653

Index